W9-BKD-848

PORTAL TO AMERICA: THE LOWER EAST SIDE 1870-1925

EDITED BY ALLON SCHOENER

PORTAL TO AMERICA: THE LOWER EAST SIDE 1870-1925

EDITED BY ALLON SCHOENER

HOLT, RINEHART AND WINSTON
NEW YORK, CHICAGO, SAN FRANCISCO

Published simultaneously in Canada by Holt, Rinehart and Winston of Canada, Limited

Library of Congress Catalog Card Number: 67-19055

Chapter I (pp. 85-92) in Book V, "I Discover America," from The Rise of David Levinsky, by Abraham Cahan. Copyright 1917, 1945 by Abraham Cahan. Reprinted by permission of Harper & Row, Publishers, New York.

Material from The Spirit of the Ghetto, by Hutchins Hapgood, is reprinted here by permission of the publishers, Funk & Wagnalls, New York.

Lillian D. Wald's case notes for July 1893 are reproduced here by permission of The Research Libraries of the New York Public Library.

Materials reprinted from the New York World and the New York Tribune appear here by permission of the World Journal Tribune, New York.

"60,000 Children in Sweatshops," by Edwin Markham (Cosmopolitan Magazine, January, 1907). Copyright 1907, 1935 by Edwin Markham. Reprinted by permission of A. Watkins, Inc.

Art Direction: Harris Lewine
Design: Herb Lubalin

First Edition

PRINTED IN THE UNITED STATES OF AMERICA   8655557

To my father, who was a Lower East Side boy, and to my mother, who, as I did, learned about the Lower East Side from my father.

Contents:

In the East Side Cafés, New York Tribune, September 30, 1900
Yiddish Theater, Hutchins Hapgood (The Spirit of the Ghetto)

Preface: When I joined the staff of The Jewish Museum in 1965, I was offered the opportunity to create an exhibition dealing with New York's Lower East Side. As an art historian specializing in twentieth-century environmental criticism, American-Jewish history was hardly my province. The exhibition appealed to me because it provided me with the opportunity to discover my heritage. I was born and raised in Cleveland; I never knew the Lower East Side until I went to college. When I came to New York on weekends from New Haven, I found myself roaming around Delancey Street and Second Avenue eating food that my mother had never cooked and trying to find the world of my father's youth. By the time I started to look, it was gone. The exhibition and book have permitted me to explore this vanished world in libraries and archives. The book is the summation of my discoveries.

Throughout my research many people have been very helpful. In particular, I would like to express my appreciation to Robert Doty, Daniel W. Jones, Miss Grace Mayer, Zero Mostel, Miss Claire Rosenstein, Leon Stein, and finally, my wife Mary, who always helps me.

Allon Schoener
NEW YORK CITY, JANUARY 1967

Introduction:

Landing places—Plymouth, Jamestown, New Amsterdam, Philadelphia—symbolize American history. For a period of fifty years, during the last quarter of the nineteenth century, and the first quarter of the twentieth century, New York's Lower East Side was the first America for millions of immigrants. As a portal, the Lower East Side prepared Jews, Italians, Irish, Chinese, and Poles for adaptation to American life. Escaping from persecution and economic hardship, a continuous stream of Eastern European Jews settled on the Lower East Side and transformed this area of downtown New York—bounded by the Brooklyn Bridge on the south, Fourteenth Street on the north, Broadway on the west and the East River on the east—into their domain. Although Jews spread throughout the entire geographical area, they tended to concentrate between East Broadway and Houston Street.

Two worlds—the old imported from Eastern Europe and the new found in America—confronted each other in a daily struggle for dominance. The experiences of the Lower East Side are particular to American Jews; however, they belong to the pattern of twentieth-century social evolution in which impoverished immigrants were able to reach a higher standard of living. A rich inheritance of ideas, images, stories, personalities, mores, and attitudes emerged from the Lower East Side. This Lower East Side, which no longer exists, has become a complex historical idea embroidered with emotional overtones. As in so much Jewish history, no roots with enduring continuity were planted. The reality of the Lower East Side is the memory.

Since the first settlers arrived in the seventeenth century, America has been a hostile environment for every immigrant. Adaptation involved conquering animals, wilderness, language, and economic hardship. By 1875, American destiny was shifting from the agrarian economy of the frontier to the industrial economy of rapidly expanding urban centers. Hundreds of thousands of immigrants came from Southern and Eastern Europe to the United States as industrial workers. New York was their chief port of entry and first stopping place. Until the restrictive immigration laws of the 1920's were passed, the tidal wave of immigration continued.

The Lower East Side symbolizes the epic of Jewish adaptation to America. Life was a panorama of hardship, misery, poverty, crowding, filth, uncertainty, alienation, joy, love, and devotion. Much of this was documented fully by journalists, photographers, and social workers. The American press saw immigrants as a curiosity deviating from accepted Anglo-Saxon standards. Reporters for the New York *Times,* New York *Tribune, Evening Post,* and other newspapers assiduously examined every detail of Lower East Side life from food to the wigs worn by women. They saw the Lower East Side as it was and reported what they found. Accounts of their visits to the Lower East Side create an immediacy that can be equaled only by the photographs of Byron, Hine, Riis, and numerous other documentary photographers, who created a vivid pictorial legacy of the difficult environment in which immigrant Jews found themselves upon landing in America. Jacob Riis generated a profound awareness and understanding of Lower East Side living conditions with his documentary photographic reports. Riis came to New York in 1870 from Denmark. As a newspaper reporter and photographer, he used both words and pictures to tell about the tenements, the markets, the sweatshops, and the people of the Lower East Side. Riis's interest in the raw conditions of urban and industrial life made him one of the most effective civic reformers of the period. Lewis Hine was a sociologist who found the camera to be a powerful research tool. His training enabled him to comprehend the background and social implications of a situation. He was the first to use the term "photo story" to describe his work. For many years, immigration and Lower East Side tenements and sweatshops were his concern. Social workers like Lillian Wald of the Henry Street Settlement documented miserable living conditions in the tenements and working conditions in the sweatshops. Her knowledge stemmed from direct contact with Lower East Side life; she moved to the Lower East Side and lived there. Through their own energy, social workers attempted to improve what they could. Beyond this, they created awareness throughout the rest of the community with the hope that amelioration would result.

The Yiddish press provided the immigrants with an opportunity to view themselves with different eyes from the Americans who saw them as curiosities and social problems. The Jews saw themselves in relation to the struggle to adapt. Everyone who came to the Lower East Side had to become an American. Americanization involved discarding old values and accepting new ones. The culture of the *shtetl* (the small town Jewish community of Eastern Europe) represented the Old World. Like all of the non-Anglo-Saxon traditions imported to this country, the way of the *shtetl* was submerged by the pressure to adapt to the new environment. The Lower East Side was the scene of this transformation. Through the "Bintel Brief" letters to the editor of the *Jewish Daily Forward* a collective consciousness was exposed. Marriage, mothers-in-law, socialism, bosses, exploitation, children, religion, health, and education were discussed. The "Bintel Briefs" provide one of the most sensitive and vivid records of the trials and tribulations of adaptation from the immigrant point of view. Although Yiddish continued to be the principal language of the first generation of immigrants, achievement in English was the measure of successful adaptation. Like all other immigrant groups, the second and third generations were discouraged from learning their father's native language.

Thirst for knowledge and the world of ideas were integral parts of a daily life that was dominated by hardship and poverty. The Yiddish theater was intellectual theater at the turn of the century when the American theater was not. Adaptations of Goethe, Shakespeare, Ibsen, Gorky, and Hauptmann were performed. Sweatshop workers avidly read the great nineteenth-century novelists; children swarmed to the public libraries; hundreds of coffeehouses served as social centers where anarchists, socialists, actors, writers, labor leaders, and workers met to discuss the problems of the world. An intellectual working class—a phenomenon never to be repeated in this country—emerged from the Lower East Side.

The dialogue between the old and the new was ever present. Jewish religious institutions continued the traditions of the Old World. Young boys were taught Hebrew and attended *cheders* (Hebrew schools). *Landsmanschft* (benevolent societies), where immigrants from the same town or village gathered for religious and social activities, provided a sense of group security. The older generation held on to their European heritage with tenacity; they made it part of the new life that was evolving among their progeny. Social service organizations like the Educational Alliance, Henry Street Settlement, University Settlement, Baron de Hirsch Fund, and Hebrew Immigrant Aid Society (HIAS) prepared both the young and the old for life in America.

At the same time as uptown Jews, reformers, and social workers were ministering to their plight, the East Side tenement dwellers and sweatshop workers were doing something for themselves. Abuse provoked protest. Strikes were an everyday experience. Tenants and workers struck against the exploitation of landlords and sweatshop operators. Many of the liberal and progressive principles of housing reform, collective bargaining, and labor legislation which are now accepted as part of our national tradition stem from the Lower East Side.

A rich tradition of aspiration and achievement belongs to everyone associated with the Lower East Side. Immigrants became peddlers, sweatshop workers, and small shopkeepers. Economic opportunities permitted many of them and their children to become successful businessmen, lawyers, doctors, and intellectuals. The American melting-pot philosophy encouraged social mobility. The Lower East Side was an open-end ghetto; it was a stopping-off place, where you lived until you could afford to go to Harlem, the Upper East Side, the Upper West Side, the Bronx, Brooklyn, or out of town. Getting out was the hallmark of success. People who came from the Lower East Side—artists, entertainers, politicians, and businessmen like Irving Berlin, Eddie Cantor, Jimmy Durante, Jacob Epstein, Jacob Javits, David Sarnoff, and Al Smith—illustrate the contribution that the Lower East Side has made to the mainstream of American life. It was a creative crucible which gave birth to great ideas and great men.

The Lower East Side of today is not the Lower East Side of yesterday. It continues to be a Jewish community. Thousands of Jews live in large, new, union-financed, cooperative apartment buildings, which are surrounded by trees and grass. Many of the tenements in which thousands of Jewish immigrants suffered sixty years ago are standing. Although they may now have electricity and running water, they are still rat and roach infested. Nothing has been done to overcome insufficient light and air. These miserable old tenements have been inherited by Puerto Ricans—New York's newest immigrants. Their lives are not so different from the lives of Eastern European Jews of sixty years ago. America may be the land of opportunity, but achievement is a long, hard struggle.

Today, New York's Lower East Side—the East Village—is the leading avant-garde art center in the United States. It promises to exert a dynamic influence on many aspects of future American culture. The East Village is characterized by youth, bohemian rebellion, and open defiance of middle-class professional success. At the turn of the century, the Lower East Side was a thriving economic center. Grand Street had stores like Lord & Taylor, and the men's and women's clothing industries were located on Broadway below Houston Street. Since that time, commerce and industry have moved uptown. None of Manhattan's real estate, commercial, and industrial booms has affected the Lower East Side. The combination of population mobility and geography—the Lower East Side is a hook at the southeast corner of Manhattan—has left it as a by-passed area. The artists who live and work in the East Village find it a compatible environment because of its isolation from the rest of New York. Predominantly residential, the hustle and bustle of downtown, midtown, and uptown are absent. An Old World, turn-of-the-century pace is to be found here.

The Lower East Side recalls a wonderfully rich and fruitful period of American history in which millions of Jews came to the United States through a small portal and spread across the entire country making their contributions to the total fabric of American life. There is pride that so much came out of it. Many of those who participated in the Lower East Side experience are in the prime of life. Their memories are strong. For others, the Lower East Side is a place they have heard about from parents and grandparents. For American Jews, the Lower East Side is a powerful symbol—their heritage.

I Discover America

I was one of a multitude of steerage passengers on a Bremen steamship on my way to New York. Who can depict the feeling of desolation, home-sickness, uncertainty, and anxiety with which an emigrant makes his first voyage across the ocean? I proved to be a good sailor, but the sea frightened me. The thumping of the engines was drumming a ghastly accompaniment to the awesome whisper of the waves. I felt in the embrace of a vast, uncanny force. And echoing through it all were the heart-lashing words: "Are you crazy? You forget your place, young man!"

When Columbus was crossing the Atlantic, on his first great voyage, his men doubted whether they would ever reach land. So does many an America-bound emigrant to this day. Such, at least, was the feeling that was lurking in my heart while the Bremen steamer was carrying me to New York. Day after day passes, and all you see about you is an unbroken waste of water, an unrelieved, a hopeless monotony of water. You know that a change will come, but this knowledge is confined to your brain. Your senses are skeptical.

In my devotions, which I performed three times a day, without counting a benediction before every meal and every drink of water, grace after every meal and a prayer before going to sleep, I would mentally plead for the safety of the ship and for a speedy sight of land. My scanty luggage included a pair of phylacteries and a plump little prayer book, with the *Book of Psalms* at the end. The prayers I knew by heart, but I now often said psalms, in addition, particularly when the sea looked angry and the pitching or rolling was unusually violent. I would read all kinds of

psalms, but my favorite among them was the 104th, generally referred to by our people as "Bless the Lord, O my soul," its opening words in the original Hebrew. It is a poem on the power and wisdom of God as manifested in the wonders of nature, some of its verses dealing with the sea. It is said by the faithful every Saturday afternoon during the fall and winter; so I could have recited it from memory; but I preferred to read it in my prayer book. For it seemed as though the familiar words had changed their identity and meaning, especially those concerned with the sea. Their divine inspiration was now something visible and audible. It was not I who was reading them. It was as though the waves and the clouds, the whole far-flung scene of restlessness and mystery, were whispering to me:

"Thou who coverest thyself with light as with a garment, who stretchest out the heavens like a curtain: who layeth the beams of his chambers in the waters: who maketh the clouds his chariot: who walketh upon the wings of the wind . . . So is this great and wide sea wherein are things creeping innumerable, both small and great beasts. There go the ships: there is that leviathan whom thou hast made to play therein . . ."

When the discoverers of America saw land at last they fell on their knees and a hymn of thanksgiving burst from their souls. The scene, which is one of the most thrilling in history, repeats itself in the heart of every immigrant as he comes in sight of the American shores. I am at a loss to convey the peculiar state of mind that the experience created in me.

When the ship reached Sandy Hook I was literally overcome with the beauty of the landscape.

The immigrant's arrival in his new home is like a second birth to him. Imagine a new-born babe in possession of a fully developed intellect. Would it ever forget its entry into the world? Neither does the immigrant ever forget his entry into a country which is, to him, a new world in the profoundest sense of the term and in which he expects to pass the rest of his life. I conjure up the gorgeousness of the spectacle as it appeared to me on that clear June morning: the magnificent verdure of Staten Island, the tender blue of sea and sky, the dignified bustle of passing craft—above all, those floating, squatting, multitudinously windowed palaces which I subsequently learned to call ferries. It was all so utterly unlike anything I had ever seen or dreamed of before. It unfolded itself like a divine revelation. I was in a trance or in something closely resembling one.

"This, then, is America!" I exclaimed, mutely. The notion of something enchanted which the name had always evoked in me now seemed fully borne out.

In my ecstacy I could not help thinking of "Psalm 104," and, opening my little prayer book, I glanced over those of its verses that speak of hills and rocks, of grass and trees and birds.

My transport of admiration, however, only added to my sense of helplessness and awe. Here, on shipboard, I was sure of my shelter and food, at least. How was I going to procure my sustenance on those magic shores? I wished the remaining hour could be prolonged indefinitely.

"Psalm 104" spoke reassuringly to me. It reminded me of the way God took care of man and beast: "Thou openest thine hand and they are filled with good." But then the very next verse warned me that "Thou hidest thy face, they are troubled: thou takest away their breath, they die." So I was praying God not to hide His face from me, but to open His hand to me; to remember that my mother had been murdered by Gentiles and that I was going to a strange land. When I reached the words, "I will sing unto the Lord as long as I live: I will sing praise to my God while I have my being," I uttered them in a fervent whisper. . . .

One of my fellow passengers was a young Yiddish-speaking tailor named Gitelson. He was about twenty-four years old, yet his forelock was gray, just his forelock, the rest of his hair being a fine, glossy brown. His own cap had been blown into the sea, and the one he had obtained from the steerage steward was too small for him, so that gray tuft of his was always out like a plume. We had not been acquainted more than a few hours, in fact, for he had been seasick throughout the voyage and this was the first day he had been up and about. But then I had seen him on the day of our sailing and subsequently, many times, as he wretchedly lay in his berth. He was literally in tatters. He clung to me like a lover, but we spoke very little. Our hearts were too full for words.

As I thus stood at the railing, prayer book in hand, he took a look at the page. The most ignorant "man of the earth" among our people can read holy tongue (Hebrew), though he may not understand the meaning of the words. This was the case with Gitelson.

"Saying, 'Bless the Lord, O my soul'?" he asked, reverently. "Why this chapter of all others?"

"Because—Why, just listen." With which I took to translating the Hebrew text into Yiddish for him.

He listened with devout mien. I was not sure that he understood it even in his native tongue, but, whether he did or not, his beaming, wistful look and the deep sigh he emitted indicated that he was in a state similar to mine.

When I say that my first view of New York bay struck me as something not of this earth, it is not a mere figure of speech. I vividly recall the feeling, for example, with which I greeted the first cat I saw on American soil. It was on the Hoboken pier, while the steerage passengers were being marched to the ferry. A large, black, well-fed feline stood in a corner, eyeing the crowd of newcomers. The sight of it gave me a thrill of joy. "Look! there is a cat!" I said to Gitelson. And in my heart I added, "Just like those at home!" For the moment the little animal made America real to me. At the same time it seemed unreal itself. I was tempted to feel its fur to ascertain whether it was actually the kind of creature I took it for.

We were ferried over to Castle Garden. One of the things that caught my eye as I entered the vast rotunda was an iron staircase rising diagonally against one of the inner walls. A uniformed man, with some papers in his hands, ascended it with brisk, resounding steps till he disappeared through a door not many inches from the ceiling. It may seem odd, but I can never think of my arrival in this country without hearing the ringing footfalls of this official and beholding the yellow eyes of the black cat which stared at us at the Hoboken pier.

The harsh manner of the immigration officers was a grievous surprise to me. As contrasted with the officials of my despotic country, those of a republic had been portrayed in my mind as paragons of refinement and cordiality. My anticipations were rudely belied. "They are not a bit better than Cossacks," I remarked to Gitelson. But they neither looked nor spoke like Cossacks; so their gruff voices were part of the uncanny scheme of things that surrounded me. These unfriendly voices flavored all America with a spirit of icy inhospitality that sent a chill through my very soul.

The stringent immigration laws that were passed some years later had not yet come into existence. We had no difficulty in being admitted to the United States, and when I was, I was loath to leave the Garden.

Many of the other immigrants were met by relatives, friends. There were cries of joy, tears, embraces, kisses. All of which intensified my sense of loneliness and dread of the New World. The agencies which two Jewish charity organizations now maintain at the Immigrant Station had not yet been established. Gitelson, who like myself had no friends in New York, never left my side. He was even more timid than I. It seemed as though he were holding on to me for dear life. This had the effect of putting me on my mettle.

"Cheer up, old man!" I said, with bravado. "America is not the place to be a ninny in. Come, pull yourself together."

In truth, I addressed these exhortations as much to myself as to him; and so far, at least, as I was concerned, my words had the desired effect.

I led the way out of the big Immigrant Station. As we reached the park outside we were pounced down upon by two evil-looking men, representatives of boarding houses for immigrants. They pulled us so roughly and their general appearance and manner were so uninviting that we struggled and protested until they let us go— not without some parting curses. Then I led the way across Battery Park and under the elevated railway to State Street. A train hurtling and panting along overhead produced a bewildering, a daunting effect on me. The active life of the great strange city made me feel like one abandoned in the midst of a jungle. Where were we to go? What were we to do? But the presence of Gitelson continued to act as a spur on me. I mustered courage to approach a policeman, something I should never have been bold enough to do at home. As a matter of fact, I scarcely had an idea what his function was. To me he looked like some uniformed nobleman—an impression that in itself was enough to intimidate me. With his coat of blue cloth, starched linen collar, and white gloves, he reminded me of anything but the policemen of my town. I addressed him in Yiddish, making it as near an approach to German as I knew how, but my efforts were lost on him. He shook his head. With a witheringly dignified grimace he then pointed his club in the direction of Broadway and strutted off majestically.

"He's not better than a Cossack, either," was my verdict.

At this moment a voice hailed us in Yiddish. Facing about, we beheld a middle-aged man with huge, round, perpendicular nostrils and a huge, round, deep dimple in his chin that looked like a third nostril. Prosperity was written all over his smooth-shaven face and broad-shouldered, stocky figure. He was literally aglow with diamonds and self-satisfaction. But he was unmistakably one of our people. It was like coming across a human being in the jungle.

Moreover, his very diamonds somehow told a tale of former want, of a time when he had landed, an impecunious immigrant like myself; and this made him a living source of encouragement to me.

"God Himself has sent you to us," I began acting as the spokesman; but he gave no heed to me. His eyes were eagerly fixed on Gitelson and his tatters.

"You're a tailor, aren't you?" he questioned him.

My steerage companion nodded. "I'm a ladies' tailor, but I have worked on men's clothing, too," he said.

"A ladies' tailor?" the well-dressed stranger echoed, with ill-concealed delight. "Very well; come along. I have work for you."

That he should have been able to read Gitelson's trade in his face and figure scarcely surprised me. In my native place it seemed to be a matter of course that one could tell a tailor by his general appearance and walk. Besides, had I not divined the occupation of my fellow passenger the moment I saw him on deck?

As I learned subsequently, the man who accosted us on State Street was a cloak contractor, and his presence in the neighborhood of Castle Garden was anything but a matter of chance. He came there quite often, in fact, his purpose being to angle for cheap labor among the newly arrived immigrants.

We paused near Bowling Green. The contractor and my fellow passenger were absorbed in a conversation full of sartorial technicalities which were Greek to me but which brought a gleam of joy into Gitelson's eye. My former companion seemed to have become oblivious of my existence.

As we resumed our walk up Broadway the bejeweled man turned to me.

"And what was your occupation? You have no trade, have you?"

"I read Talmud," I said, confusedly.

"I see, but that's no business in America," he declared. "Any relatives here?"

"No."

"Well, don't worry. You will be all right. If a fellow isn't lazy nor a fool he has no reason to be sorry he came to America. It'll be all right."

"All right" he said in English, and I conjectured what it meant from the context. In the course of the minute or two which he bestowed upon me he uttered it so many times that the phrase engraved itself upon my memory. It was the first bit of English I ever acquired.

The well-dressed, trim-looking crowds of lower Broadway impressed me as a multitude of counts, barons, princes. I was puzzled by their preoccupied faces and hurried step. It seemed to comport ill with their baronial dress and general high-born appearance.

In a vague way all this helped to confirm my conception of America as a unique country, unlike the rest of the world.

When we reached the General Post Office, at the end of the Third Avenue surface line, our guide bade us stop.

"Walk straight ahead," he said to me, waving his hand toward Park Row. "Just keep walking until you see a lot of Jewish people. It isn't far from here." With which he slipped a silver quarter into my hand and made Gitelson bid me good-by.

The two then boarded a big red horse-car.

I was left with a sickening sense of having been tricked, cast off, and abandoned. I stood watching the receding public vehicle, as though its scarlet hue were my last gleam of hope in the world. When it finally disappeared from view my heart sank within me. I may safely say that the half-hour that followed is one of the worst I experienced in all the thirty-odd years of my life in this country.

The big, round nostrils of the contractor and the gray forelock of my young steerage-fellow haunted my brain as hideous symbols of treachery.

With twenty-nine cents in my pocket . . . I set forth in the direction of East Broadway.

The History of American Immigration

In the good old days before New Amsterdam had become New York, and before New York had extended its northern boundary beyond what is now Chambers Street, indiscriminate immigration was favored by the authorities of the colony of New York and of this city. It mattered not whether the immigrants that reached this port came of their own volition or were kidnaped on the other side and brought here by men who made a business of supplying the colonists with laborers, white and black.

Those who purchased the laborers after they arrived here cared little or nothing about their pecuniary wealth. Paupers were then made welcome, whereas now efforts are made to keep persons of this class from coming to these shores.

If the immigrants of those days had not sufficient money with which to pay for a passage across the ocean, or had been kidnaped, an enterprising sea captain was always to be found who was willing to risk the expense of bringing them here. He well knowing that if he once got them here he would receive money enough to compensate him for his trouble, and a handsome bonus besides, by selling their labor for a number of years to some colonist. And so the early pauper immigrants were usually sold and held in bondage until they had worked out the sum that had been paid for their passage. The working-out process was usually prolonged as much as possible, and until the period of bondage had expired the immigrants could be sold and resold any number of times. There was always a profit in the transaction for all concerned but the hapless immigrant—unless, soon after getting here, he was fortunate enough to run away and elude capture.

Since the early Colonial days immigration has undergone various phases, and, whereas at times in the past any one was welcomed, great restrictions are now being placed on those who seek this country for a new home. The Colonial period may be said to have ended and the period of immigration to have begun with the close of the Revolutionary War, in 1783. Decennial censuses were taken in 1790, 1800, and 1810, but no immigration statistics were gathered until 1820. The accepted estimate for the period is 250,000. From 1820 to 1856 no distinction was made in the returns between settlers and travelers. From 1856 to 1868 settlers were distinguished from travelers, but the number of immigrants of each nationality was not displayed separately from the number of travelers of that nationality. Since 1885 immigrants from the British North American possessions and from Mexico have not been included, and in 1894 the Commissioner General of Immigration presented for the first time the number of European immigrants arriving in the Dominion of Canada destined for the United States.

The immigration records were never before kept as carefully and with as much detail as they are today, but, according to those which are in existence, it is shown that up to the end of the last governmental fiscal year, June 30, 1896, the total immigration since 1783 was 17,813,750. By decades, from 1820 to 1890, and from 1890 to 1896, it was as follows: 1820–1830, 128,393; 1830–1840, 539,391; 1840–1850, 1,423,337; 1850–1860, 2,799,423; 1860–1870, 1,964,061; 1870–1880, 2,834,040; 1880–1890, 5,246,613; 1890–1896, 2,878,492. It will be noticed that from 1880 to 1890, it was nearly twice as much as it had been for any previous decade, and over two-thirds what it was for the entire period. In fact, nearly two-thirds of the entire immigration movement of the world in 1890 was directed to the United States.

The commercial depression of 1826–27 in England was accompanied by a decided increase in the number of immigrants to this country. In 1827 there were 18,875, almost twice as many as in any previous year, and in 1828, 27,382, a figure that was not reached again for some time. The American panic of 1837 registered itself in the immigration returns for 1838, when the number was less than it had been for any year since 1831 and was only about half of what it had been for the two years previous. The years 1848 to 1854 were marked by an enormous increase, culminating in the latter year, when the arrivals were 427,833, the largest number recorded until after the close of the Civil War. Three principal things contributing to the change were the bad times in Germany, the famine in Ireland, and the discovery of gold in California. The financial depression of 1857 was followed by another decrease, the number for each of the years 1858 and 1859 being less than 120,000. The Civil War naturally checked the incoming movement still further; then the immense business activity of the years following (when transportation facilities were being speedily improved and the West was being opened up) was coincident with another increase in immigration, as the hard times of the later seventies were with another falling away. The return to prosperity after 1879 brought with it an enormous immigration (788,992 in 1882 alone). Finally, the recent depression (1893–95) was accompanied by a most significant decrease. For 1894 the immigrant arrivals were only 285,631, and for 1895 only 258,536, and for several months of this period the outflow of steerage passengers, almost exclusively foreign-born, from American ports actually exceeded the inflow—an unprecedented condition. The gradual return to prosperity is already observable in the immigration figures. For the period from January 1 to September 1, 1895, for example, there was an increase of 36,270 at the Port of New York over the same period of 1894. Furthermore, returns show an increase of 51 per cent, for the month of July, 1895, over July, 1894; of a little over 60 per cent for August, 1895, over August, 1894, and of more than 55 per cent for September, 1895, over September, 1894. From 1820 to 1840 the immigration was almost entirely from Great Britain and Ireland. During the decade ending with 1840 German immigration first became noticeable, and this steadily increased until, in the decade ending with 1890, it amounted to nearly 1,500,000, about the same as that from the whole United Kingdom. Norway and Sweden first made themselves felt in the returns for the decade ending 1870 with over 100,000 arrivals, a number which increased to over 500,000 during the decade ending with 1890. The last decade, however, is even more notable for an enormous increase in the immigration from Austria, Hungary, Italy, Russia, and Poland.

The first national immigration law was passed by Congress in July, 1864. It was for the purpose of encouraging immigration, all immigration theretofore having been cared for by the individual states. The passage of the act was due in part to the absence in the army of the large bodies of wage earners who had been employed in important industries, and it encouraged indiscriminate immigration. No safeguards were provided against the worst classes of foreign population, and idiots, criminals, paupers, etc. were admitted without inspection or examination. "Contract labor" was encouraged under this act. The law of 1864 was repealed in 1868, and from that time until 1882 there was no United States statute bearing on immigration. The law of 1882 instead of encouraging immigration was passed to restrict it. Since 1882 other laws and amendments to laws have been passed, and now the immigration officials exercise a power that permits them to stand between the objectionable persons in other countries and the people of their own. The laws declare who shall not be permitted to land, and their provisions are very broad.

A great percentage of the immigrants who enter this country enter by way of New York, and consequently the history of immigration at this port is of much interest. For many years the New York State officials had entire charge of immigration matters in this port. They used Castle Garden for their purposes, and there all immigrants were landed. For a time after the first federal laws affecting immigration were passed, the federal and state officials worked together, the state officials doing the work under contract with the Nation. It was discovered, however, that the state officials were misusing their power and were using the bureau for political purposes to the injury of the immigrants. By the federal act of 1891 the Immigration Bureau was placed exclusively in the charge of federal officials. Thereafter Castle Gardens was used for a time; then the Barge Office at the Battery was used, and then Ellis Island. There the Commissioner of Immigration now has his office, and there the federal government has a valuable and almost perfect plant for the purpose of inspecting and caring for all immigrants who come to this port. Immigrants have been landed there since January 1, 1892. All passenger vessels are boarded at Quarantine by inspectors from the Immigration Bureau. As the vessels proceed to their docks the passenger lists are examined by the inspectors. Cabin passengers' tickets and declarations are scrutinized as well as steerage passengers and if any cabin passenger is thought to be a person who comes within the restrictive clauses of the law he is compelled to go to Ellis Island and await investigation. When the vessel has reached her dock the immigrants and their baggage are taken by barge to Ellis Island and there they are all inspected and their baggage is examined.

The main building on the island has a great room on the ground floor, into which the baggage is taken, and rooms on the upper floor, into which the immigrants are sent. Every immigrant is numbered and tagged, and 240 at a time, in groups of 30, are examined by the men and women inspectors before whom they are compelled to pass and to whom they make their declarations. If any immigrant fails to pass an inspector, he or she is at once sent before the Board of Special Inquiry for fur-

ther examination; if the board finds that the immigrant should not be allowed to land, he or she is put in the detention pen to await a re-examination for his or her return to the place from which he or she came. Every immigrant who is found ineligible to land is detained on the island and returned to his or her home at the expense of the steamship company that brought him or her here.

The immigration officials are familiar with the ways of those who would prey upon the newcomers, and every effort is made to protect the men, women, and children. They are particularly solicitous about women and children, and hedge them around with the safeguards of the law and of the church to which they belong. If a woman or a child is not met by friends or relatives, she is detained until someone whom she names can be communicated with and until it is determined to be safe for her to land. In such instances the missionary societies aid the immigration officials.

As an instance of the care that is exercised to prevent improper persons from landing, statistics show that as many as 800 immigrants have been detained and returned to their homes in Italy in one month.

There is a well-conducted hospital on Ellis Island, and in it all ill immigrants are placed and kept until returned or allowed to land. The Immigration Bureau's care of an immigrant does not end with his landing, for every immigrant who becomes ill or unable to care for himself during the first year ashore must be cared for at Ellis Island. Those who are ill are cared for in the hospital, the others in the dormitories.

As it is possible to inspect and pass 5,000 immigrants in a day, it is seldom that there are many of them at the island overnight. For those who are there, however, ample provision has been made, and wholesome food and clean beds are provided. The dormitories, which will accommodate 475 persons, are well lighted and ventilated and are kept in an odorless condition. Separate rooms are provided for the men and for the women and children. Every immigrant is permitted to land in this city as soon as possible after he has disembarked from his ship. All come ashore at the Barge Office at the Battery.

THE NEW YORK TIMES, DECEMBER 3, 1900

Ellis Island, New Buildings

The Bureau of Immigration will be transferred from its present quarters to the new station on Ellis Island the 15th of this month. The transition from the cramped and badly arranged quarters which the bureau has occupied since the fire that destroyed the old station on the island in 1897 will be marked. One has only to remember the old ramshackle structure to be able to appreciate the magnificent and admirably arranged new quarters. Situated on one of the most prominent locations in the harbor, the new station is an imposing as well as a pleasing addition to the picturesque water front of the metropolis. The plans and specifications for the new structure were selected from the designs submitted by the architectural firm of Boring & Tilton of this city. The judges upon whose recommendation the designs were accepted were Robert S. Peabody of Boston, T. P. Chandler of Philadelphia, and James Knox Taylor, Supervising Architect of the Treasury Department at Washington, all of whom are among the leading members of the American Institute of Architects. The wisdom of their choice of plans can be best understood by studying a description of the station. The main building, situated in the center of the island, is 385 feet in length and 165 feet in width. The body of the building is 62 feet high, while the four towers at each corner are 100 feet from the ground to the top of the domes.

The style is a conglomeration of several styles of architecture, the predominating style being that of the French Renaissance. The material used in the construction is brick with light stone trimmings, harmonized so as to make the general effect as attractive in appearance as possible. The spires of the towers are copper-covered, and in the top of each is an observatory from which a splendid view of the harbor and city may be had. On the western and eastern sides of the building are the main entrances, massive arches which extend well into the second story. Over the arch in concrete work appears the national coat of arms, while eagles of the same material make the general effect still more attractive.

But the interior arrangements are what, after all, makes the station a model of completeness. Every detail of the exacting and confusing service to which its uses are to be dedicated were considered in perfecting the interior plans. The transportation, examining, medical, inquiry, and various other departments of the service are being assigned quarters that, while they are practically separate in every detail, yet are so arranged as to follow one after the other according to its proper place in the department. Thus from the office of the Commissioner the doors lead to the quarters of his assistant, and then, according to rank, come the medical, financial, examining, railroad, inquiry, and other branches of the service. When the immigrant is landed from the barges, he will pass through an imposing private entrance, made as nearly as possible free from the observation of the curious, besides protecting him during bad weather. He then goes to the second floor, the entire center of which is given up to the examining department, where he is inspected by the medical authorities, and to the officials of the other branches of the service who pass upon his eligibility to land. Every inch of space on this floor is utilized. The railings forming the network of the aisles in which the immigrants are placed in alphabetical order, according to nationality, gives the great amphitheatre the appearance of an immense spider web. Two shiploads can be handled easily, and two more in an emergency by the inspectors and other attachés. It is estimated that 5,000 persons can be thoroughly examined with perfect ease, and in an emergency 3,000 more, by the application of a little added energy on the part of the examiners. Surrounding this room from the third floor is the observation gallery, where visitors can watch the inspectors at work. The dormitories are entered from doors on the gallery. There are two main apartments which can accommodate about 600 sleepers comfortably.

The southwestern corner of the second floor has been assigned to "that terror of the immigrant," the Board of Special Inquiry. Adjoining this department is the dormitory for the unfortunates labeled "excluded." There is a telegraph and railroad office also on this floor, the latter service also having a large division on the southern end of the ground floor, where the principal agencies will be located. Iron stairways lead from the private quarters of the immigrants to the roofs on either end of the building, which have been dubbed "roof gardens" and "pavilion roofs." The former name being the name given by the immigration authorities, while the latter is a title conferred by the construction forces. Whether there are to be vaudeville or other entertainments, the authorities so far have failed to state. But it can be said, with some degree of authority, that such entertainments as will take place will be given by "stage folk" and other artists who of necessity will have to pass under the supervision of the department. The administration offices and baggage room, together with the railroad departments, occupy the ground floor.

Convenient apartments have been assigned to the Bureau of Information with private rooms for the inspectors, matrons, clerks and other attachés. One of the greatest of the improvements will be the bathing house, where 200 immigrants can be bathed at a time, 8,000 being about the number that can be thus refreshed during an ordinary day. "We expect to wash them once a day, and they will land on American soil clean, if nothing more." said Assistant Commissioner McSweeney a few days ago. This improvement will not be ready for use, however, until the beginning of the new year. The baths will be of the "shower" variety. The restaurant and the laundry, where thousands of pieces of linen and other fabrics can be cleansed daily, besides other routine necessities, will also have a separate pavilion.

The next building in importance to the main one is the hospital situated opposite Governors Island. This structure, while plain in plan, is arranged with perfect details for the purpose for which is to serve. All of the structures on the island are absolutely fireproof, the only inflammable material being the office furniture. The floors are of concrete and slate, the railings of iron, while the beds are combinations of iron and wire netting. The completion of the station will eliminate practically all of the unpleasant and irritating features connected with the Barge Office at the Battery. No longer will the immigrant be defrauded by the boarding-house shark and the faker. The crowd of foreigners who besiege the present quarters every day, making life hideous with their quarrels or cursing the guards and gatemen in a babel of tongues, will be things of the past. At the new station, while everything will be arranged so as to permit the friends of immigrants to see them or visitors to inspect the department, this eliminating of the hoodlum and faker element is to the authorities one of the pleasantest anticipations connected with the transfer so soon to take place. New ferryboats are to be added, better and more substantial docks to be built, and the official force will probably be increased. The spending of the million and a half dollars by the government on Ellis Island will be, according to those best fitted to judge, the beginning of a new era in the complicated system of the immigration service.

EVENING POST,
JANUARY 7, 1905

Influx of Jewish Immigrants

In all probability, when the returns for December are in, the aggregate from Russia alone for 1904 will surpass all previous totals for both the Russian empire and Finland. The greatest element in this immigration, as always, is the Jewish. In general, about 70 per cent of all immigrating Russians are Jews. At this rate, this year's Jewish arrivals from Russia alone promise to be about 100,000. The total Hebrew immigration last year was 106,000 of which 20,000 came from Austria-Hungary and 6,000 from Rumania. The statement, therefore, that Jewish immigration for 1904 will be the greatest on record seems amply warranted. Nor is it surprising. It is caused chiefly by two circumstances—the revival of persecution reaching its most intolerable manifestation in Kishinev and the desire to escape service in the Japanese war. Russia, while denying her Jewish subjects all civil rights, does not object to sending them to Manchuria to stop Japanese bullets. For the Jew, however, even military glory is denied as he is not permitted to rise in the ranks. It is not strange, therefore, that the war does not arouse any sentiments of patriotism and that he should instead think it a particularly auspicious time to seek the land of freedom.

No immigration is more sensitive to economic and political conditions than that of the Russian Jew. Had it not been for the revival of the medieval spirit of persecution in Russia and Austria, the Jewish population of the United States would be comparatively slight. It is from these countries only that Jews in large enough numbers to affect materially our population could be drawn. There are probably not more than 9,000,000 or 10,000,000 Jews in the world of which from 6,000,000 to 7,000,000 are in the old Polish provinces of Russia. Up to 1882, however, they hardly came to this country at all. The reason is that during the reign of Alexander II, from 1855 to 1881, the Jews enjoyed comparative quiet—that is, for Jews. The Czar abandoned the hard policy of Nicholas, encouraged Jewish settlement outside of the Pale, and removed numerous disabilities. The period of Alexander II's reign is still referred to by Jews as their "golden age." Consequently, there was very little immigration during these twenty-six years. Thus, in 1857, at the beginning of the reign, only seventy-four Russians emigrated. In 1870 only a few more than 1,000 came. In the latter years of the reign it increased somewhat as the peace of the Jews began to be disturbed.

In the early eighties came the May Laws, according to which the Jews in the Pale were forced to leave the country and settle in the cities, a regulation that wrought much misery. Thus, in 1882, Russian immigration suddenly jumps to 21,000 and by 1890 had increased to 35,000. In 1891 came perhaps the most serious persecution of all. Jews were forced to leave Russia itself and settle in the Pale. The midnight expulsions from Moscow, the awful sufferings at St. Petersburg and Kiev, the miserable *étapes* of Jews from all the Russian cities and towns, driven into the densely populated districts of the fifteen provinces—all this was reflected in the immigration figures. In 1890, before the outrages began, 35,000 Russians landed in America. In 1892, a year after, 81,000 came over. Thus, the policy of the Russian government reacts immediately upon conditions here. It is not too much to say that the local tenement problem, which is largely a Jewish question, is caused in some measure by the domestic policy of the Czar. The story of Jewish immigration shows that the Jew is naturally homekeeping and that he leaves Russia only under the strongest provocation.

Those who are now leaving to escape military service have to do so, of course, surreptitiously. They have no passports, and must steal across the border into Austria and Germany. From long years of experience, however, they know how to manage that. If they are caught, a few coins placed in proper hands usually insure their escape. Indeed their whole passage through the Russian empire is obtained by wholesale bribery. It is said that there are many Russian officials who do a thriving business smuggling Jews across the frontier. For $10, it is reported, they will agree to get any young man of military age where the recruiting officer will not find him. This custom of buying their way is familiar enough to the Russian Jews in other matters. With the thousands of restrictive laws against them, they are ready victims to the blackmailing propensities of Russian officials. Nearly all the privileges they enjoy they get by purchase. It is frequently said that the police on the East Side debauch the civic morals of the Jew. Even Tammany at its worst, however, can probably teach him nothing new in official corruption. The blackmail which he has submitted to as a pushcart man and small merchant is only a continuation of the extortion to which he has always been accustomed. According to all reports, the Jews who come to escape conscription are most desirable immigrants. They are able-bodied young men, between eighteen and thirty, clean and fairly well supplied with money—as they must be to get here. In the latest report of the Immigration Bureau they are well spoken of.

THE NEW YORK TIMES, JANUARY 29, 1905

Are We Facing an Immigration Peril?

They never know on Ellis Island when the Commissioner General of Immigration is coming. But they always know when he is there. His name, which was received in Vermont some forty-five years ago and borne to Arizona as a young man beginning a hard-working career in railroading, is Frank P. Sargent. Sometimes he is addressed as Grover Cleveland by mistake. Any caricature of Commissioner General Sargent is likely to resemble the Sage of Princeton, and here the resemblance abruptly ends. For while the one is disposed to move more slowly and seldom, the other is as uncertain in his movements as the gyrations of an automobile or the appearance of a funnel-shaped cloud. His official territory embracing every highway into the United States—at the gates of which more than a million aliens during the waning fiscal year will have knocked for admission by or before June 30—his appearance here or there is governed generally by the loudness of the knocking. This brought him to Ellis Island a few days ago, when nearly five thousand immigrants were clamoring for admission in a dozen tongues and thronging the great double doors of the metropolis. The grave and growing importance of the immigration problem is based upon positive assurances that upward of a million aliens will this year be added to the population of the United States—a record-breaking year. To the vast tidal wave of controversy which the existing situation has let loose over the country, the declaration of Commissioner General Sargent that the United States is swiftly approaching, or already faces one of the gravest crises of its history—a crisis which he believes can only be met and mastered by immediate remedial legislation tending to restrict immigration and also to deflect it toward the more sparsely settled sections. He foresees a gigantic western immigration movement by reason of the gathering revolution in Russia, and he strongly advises congressional action tending to strengthen the hands of the Immigration Bureau in coping adequately with the situation. Vast hordes of fear-driven, poverty-stricken Russians, especially of southern Russia, are pouring through every loophole of escape to this country according to information in his possession, and scores of secret agencies in London,

Paris, Berlin, and Vienna are daily stimulating the movement at an average fee of $10 a person.

Commissioner General Sargent was seated in his office, the windows of which command a sweeping view of the harbor. Physically large and of a girth partly inherited and partly acquired from a hearty fondness for life and the things which make it worth living, he occupies one of the amplest seats of the mighty under the present administration. Crude fighting power is boldly written about the jaw and base of the brain, just as kindliness and a sense of humor are traceable in the lines radiating from the corners of the shrewd gray eyes. Piecing these characteristics together a solid, perhaps stolid Scotch–Irish ancestry is revealed with an added sharpness of expression attributable to the Vermont grindstone which the Commissioner General turned as a lad. One might travel far and fail of finding a more representative American.

"By present conditions," he explained, "present laws or rather legal restrictions are meant. Put me down in the beginning as being fairly and unalterably opposed to what has been called the open door, for the time has come when every American citizen who is ambitious for the national future must regard with grave misgiving the mighty tide of immigration that, unless something is done, will soon poison or at least pollute the very fountainhead of American life and progress. Big as we are and blessed with an iron constitution, we cannot safely swallow such an endless-course dinner, so to say, without getting indigestion and perhaps national appendicitis."

"Do you mean that the danger is immediate or prospective?" was asked.

"Both," he replied promptly. "Today there is an enormous alien population in our larger cities which is breeding crime and disease at a rate all the more dangerous because it is more or less hidden and insidious. But the greatest source of uneasiness has to do with the future. Under present conditions nearly one-half the immigrants who pass through this port never get beyond New York City and State, or the immediately contiguous territory. Unless something is done to discourage this gradual consolidation, it is my fear and belief that within five years the alien population of the country, or rather cities, will constitute a downright peril.

"On the other hand," continued the Commissioner General, "the South, the Southwest, and the great West are rapidly opening up new industries, tapping new industrial fields at such a rate as demands more labor. Hardly a day passes but that scores of letters are received at my office in Washington calling for the better class of immigrant labor in those sections, and we are doing everything possible to encourage immigration in that direction.

"But," sweeping his hand toward Washington, "Congress must untie and strengthen our hands before we can accomplish anything adequate in the premises. For in order to grapple with the situation properly it will be necessary to establish bureaus of information at each immigration office to acquaint the newcomers with the need for various classes of labor in the national suburbs, so to say. It is my earnest wish and ambition to see such a bureau established in the immediate future," was added in a tone calculated to carry past the Capitol building to the White House.

"There is an unfounded idea," pursued Commissioner General Sargent, "that an immigrant must have $100 as a financial credential. Under present regulations no money at all is required, the question of eligibility being left entirely to the judges of inspection. Frequently," was admitted, "we are warranted in passing persons, particularly young men of unblemished physique and mental equipment, who are without a dollar on earth. Several such instances have come to my notice where newcomers have secured work and become useful citizens.

"But," gripping the adjoining table with a hand capable of making anything save dry wood wince, "there would be few utterly destitute immigrants were it not for the pernicious soliciting system practiced by certain transportation companies. We would today have an immeasurably higher type of immigration but for such grasping corporations or rather their agents, who, for a small commission, are scouring Europe for steerage passengers. Last year over 8,000 aliens were deported, and it would melt a heart of stone to see them. Come with me," he added, rising and leading the way through corridor after corridor, past men, women and children herded like cattle and hardly more intelligent, until, throwing open a door at the far end of the building, a motley assemblage of vice-ridden, stolid, bovine parodies of manhood was disclosed.

Passing out again, the Commissioner continued: "Nine-tenths of them are not here of their own volition. They were encouraged to come by irresponsible criminal agents or solicitors, such as many steamship companies maintain abroad. Of course," by way of parenthesis, as he opened the door to what is known as the first-degree examination room, "the steamship companies which brought them here must maintain them and stand the expense of taking them back. Doubting Thomases sometimes inquire how the steamship companies can afford to bring over such creatures on the hazard of deporting them. My answer is that a steerage passenger can be brought over and taken back and the company will still have pocketed a profit of 33 per cent on the transaction. This despite fines aggregating $31,000 imposed upon the steamship companies last year. It is infamous, outrageous, and it should be made a subject of international inquiry," declared the Commissioner vehemently.

Advancing to a position within the railing, it was seen that a woman, accompanied by seven children ranging from a babe in arms to a daughter quite as old as the mother in appearance, was being examined. Commissioner Sargent explained that visitors were seldom or never permitted to witness this first degree. Only at the second, third, and fourth examina-

tions are spectators allowed. This was the tribunal frequently criticized as being a sort of inquisition. Crowding the benches outside the railing were specimens of nearly every nationality under the sun. Chinamen elbowed Magyars; Celts and Teutons rubbed shoulders with Gauls and Latins; Russians, resembling so many John the Baptists in their primitive sheepskin coats, trod the heels of ale-hued Turks; screaming children, scowling men, and patient, resigned women made up the curious ensemble. Asked how much money she and her children had, the woman under examination signaled to her daughers, and each, stooping, produced a handful of silver and copper—enough to get them to West Virginia, where the woman said she had a son. His address being learned, a telegram was dispatched to him, and the family was remanded to the waiting room pending an answer. Four in twelve of those examined were ticketed for deportation, two being afflicted with trachoma, one with tuberculosis, and one with friendless poverty, cloaking general debility.

"This is a fair sample of the immigrants we are getting," commented the Commissioner. "During the present month all records for deportation have been broken, over a thousand immigrants having been ineligible for admission into the country. What is the principal reason for their ineligibility?" he repeated. "Disease and destitution. Since the outbreak of the Russo-Japanese war thousands and thousands of Russian Jews are fleeing here to escape conscription. Poor fellows, most of them are hardly more than food for powder, having been ill-fed, ill-housed, and ill-clad all their lives, and the impromptu accommodations here on the island are amazing luxuries to them. Others who are being deported today are contract laborers and decrepit men and women inveigled by steamship agents who have willfully disregarded the law."

Probing on into the subject with savage jabs, as though it were a sore that needed a thorough amputation, the Commissioner General declared that the appearance in the United States of a sweeping plague—especially on the east sides of our cities—of European importation would surprise no medical man familiar with foreign conditions and in touch with the swollen tide of immigration flowing towards us from sources beyond the jurisdiction of modern sanitation. Hardly a month passes, he continued, but that evidences of cholera and bubonic plague are discovered at one or more seaports of southern Europe. Trachoma, an insidious and disabling eye disease is now sweeping from Spain to Constantinople, nearly 20,000 intending immigrants having been rejected last year at Naples because of trachoma.

"But is it not possible of detection before the diseased immigrant is permitted entrance into the country?" was asked.

For reply, it was admitted that in advanced stages of the affliction, this could be and is being done. "But," the Commissioner went on, "it is contagious, and where afflicted persons are confined for days in congested steerages, others contract it, only to discover their condition after being admitted into the country. Cooped up in narrow quarters, unable to exercise even the most ordinary requirements of cleanliness, immigrant passengers are exposed by wholesale to whatever disease may be in circulation. Hence it is now my earnest endeavor to have Congress take action tending to establish marine hospital agencies at the leading ports of Europe and Asia where immigrants embark for the United States. While they would not have authority, save by international legislation, to exclude people from foreign ships at foreign ports, if any steamship company insisted upon taking a man whose rejection had been advised by the American physician, we over here would be warned in time to act upon advices received and so detain the exposed persons until such time as it could be shown that they had not contracted disease. This system is now working admirably at a few ports where our examiners are stationed, and it should most emphatically be practiced everywhere."

Leading the way to another section of the great barn-like but admirably equipped structure, the Commissioner entered a room filled almost entirely with boys ranging from ten to fourteen years of age. A major part of them, he explained, were Armenians and Greeks, who had been brought over to be farmed out as bootblacks, newsboys, and barber-shop attendants. Sweeping the motley company with his eyes, as though weighing and finding them wanting, the Commissioner General vouchsafed that hardly one in twenty of them had left home voluntarily and that unless they could satisfy the inspectors that they had relatives amply qualified to care for them they would one and all be deported. Speaking earnestly and forcefully as he passed into another corridor leading to a large room congested with detained women and girls, the Commissioner arraigned what he called the European slave traders who traffic in flesh and blood by bringing not only girls under age but immoral women, confirmed invalids, and criminals to the United States. "During the past year there has been a notable increase in the number of criminals coming over here," he continued, "some of them being the worst criminals of Europe. There is no question about it, for we have positive evidence of the fact. In short, the time has come for the country to demand to know the character of immigrants that Europe is shedding or trying to shed."

Continuing, the Commissioner stated that in several European cities, with or without the connivance of the authorities, inmates of hospitals and almshouses were, there was reason to believe, being provided with tickets and means of reaching Ellis Island. Approximately 5 per cent of deportation cases come under this class, he estimated.

EDWIN LEVICK/IMMIGRANTS ON ATLANTIC LINER, c. 1906/LIBRARY OF CONGRESS

BYRON/STEERAGE DECK OF THE SS *PENNLAND*, c. 1893
THE BYRON COLLECTION, MUSEUM OF THE CITY OF NEW YORK

UNKNOWN PHOTOGRAPHER/ELLIS ISLAND, c. 1905/CULVER PICTURES, INC.

LEWIS W. HINE/ITALIAN IMMIGRANTS ON FERRY, 1905/GEORGE EASTMAN HOUSE

UNKNOWN PHOTOGRAPHER/SLOVAK WOMEN,
ELLIS ISLAND, WINTER, 1907/BROWN BROTHERS

UNKNOWN PHOTOGRAPHER/IMMIGRANTS ARRIVING AT ELLIS ISLAND, c. 1905/CULVER PICTURES, INC.

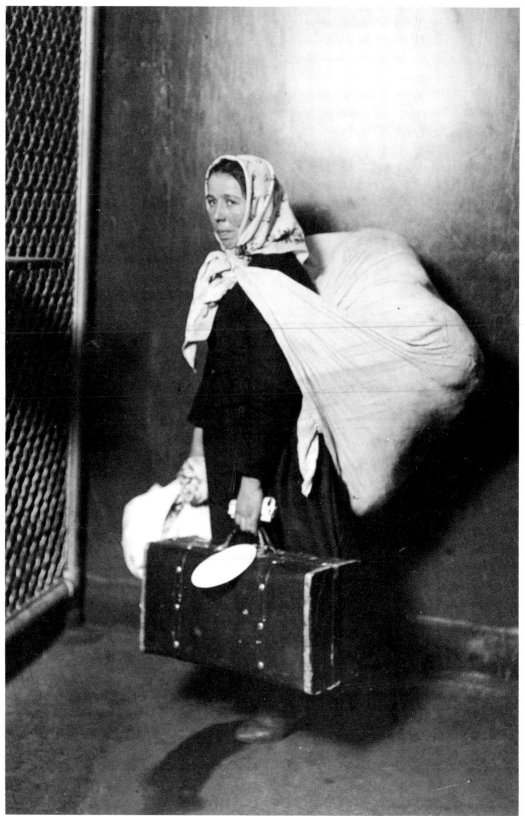

LEWIS W. HINE/SLOVAK WOMAN, ELLIS ISLAND, 1905/GEORGE EASTMAN HOUSE

UNKNOWN PHOTOGRAPHER/ITALIAN IMMIGRANTS FROM THE S.S. *PRINCESS IRENE* ON THEIR WAY TO ELLIS ISLAND,
c. 1905/THE GRANGER COLLECTION

LEWIS W. HINE/ITALIAN IMMIGRANTS, ELLIS ISLAND,
1905/GEORGE EASTMAN HOUSE

UNDERWOOD & UNDERWOOD/EXAMINING EYES, ELLIS ISLAND, 1913/LIBRARY OF CONGRESS

UNKNOWN PHOTOGRAPHER/WAITING AND PROCESSING, ELLIS ISLAND, c. 1910/NEW YORK PUBLIC LIBRARY

UNKNOWN PHOTOGRAPHER/PROCESSING IMMIGRANTS
AT ELLIS ISLAND, c. 1905/CULVER PICTURES, INC.

UNKNOWN PHOTOGRAPHER/DINING ROOM AT ELLIS ISLAND, c. 1905/CULVER PICTURES, INC.

UNKNOWN PHOTOGRAPHER/MEN'S DORMITORY, ELLIS ISLAND, c. 1920/UNDERWOOD & UNDERWOOD

UNKNOWN PHOTOGRAPHER/ELLIS ISLAND CLASSROOM, c. 1924/UNDERWOOD & UNDERWOOD

UNKNOWN PHOTOGRAPHER/JEWISH IMMIGRANT, c. 1905/CULVER PICTURES, INC.

UNKNOWN PHOTOGRAPHER/IMMIGRANTS AT ELLIS ISLAND, c. 1905/BROWN BROTHERS

UNKNOWN PHOTOGRAPHER/ITALIAN MOTHER AND CHILD IN DINING ROOM AT ELLIS ISLAND,
c. 1905/BROWN BROTHERS

LEWIS W. HINE/JEWISH IMMIGRANT, c. 1915/GEORGE EASTMAN HOUSE

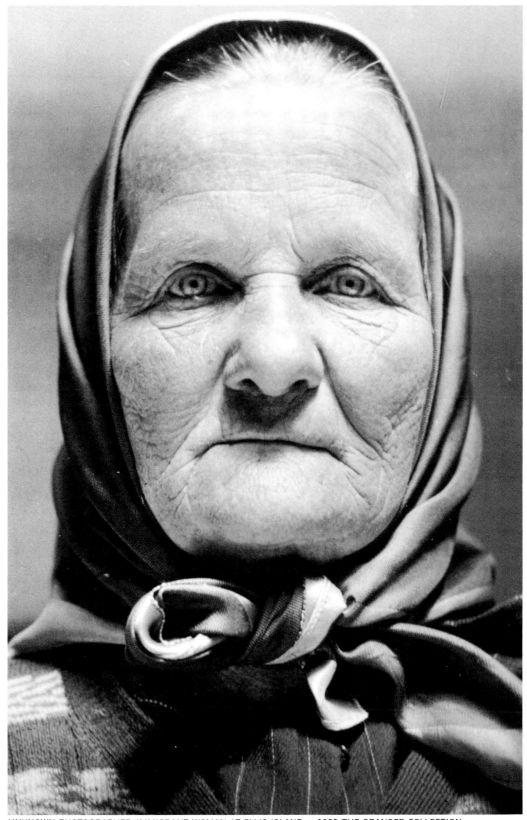

UNKNOWN PHOTOGRAPHER/IMMIGRANT WOMAN AT ELLIS ISLAND, c. 1920/THE GRANGER COLLECTION

LEWIS W. HINE/ARMENIAN JEW, ELLIS ISLAND, c. 1924/PHOTO LEAGUE ARCHIVE, NEW YORK PUBLIC LIBRARY

LEWIS W. HINE/GRANDMOTHER, ELLIS ISLAND, c. 1924/GEORGE EASTMAN HOUSE

UNKNOWN PHOTOGRAPHER/MAN IN BOOTS, c. 1910/ NEW YORK PUBLIC LIBRARY

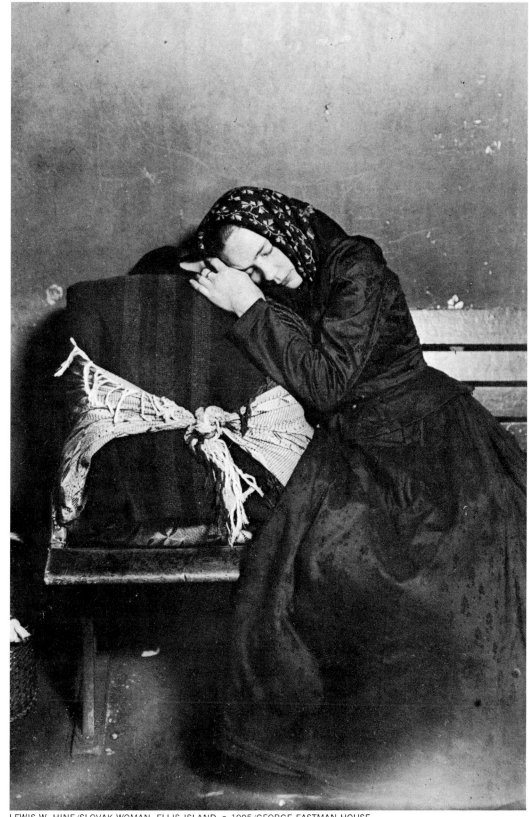

LEWIS W. HINE/SLOVAK WOMAN, ELLIS ISLAND, c.1905/GEORGE EASTMAN HOUSE

UNKNOWN PHOTOGRAPHER/NEW YORK SKYLINE, 1883
THE NEW YORK HISTORICAL SOCIETY

UNKNOWN PHOTOGRAPHER/IMMIGRANTS ARRIVING MANHATTAN, c. 1905/CULVER PICTURES, INC.

UNKOWN PHOTOGRAPHER/ARRIVING, BARGE OFFICE, c. 1900/LIBRARY OF CONGRESS

R. F. TURNBULL/RUSSIAN IMMIGRANT, 1900/LIBRARY OF CONGRESS

THE NEW YORK TIMES,
NOVEMBER 14, 1897

The Ghetto Market, Hester Street

It is quite unnecessary to go to Europe in order to see a genuine Jewish ghetto. There is one, a large one, the largest in the New World, in fact, right here in New York. It is true that the New York ghetto is not as interesting from a purely historical point of view as those which are to be found in Vienna and in Rome and which date back to and are historic survivals of the Middle Ages. But the New York ghetto is an inexhaustible mine of interest and information for those who delight in studying the life, manners, and customs of a race which is unique among the races of the globe. The Russian–Jewish inhabitants of the New York ghetto, while certainly somewhat affected by Americanizing influences, live together in such numbers that they have to a large extent retained their own peculiar modes of life. Many a striking picture is presented to the view of the interested observer who walks through the section of New York south of Houston Street and east of the Bowery.

No expensive steamship fares need be paid in order to visit this American ghetto. Step off a Third Avenue car at the corner of Hester Street and the Bowery some Friday morning and walk east along the former street. I say "Friday morning" because the market, striking and characteristic of the ghetto and its life, is held on that day. This is done so that an ample store of eatables may be laid in for *Shabbes* (the Jewish Sabbath) on the morrow. The most orthodox of these Russian Jews and those who wish to observe the religion of their fathers strictly must do all their cooking and preparing for *Shabbes* before the first three stars appear in the Friday eve sky. Not even a match may be lighted, not a bit of paper torn, or

a line written if the holy day is to be properly observed. So Friday is a busy day, with its marketing, its cooking, its cleaning, and the other preparations for the Sabbath.

It is indeed worth-while going a few blocks out of one's way to see this Friday morning scene. The pavements along both sides of Hester Street are lined by a continuous double row of pushcarts filled with eatables of every kind agreeable to the palate of the Russian Jew. The latecomers among the vendors, no longer able to secure a place for their carts along the main avenue of the market, form an overflow market along the pavements of the side streets—Ludlow, Essex, Norfolk, and Suffolk. Here is a cart laden with grapes and pears, and the fruit merchant, a short, dark-complexioned, bearded fellow, clad as to outer garments in an old cap, a dark-blue sweater, and a nondescript pair of dirty-hued trousers, is shrieking at the top of his voice: *"Gutes frucht! Gutes frucht! Metziehs! Drei pennies die whole lot."* ("Good fruit! Good fruit! Bargains! Three pennies a whole lot.") Such a vendor's call is fairly indicative of the sort of jargon that passes current as the common language of the ghetto. In the few words that the fruit peddler has bawled out in order to attract the bewigged women to his cart, he has managed to introduce some bad German, a Hebrew word, and a hybrid phrase of German and English parentage. Sometimes there are a few words of Russian, Hungarian, or Rumanian mingled in the phrases, acording to the particular country of which the speaker is a native. For, although the Russians constitute the very large majority of the residents of this district, there are immigrants from all parts of Austria, from Germany, from Rumania, and from Turkey as well living here in this cosmopolitan ghetto.

The numbers of bewigged women seem to be continually increasing, and the street becomes more and more crowded. Bewigged these women are because they are married. The theory is that after marriage a woman should be attractive to her lord and master alone and that if she once cuts her hair and wears a wig, it will be not only for a sign that she is no longer fancy-free but will also serve to make her unattractive to other men than her husband. What effect such a "wigging" has upon the husband's admiration of his wife is, it seems, a matter of no importance.

Instead of heeding the hoarse, guttural cries of the fruit merchant and his fellow vendors close by, women and market baskets swarm and push and jostle around some pushcarts at the lower end of the street, the contents of which seem to possess a peculiar power of attraction. It is not necessary to get even within seeing distance to tell what the magnet is. Another organ of sense besides the eye informs one that it is fish—big fish and little fish, light fish and dark fish, bluefish and whitefish, fresh fish and fish not quite so fresh—which form the centers of the little eager groups. These people love fish, and that dish is generally the *pièce de résistance* of the Friday evening meal. *Shabbes* fish, *gefuellte* fish, fish cooked sweet and sour, indeed, fish prepared in all the ways imaginable and in some ways quite beyond the realms of the ordinary imagination are the noble ends appointed for these finny treasures of the sea. For fish is good *kosher* (clean) food, and a particularly appropriate viand with which to usher in the Sabbath.

But these women who jabber and jostle and haggle with the vendors and paw over the wet and glistening and silvery piles upon the carts and finally go off the triumphant owners of particularly desirable bargains do not think of this as a reason for their purchases. They know that *mei mann* is very fond of a fish supper, as well as "Mosche" and "Rachele" and little "Smulche," and all the rest of the multitudinous ghetto household. And so that noisy market goes merrily on. After the fish have been bought and the other vendors get their share of the trade, buyers and sellers depart well satisfied until next Friday, when the whole living picture will again appear at the same place.

A result of the mighty economic forces that shape men's lives is an elderly, bearded man who is hung about with his stock in trade—his suspenders, his shoestrings, and his gaily colored handkerchiefs. A walking shop, he will never be able to change his condition. Unlike the many thousands of his younger fellow countrymen and coreligionists who, upon their arrival in this country, set about learning to make coats, pantaloons, vests, shirts, etc., he was too old to learn a new trade. He had not capital enough to open a shop, not even a very small one. There was but one resource left to him whereby to make a living: he must peddle. And so he invested in a small stock of cheap goods; now, if business is good, he is able to eke out a bare existence. Cigarette in hand or mouth, he shuffles along the street or haunts the Bowery or the Friday morning market in the ghetto, and his cry of "Suspen'ehs! Cullah Bottens!" is a familiar one in and about the Jewish quarter. He loves dearly to stop and chat (*Schmoos,* he calls it,) with some old crony, to retail the small talk of the quarter which he has gathered during his transactions with his customers, or to exchange *mayselakh,* or anecdotes, with a kindred soul. The cigarette is his constant companion and friend, and he puffs at it with all the keen delight of a callow collegian.

Aye, so are all these people human, intensely so, and many are the sides upon which their lives are keenly interesting, because, while somewhat strange to us, they have the "touch of nature that makes the whole world kin," and the very strangeness lends an additional charm and attractiveness to the student of mankind. There are the manifold scenes in the synagogue and the domestic life of this pious and home-loving people, those interesting glimpses of typical Russo-Jewish life to be found at the theaters, the weddings and merrymakings, and finally the funerals of these people. Even the daily drudgery and toil of these immigrants is worth the study of the careful student of humanity.

East Side
Street Vendors

We take everything in sight," said a Russian fish vendor to a reporter for the New York *Times* yesterday, at Essex and Hester Streets. "What difference does it make if we take up the street with our carts? There is nobody in this neighborhood but Russians, and I am sure none of them complain." This vendor was one of the many who obstruct the streets in the old Seventh Ward, making Ludlow, Suffolk, Hester, and Canal Streets almost impassible for pedestrians. The claim of the vendor that Russians and Polanders in the neighborhood did not complain was evidently true. The streets thereabout swarm with people with pushcarts and stands. Early in the morning the people start out to buy food for the day. The street stands are piled high with food, but it is food that would make the average citizen turn his nose high in the air.

A bread stand first attracted the reporter's attention. "The bread," said the woman attendant, "is called Polish bread." It is made up of huge loaves as black as tar. Next to the bread stand was a fish stand, attended by two stalwart Rumanians. Every time the Rumanians handled a fish they made movements which threw fish scales and slime on the loaves of bread on the next stand. This they did not seem to mind; neither did they notice the horrible stench that came from the putrid fish. A little way from the fish stand was another pushcart, on which were pieces of fresh meat and dead fowl. A huge swarm of great blue flies buzzed about and laid their eggs on the meat, which was already alive with the larvae of insects. Another stand had cheese for sale. A slatternly young woman, who had a scarcity of cloth-ing and who was tending the stand, called it *käse*. It did not require a microscope to detect the mites, for they were large and lively. The reporter got to the windward of the stand and received such a shock from the powerful odor thrown out that he almost had a spasm. Phew, how that cheese did smell! Yet, in spite of the fact that the cheese was a reeking mass of rottenness and alive with worms, the long whiskered descendants of Abraham, Isaac, Jacob, and Judah on the East Side would put their fingers in it and then suck them with great and evident relish.

Nearby was a soda fountain, from which a dirty boy, about fifteen years of age, was drawing a turbid liquor which he called "Jewish beer." This was drunk by the vendors with great gusto and smacking of lips. After the vendors had swallowed their beer the attendant would give the tumblers a hurried rinse in a pail of water which looked as if it had been used to mop out a cow stable. Then the glass, dirty and foul, would be ready for the next customer for "Jewish beer."

A writer might go on for a week reciting the abominations of these people and still have much to tell. One of their greatest faults is that they have an utter disregard for law. There is a certain hour when they are required to set out their garbage and ash cans, but they pay no attention to that. The ash cart comes along and takes what is in sight, and perhaps five minutes later some of these people will empty pail after pail of household ashes and garbage into the middle of the street. If they are arrested for this or any other offense, hundreds of their compatriots and coreligionists follow them to the courts and stand ready to swear in their favor. Filthy persons and clothing reeking with vermin are seen on every side. Many of these people are afflicted with diseases of the skin. Children are covered with sores, and hundreds of them are nearly blind with sore eyes. There is hardly a person among the whole crowd of street vendors who has not sores underneath the finger nails and between the fingers. Some time ago the city government decided to help these people to keep clean. Asphalt pavements were laid in the district with the hope that the streets would be kept cleaner, but they are now a sight to behold, being filthier than the old block pavement ever was.

The neighborhood where these people live is absolutely impassable for wheeled vehicles other than their pushcarts. If a truck driver tries to get through where their pushcarts are standing they apply to him all kinds of vile and indecent epithets. The driver is fortunate if he gets out of the street without being hit with a stone or having a putrid fish or piece of meat thrown in his face. This neighborhood, peopled almost entirely by the people who claim to have been driven from Poland and Russia, is the eyesore of New York and perhaps the filthiest place on the western continent. It is impossible for a Christian to live there because he will be driven out, either by blows or the dirt and stench. Cleanliness is an unknown quantity to these people. They cannot be lifted up to a higher plane because they do not want to be. If the cholera should ever get among these people, they would scatter its germs as a sower does grain.

NEW YORK TRIBUNE, SEPTEMBER 15, 1898

Thursday in Hester Street

The neighborhood of Hester, Norfolk and Essex Streets presents a quaint scene. The streets are black with purchasers, and bright with the glare of hundreds of torches from the pushcarts. The faces are markedly of a Oriental type; and the voices of the peddlers crying their wares, the expostulations of the purchasers, the mingling of the "Yiddish," of the elders with the English of the young people, make a strange medley of sounds.

Great is the variety of wares to be seen on the carts. Dr. Wolborst, who is much interested in the peddlers, has stated that what cannot be bought in the pushcart market cannot easily be bought in New York. A friend of his wanted to match some draperies. After visiting the best stores uptown she inspected the wares of some Hester Street peddlers and found what she required. The dry goods peddlers buy remnants, odd pieces and samples from wholesale houses at low prices. A woman bought a remnant of valuable lace from the peddler. A pair of curtains of similar lace would have cost $75. She paid 50 cents. A friend of hers begged her to sell the piece for $20. She did so, returned to the peddler and invested in a sufficient number of similar remnants to make vestibule curtains and other lace furnishings for all the rooms in her house. From bits of lace, bought for a trifle from the peddlers, other women have made fichus, capes, overskirts, etc. Pieces of fine cloth in sizes from half a yard to several yards are often sold at low rates. Squares of carpets such as the sales-men take out on the road as samples have been bought from the peddlers for a trifle and converted into handsome rugs. One ingenious woman carpeted a large room by joining a number of squares of harmonious pattern and color. She called it a "harlequin carpet" and it was much admired.

But the peddlers who vend such materials are not numerous. Most of the goods are of ordinary quality. Stockings may be bought for 6 cents a pair, children's undergarments for 5 cents apiece. Many of the carts are filled with rolls of oilcloth or wallpapers. The smaller articles of household furniture—crockery, glassware, tins, etc.—are displayed. Ready-made clothing is cheap. Each cart has its specialty, but in the line of carts there is a strange medley. Dried fruits, fresh fruit, pickles, preserves, vegetables, meat and fish alternate with household utensils, boots and shoes, jewelry and clothing, books and stationery.

The fish carts are largely in the majority. The wholesale merchants sell the fish at auction to the peddlers who go in crowds to the stores of the dealers and have a lively but anxious time in trying to outbid one another. Sometimes the fish is condemned by the Health Department, to the great loss of the peddlers. As many as fifty tons of fish are sometimes seized from them in a day. Charles B. Stover and other members of the Social Reform Club have taken up the cause of the fish peddlers and are trying to remedy some of the ills from which they suffer. It is proposed to utilize a part of the Hester Street Park for a fish market in the mornings, the building to be used for other purposes later in the day. In this way the peddlers would be relieved from paying tribute to the police which they do in order to avoid arrests for obstructing the streets. Those who pay regularly are not molested.

It is estimated that there are 1,500 peddlers of various wares in that vicinity. The regular peddler pays $25 a year for his license with the additional fees to the police. He can hardly earn more than $5 a week so he often hires a pushcart for his wife, and sometimes the children too are brought into the service. The rent of a pushcart is 10 cents a day. Many of the peddlers are only temporarily in the trade. Tailors or mechanics who are out of work hire a pushcart until they find a position. Recently landed immigrants are advised by their friends to take a pushcart until they can establish themselves in some business.

NEW YORK TRIBUNE,
JULY 28, 1901

The Delights of Haggling

It is generally conceded that to practice properly the art of shopping in any place at any time requires leisure and experience, and if this is true of the great stores, it is infinitely more pithy in regard to many of the smaller establishments on the East Side. To decide on the style and quality one wants and on the price one is prepared to pay may be the only tasks of the well-to-do shopper, but in out-of-the-way parts of the city the element of bargaining enters into the transaction further to complicate the affair. The would-be purchaser must have not only a clear idea of what he wants, but also a knowledge of the value of the various prices of goods which are set before him. The price asked by the storekeeper is certainly not what he will be willing to accept under proper moral suasion, and it is necessary for the buyer to judge just how far it is safe to push the seller without bringing on himself a torrent of abusive language and prematurely closing the deal. In many of the smaller East Side shops it is safe to assume that the seller will accept about one-half of the price he asks at first. To accomplish this, however, great tact and patience are required. The worm is likely to turn, and, after all, time, even on the East Side, has a certain value.

It is not uncommon to see two men in some small shop haggling for ten or fifteen minutes over the price of a suit of clothes, for instance. Eight dollars is the price demanded by the shopkeeper. The buyer laughs pleasantly and suggests that he means four dollars. With indignation in his honest eye the storekeeper states emphatically that he means what he said, that he sells his goods as cheaply as anybody, and that the clothes cost him $7.50, anyway. Automatically, the customer repeats, "Four dollars," and he gazes calmly while the man rages. This sort of thing will be kept up for ten minutes or so. Finally the situation is that the one has gone up to $4.50 and the other has come down to $6. About this time the customer will shake his head, apparently wondering at the depravity of traders in general, and will leave the place. Then the storekeeper rushes to the door and shouts, "Five an' a half!" The departing purchaser, whose walk has been suspiciously slow, will return and say, with an engaging smile, "Five," and the deal will be closed.

The whole transaction, irrespective of the choosing of the suit, has taken perhaps fifteen minutes. Neither grudges the time for the whole thing is sport to them—a case of finding foemen worthy of their steel —and they have enjoyed the combat. The "one-price" stores are tame in comparison; anybody can shop in them, even the women from uptown, who always hand over what is asked and have no spirit of sportiness discernible. Some good citizens of the East Side come, in time, to win a local reputation for their bargaining ability, and are sought after by their friends when there is any purchasing to be done.

Besides the bargaining, East Side shopping has much that is picturesque to recommend it. The vast majority of small shops have at the back a room or two in which the family lives. Without any eavesdropping it is possible to see much of the family life; indeed, not to see it one would have to be deaf and blind. On winter days, when the entrance of a breath of fresh air has been guarded against as if it entailed the plague, the odors of the last week's meals make a detective of another sense as well. In some of the shops, especially in neighborhoods which cherish the herring and the national sauerkraut, intending purchasers who may have some slight prejudice against these honest articles of diet have to make their purchases between gasps, as it were, retreating to the door like whales, when it is absolutely imperative to draw breath. The worst of it is that to any person sentimentally inclined the poverty of the little household and its evident need of every cent that can be coaxed its way overbalances the discomfort of such shopping and lure the feet of dwellers on the East Side into these strongholds of unsavoriness.

It is not true that all these tiny shops are unpleasant to visit. In some of them one gets delightful glimpses of a well–ordered and happy household. One shoe-store, in particular, is a spot for pessimists to visit when they despair of humanity. A settlement woman discovered the place and spread the knowledge of it among her friends. She had taken a boot there for some mending, being of an economical turn of mind, and the keeper of the store had said that the work would cost 25 cents, which seemed entirely reasonable. When she returned for the boot she put down the quarter and was struck dumb with astonishment to have the man hand her a nickel, with the remark: "There wasn't as much work on it as I thought there would be. 'Taint worth a quarter." As she said afterward, it seemed like spoiling an idyl to make him take the money; so she pocketed the nickel and went on her way wondering.

Of course, virtue had its reward, and some evil–minded persons suggest that the man knew he would secure her patronage forever and a day at the cost of a nickel. She stoutly maintains that this is a libel, for he could not possibly have realized the extent of the sentimentality of the person with whom he was dealing. It is a trifle uncomfortable at times to be restricted to one small East Side shoeshop, but she declares that she feels quite like a criminal if she wanders away to the abodes of fashion on the West Side. The honesty of the proprietor is not the only attraction she has found in the little shop. The wife is a comfortable woman of generous proportions, and the name of her family is legion. As she tries on the shoes of the customers, she shouts directions of a domestic nature back into the obscurity of the rear room, and she never fails to accompany the order with a term of endearment. "Keep that baby away from the stove, my love," she will direct, and a sweet little maiden will appear and grasp the wandering youngest scion of the house. Or it will be "Julius, dear, look that the soup won't burn," and so on. Everybody is invariably cheery and affectionate. It is a real tonic to a jaded soul just to step into the small shop.

One woman who has shopped a good deal on the East Side says there is more occasion for gratified vanity in an hour among these small shops than in any other occupation she knows of. "You walk in," she explained, "and you say, in a queenly fashion, that you want an umbrella, adding,

'The best in the store,' and every member of the family will run to look at you and to seek the desired umbrella, making you feel like the most bloated kind of aristocrat. When the umbrella comes, you pay $1.69 and go away covered with glory. In the same way you step into a shop which is not one-price, ask for a handkerchief or two, and pay 15 cents apiece for them without the slightest haggling, which brings blessings on your head and gives you a fine sense of superiority. There is nothing like it "

THE NEW YORK TIMES,
MARCH 6, 1893

Streets Buried in Filth

The condition of the streets of this city has been so much written about and talked about during the past few weeks that the subject has become a bore. People have become accustomed to wading around in mixed snow and mud, and now are inclined to regard the evil as a necessary one and to believe that the only relief from it will be the coming of warm weather, which will carry the snow off. Getting about on foot during the past six weeks has been such a difficult matter that those who could have taken a conveyance, even to travel two or three blocks. Consequently it may be interesting for people, whose observation of the condition of the streets has been limited to the thoroughfares through which they have been obliged to pass in the conduct of their daily affairs, to learn something of the general state of affairs throughout the city. A general inspection made yesterday by a reporter of the New York *Times* warrants the statement that unless heroic remedies are applied immediately, the state of affairs that will prevail with the first spell of warm weather is not pleasant to anticipate. Most people are longing for the coming of gentle spring weather, March being the month when anticipation is prone to run in that line. Three or four days of warm spring weather will give most of the streets of this city the appearance of veritable mud rivers.

When men have a grievance, their first impulse is to place the responsibility for it. New York has a Street Cleaning Department. Mr. Brennan, its head, declares that the snowfall this winter has been so heavy as to give his department a task which it cannot accomplish. He says he has hired all the men and all the carts which he has been able to secure in an attempt to clean the streets of snow, but that the coming of one fall upon another has been too much for him. Accepting Mr. Brennan's statement that if he "had a half million men" and ten times as many carts as he has he could not clean out the streets does not in any degree lessen the discomfort and the danger of the situation.

A tour over the city will prove that however much or little effort may have been made by the Street Cleaning Department, the streets generally are in quite as bad a condition as if nothing had been done. The exception to this—and it is the more marked because it tends to indicate what might be done elsewhere—is the main artery of the city, represented by Broadway and Fifth Avenue and the busiest portions of a few of the main cross streets, such as Forty-second Street, Twenty-third Street, Fourteenth Street, Canal Street, and a few of the downtown streets. These are comparatively clean. All the other streets of the city might be divided into two classes, those through which streetcars pass and those through which streetcars do not pass. In the former, the snow, mixed with mud and such rubbish and filth as naturally accumulate, has been thrown up by the snow plows sent over the car lines and piled, together with the snow shoveled off the pavements, between the horsecar tracks and the curb lines. Like miniature mountain ranges these piles of dirt and filth-burdened snow run through the streets, their height varying from two or three to five or six feet, according to the amount of space adjoining that the horsecar lines and property owners had to clear off. In streets where there are no horsecar lines, the snow is not thus piled up. In the ordinary crosstown street, where the pavements are not wide, there is a depth of about two feet of well-packed snow along the curb lines, caused by the shoveling off of the sidewalks, and the middle of the street is covered with all the snow that has fallen on it during the winter, except such as has thawed, which is not much. Traffic has ground the snow and the dirt on which it fell all together, until now it looks like granulated frozen mud. Such is the prevailing condition all over the city except for one place, where it is much worse. That place is the downtown East Side tenement-house district. The conditions that prevail there are to be observed in other tenement-house districts but to a much lesser extent. In no other part of the city as in the downtown East Side do filth and garbage seem to accumulate so rapidly in the streets or are so many of the streets used by horsecar lines.

Since the streets have been blockaded with snow, the service of the dumping carts that go around to empty the ash and garbage barrels and boxes placed out on the curbstones in the mornings has been so badly interrupted that the barrels and boxes of refuse have everywhere accumulated. In the better parts of the city, householders and storekeepers have taken steps to get rid of the stuff themselves, but in the tenement-house districts these barrels and boxes of ashes and garbage have been allowed to rest until they were tipped over and their contents mixed with the snow and mud. It is in the downtown East Side district that this present offense to the eye and prospective stench to the nostrils exist to an extent that warrants alarm. Hester Street, Forsyth Street, Stanton Street, Essex Street, and others streets in that neighborhood which is largely populated by Russian and Polish Jews, Bohemians, Slavs, etc., the most unclean population which the city has, are really in a terrible condition. Every pile of snow is garnished with rubbish and decaying matter, and even the sidewalks are not clear of it. In the narrow streets of that district through which the horsecars run it looks now as though a good thaw would result in the flooding of the sidewalks and all the cellars about. In Columbia, Essex, and other like streets which the car companies' snow plows have been through, the snow is piled up between the tracks and the curb lines five or six feet as a rule.

It was noticeable, too, while going about town, that the entrance to a sewer was seldom to be seen. Though they exist to the number of two or three on nearly every block, practically all of them are buried out of sight beneath the snow. The New York *Times* some time ago suggested to Mr. Brennan that if his force could not clear the snow out of the streets it would be at least well to get down to the simpler matter of opening up the sewer entrances, so that when nature started to rid the city of the snow by melting it, the water would have opportunity to run off. Little seems to have been done in this direction. Altogether the prospect of a good thaw, while it carries with it the pleasant anticipation of clearing the streets of the snow, is not a bright one to contemplate.

THE NEW YORK TIMES,
AUGUST 15, 1893

Hester Street Enjoys a Bath

The Board of Health, the Street Cleaning Department, the Police, and the Fire Department made a combined attack yesterday on Hester Street and Mulberry Bend. When they got through, those two thoroughfares were no longer redolent with the various odors of stale fruit, flesh, and fish; they were no longer filled with a miscellaneous assortment of pushcarts and peddlers' wagons.

First, the police routed the pushcarts and wagons. Then Commissioner Andrews' carts came along by the dozen and carried off all the garbage and refuse. They were followed by squads of laborers, who swept the pavements until they were shiny with the accumulated grease and mud. After the sweepers came the firemen, who flushed the streets. Last of all were twenty experts from the sanitary squad, who marched along sniffing to the right and the left and watching for stray watermelon rinds and vagrant cabbages and herring.

This wonderful transformation was not wrought without a good deal of excitement and indignant protest on the part of the hucksters and vendors. When Officer John Kenney of the Eldridge Street squad took his stand at Eldridge and Hester Streets, it lacked three minutes of the hour set by the Board of Health for clearing the street. The street was then swarming with peddlers.

"Come, get out," said Kenney, waving his arms at an old Jew who was in the midst of a sale of pears. The Jew protested that his cart would not move. The officer took hold of the handle. Sure enough the cart was anchored fast. An investigation showed that the peddler had locked the rim of his wheel to the tailboard. The peddler giggled and then swore as the officer threatened him with arrest. Reluctantly he fished out the key from his pocket, unlocked the wheel, and moved down a side street amid the cries and jeers of a great crowd of his countrymen. On another corner was a Jew selling calico wrappers. "That wheel is broke!" he yelled, as Kenney grabbed the cart. This statement soon proved to be erroneous, and the cart was hustled off. All along the street Kenney encountered prevarications, supplications, and protestations. The wheels of many carts had been removed and hidden in the tenements. One peddler, whose cart was surmounted by an umbrella, had chained the umbrella to a lamp post, and he perspired with rage as the officer broke the chain.

There was no physical opposition to the officer, though, and in an hour Hester Street was cleared of the small carts. Street Cleaning Commissioner Andrews and Sanitary Superintendent Roberts drove through Hester Street and Mulberry Street in a carriage superintending the work. Assistant Corporation Counsel Appell was on hand to see that nothing was improperly confiscated by the city.

In Mulberry Street the Italian vendors were beside themselves with fear at the prospect of having their wares confiscated, and they were loud with supplications. They offered no opposition, though. Hereafter the police will keep Hester and Mulberry Streets clear of all peddlers and vendors after 10:00 A.M. every day.

EVENING POST,
JUNE 17, 1899

Preaching Christ to Angry Jews

On the doorpane of the old store on East Houston Street from which one Wilson W. Dunlop, a Gentile, directs an organized effort to preach Christianity to the ghetto Jews, there is painted in thin, yellow letters, in Hebrew, "The Lord, Jehovah, Jesus, the Anointed One, of the seed of the House of David, said unto Moses, 'Hear O Israel, the Lord thy God is One God.'" When on one day of the week, the mother of the youngest preacher for whom Dunlop provides, a Jew, went to the mission for the first time, yielding her countenance after long entreaty, she stopped short at the door and exclaimed: "Why, you have written here, the 'Hear, O Israel.' Your teaching can't be so very bad, then. Perhaps I have done you an injustice." Flaunting in the children's eyes, however, this familiar, sacred text under the very assertion of the quality of Jesus, whose mother they despise, with Jehovah, the One God, has so incensed the Orthodox Jews of the quarter that they break the glass, and particularly that pane upon which the name of Jesus is written in great letters.

Every child of the quarter is taught first that "the Lord thy God is One God." As a matter of course, therefore, the sustained preaching of Jesus as God, the Son of God, excites violent opposition. In these days, the ghetto is wrought up to the pitch of strange lawlessness by the persistence of the "blasphemous teaching." The three converted Jews who preach are followed by jeering mobs on their every appearance; the half-dozen young women who have a part in the work are struck and reviled; the head of the mission, Dunlop, being a paralytic, and not able to rise from his chair, is only spat upon. The youngest preacher has been stoned, knocked down, and beaten near into insensibility; this he counts "a privilege" and "glories" in, though the Jew boys he catches and carries into police court escape with nothing more than a "warning." Indeed, the young women show their bruises with pride, and all agree that to be spat upon by men and women and vilely taunted by little children is a "glory" and a "privilege." Lawlessness of this character has been going on for six months, and the police have frequently had difficulty in suppressing outbursts; so the Mayor recently threatened to revoke Dunlop's license for street preaching if the "rioting does not stop."

Bible classes are held afternoon and evening at the mission room, but the real preaching is done from a large wagon at the corners of Orchard and Rivington, Houston and Sheriff, and Grand and Sheriff Streets. The preachers have to push their way quickly across the sidewalk to the wagon when the start is made. If the policeman has his face turned away, they get blows from right and blows from left and spittle from everywhere. When the wagon drives off, it is followed by the crowd—it may be 200 persons—who groan and hiss as they follow along; the most prominently placed text on the wagon, "Jesus Christ is Lord Jehovah," keeps them always up to the point of flinging insults and stones.

"Our Redeemer," says the youngest preacher, perchance in jargon Hebrew, perchance in broken English, "the Lord of Hosts is His name—the Holy One of Israel! Dear friends, there is a mistake among you in believing that we preach that there is more than one God in existence."

The crowd gathers closely about the wagon, prepared to vent its feelings at the first mention of the name of Jesus, as the preacher and the policeman know.

"There is only one God, and that God is the God of the Jews."

The ghetto is now familiar with this, and it is greeted with derisive laughter, as it comes from the mouth of the "apostate."

"There is only one God, I say, the God of the Jews, who gave to our great teacher Moses these ever-to-be-remembered words, 'Hear, O Israel, the Lord thy God is One God.' I know that, nevertheless, you think we believe that Jesus Christ is. . ."

There is a shrill outburst of execration and derision. Meantime the preacher has to dodge whatever chances to be thrown, and his co-workers duck their heads to keep them safe from hurt.

"Jesus Christ is . . . ," the preacher begins again.

It so happened once that an urchin, with sure aim, threw a banana peel at the preacher and struck him on the check.

"Christ the Fatherless Liar!" the boy shouted, before the missile had reached its mark.

It is at such points that the policeman stops laughing and "moves on" the crowd, if he has not done so before.

"This is true, dear friends; Jesus is the Son of God," the preacher goes on through all the uproar. "If you knew more of the truth, you would believe with me. I believe in God, who gave to Moses and the prophets His will; and, believing orthodoxly in Moses and the prophets, I believe them when they spoke of Jesus as God-Man. I cannot but believe in Christ. If I did not, I should call God a liar. God was not always Jesus, but Jesus was, is, and ever shall be God."

The crowd follows the wagon back to the mission and does not leave the missionaries in peace until it is bedtime for all. The wagon stood in front of the mission yesterday afternoon. The afternoon meeting was over, and Dunlop was locked inside with his three converted Jews and the women helpers. The hostile crowd at the door was composed of boys and idle men; they kicked the door, beat the windowpanes, shouted approbrious names, and dared the preachers to come out. The youngsters swarmed over the wagon and had a good time for themselves with the books and papers they found in the locker. There were about a hundred in all, and the policeman on duty at the door said they were "quiet for that crowd." Inside, Dunlop expected that the door would be broken in or the windows smashed. Still he kept saying that he loved the ghetto Jews; else why would he devote his life and fortune to them? The youngest preacher was the least perturbed. Making himself heard above the uproar with difficulty, he said that an impression was being made on the ghetto—even that "stronghold of prejudiced Judaism." The work had been going for six months, and he could name three or four Jews who had been converted. Dunlop said it was "God's work," and he would "leave results with God." The opposition was "frenzied" and inspired by the rabbis. If only the police had not been "reached," the workers, being protected, could accomplish much more. The policeman at the door was then laughing with a young fellow, while three little girls rattled the latch and beat the glass, and two boys kicked the panels. He had the preacher's whip and flogged a youngster now and again for the fun there was in it.

"I love the Jews," said Dunlop again, sternly.

Rowdies Annoy Jews

Another instance of police inefficiency or indifference was yesterday given on the East Side where Orthodox Jews in the observance of the New Year ceremony were assaulted and mocked by gangs of ruffians along the river front. Although the Jew baiting and intermittent riots continued from two o'clock until nearly sundown, the blotter of the 7th Precinct Police Station in Madison Street showed only three arrests. Of these, two were effected by a special officer. Not only were the police precautions entirely inadequate, but the few policemen who were assigned to the work of protecting the thousands of Jews in the observance of the day refused on several occasions to make arrests.

Yesterday was the second day of the Jewish New Year, and of nine days of prayer, which will terminate at sundown next Monday. From Saturday night to Monday night the Jews celebrate *Yom Kippur*, or the Day of Atonement, when they abstain from food and water for twenty-four hours. There was not a hall on the East Side that was not crowded yesterday to its capacity by devout Jews, Orthodox and Reform. The many synagogues are altogether too few to admit one-half of the great Jewish population of the ghetto. Even restaurants were utilized for the holding of services. Two thousand tickets had been distributed gratis by the Educational Alliance to those who were too poor to pay for a chair in the usual places of worship, and services were held for them on the first floor of the Alliance Building on East Broadway. In the auditorium of the same building were 700 of the more prosperous Jews, who paid for their seats. The stage was turned into an altar.

The *Tishre* ceremony at the river front followed the services in the synagogues, which terminated with the blowing of the *shofar* or ram's horn. None of the symbolical ritualism of *Rosh Hashanah* is more interesting than *Tishre*. The Jews from now until *Yom Kippur* prepare for the forgiveness of their sins. Yesterday's ceremony in this connection consisted of casting their sins into the sea. Many of them carry with them crumbs with which to feed the fishes, and they throw these out in token of the unloading of their sins into the water.

From early afternoon until evening there was an incessant flow of the devout sons of Israel to points along the water front. Thousands of them were along the docks from the Brooklyn Bridge to Houston Street while many performed their religious duties on the two East River bridges. The even more than congested condition of the East Side streets caused by this great outpouring of worshipers made them almost impassable. It was during this part of the observance of the Jewish ritual that the Jew baiting occurred. Most of the trouble took place at Pike's Slip where members of the Cherry Hill gang pulled the beards of the worshipers and in other ways maltreated them. Other ruffians from the trestle used in extending the Delancey Street approach to the Williamsburg Bridge pelted the men, women, and children with stones. Several of them were injured. There were several fist fights, and several of the policemen who were on duty refused to make arrests when appealed to. While the rioting was at its worst, Special Officer Henry Revowitz, who was passing on a belt-line car, heard cries for help and rushed into the crowd. He was set upon by the thugs whom he beat off with his club. He arrested two Italian laborers who were charged by Harris Brown of No. 249 Cherry Street with assault. Brown bled profusely from a wound on the arm, having been apparently struck with a club. The prisoners were turned over to Detectives Wuchner and Delaney who appeared after the arrest. At the Madison Street station they said they were Frank Katso, twenty years old of 146th Street and 8th Avenue and Salvatore Mongabaro, thirty-four years old of No. 44 Oak Street.

Shortly after the arrest of these two men, Joseph Rich of No. 240 Delancey Street, who was returning to his home from the river front, was struck in the right eye at Madison and Market Streets by a stone thrown by one of three young ruffians who ran away. Patrolman Louis Levy chased the trio but caught only one of them, who, at the station, said he was Louis Russo, an Italian, sixteen years old of No. 58 James Street. Dr. Lohmiller of the Gouveneur Hospital dressed Rich's eye which was badly contused.

EVENING POST,
DECEMBER 4, 1905

50,000 Marchers Mourn Kishinev Massacre

Previous demonstrations in this city in mourning for the victims of the recent anti-Jewish outbreaks in Russia were eclipsed today by an immense parade of Jewish organizations through the East Side and the wholesale district in Broadway, ending with a meeting and the adoption of resolutions in the plaza at Union Square. The demonstration was the most impressive ever attempted by the Jews here, not excepting the great procession of mourners at the funeral of Rabbi Joseph four years ago. Nearly a hundred organizations, labor, benevolent, and charitable, religious, socialistic, and revolutionary, took part in the parade, and not less than 50,000 persons were in line. More than 10,000, it was estimated, came over the Williamsburg Bridge from Brooklyn.

The demonstration was under the direction of the Jewish Defense Association, the body which has raised a fund of above a million dollars for the relief of the Jews in Russia. The procession started at Rutgers Square at 12:30 o'clock. For an hour before, the square and Seward Park adjoining were crowded with people. The route was from Rutgers Square along East Broadway to Pike Street, to Henry Street, to Jefferson, to Hester, to Norfolk, to Broome, to Ludlow, to Rivington, to Chrystie, to Houston, to Second Avenue, to Fourth Street, to Broadway, and to Union Square, where after an open-air meeting and the adoption of resolutions denouncing the Russian antiSemitic outrages, the crowd disbanded.

Joseph Barondess, a well-known East Side labor leader, was the grand marshal. The procession was divided in eight parts, each assembling at a different point under a different marshal and falling in at the proper time. The first division, of which M. Keffier was marshal, consisted of nineteen organizations and formed at No. 98 Forsyth Street. The second division, led by Jacob Deutsch and consisting of seventeen organizations, formed on East Broadway. The third division, consisting of ten organizations and led by M. S. Weeker, assembled on Henry Street. The fourth division, led by M. Frank, was made up of twelve organizations, and assembled at Henry and Jefferson Streets. The fifth, headed by L. F. Frachtanberg and consisting of twenty-one organizations, formed on Suffolk Street. The sixth division of eleven organizations, headed by I. Rosenthal, formed on Rivington Street. The seventh division of twelve organizations in two sections, led by Michael Gold and Michael Kipp, formed in Allen Street. The eighth division, led by Marshal Rothfoord and composed of twelve organizations, formed in Delancey Street.

At the head of the parade, following a squad of mounted police, marched members of the Theatrical Musical Union, playing solemn music and accompanied by the Choristers Union, the Boy Synagogue Singers, and the Cantors Union. There was music, instrumental and vocal, in every division and all mournful and dirge-like. In line also were the Manhattan Rifles and Zion Guards, semimilitary organizations. A detachment of the Zion Guards from New Haven marched with them, and the Kishinev Organization, made up of survivors of the Kishinev massacre, was another notable part of the parade. Black and white crepe draped the houses and stores all along the line of march. The banners of the various organizations were also draped with black flags signifying mourning for the dead. American flags draped in black and the Zion flag, a blue six-pointed star on a white field, were numerous. Several times as many people as were in the parade watched its progress from sidewalks, windows, and roofs. One thousand patrolmen and 300 mounted men, under Inspectors Schmittberger and Hogan, kept the crowds in order and forced a way through the throngs. The officers and executive committee of the Jewish Defense Association inspired the demonstrations, and, headed by the chairman, Dr. J. L. Magnes, marched in the parade.

NEW YORK TRIBUNE, JULY 5, 1896

Playgrounds of Asphalt

That part of the East Side which lies between the Bowery and the river is, to a considerable extent, paved with asphalt, and the Public Works Department is planning still further extension of that system of pavement. Indeed, E. P. North, the Water Purveyor in whose direct charge this branch of municipal administration is, favors smooth streets for tenement-house regions, even if thoroughfares used by bicyclists have to be content with rough granite a few years longer. In general, the argument in favor of asphalt for streets where the population is huddled in greatest numbers is the sanitary one. That material can be kept clean so easily that the health of a neighborhood is appreciably affected by its use, and, besides, danger of an epidemic which might spread to wealthier parts of the city is averted.

This is true, but it is not all. Asphalt pavements are an important contribution to the opportunities for amusement of the East Side residents. They in a measure add to the park area of that region, serving as they do as playgrounds for the children and breathing spaces for their parents. It may be said in passing that these two classes seem to make up the population over there—early marriages are so common. It might appear that as the streets were there before, they would have served as well for playgrounds when paved with cobblestones, but such is not the case. Their superior cleanliness for one thing makes the asphalt pavements far more available. In the next place, they dry quickly after a rain, and, unless in poor condition, are not covered in spots with puddles of water.

The smoothness is perhaps the chief element in their adaptability to the sports of childhood. The boys can play marbles on them, while granite pavements are useless for this. It is lots more fun to roll a hoop, play ball or "one o' cat" or "prisoners' base" on asphalt than on rough stones, muddy, perhaps, and slippery. The little girls also find that "ring around a rosy" and other song games are much more satisfactorily played on a smooth surface. The Hebrew boys are not as much given to "prisoners' base" as those of other nationalities; neither do they play ball a great deal. There is no room for batting, and mere pitching and catching get tiresome. Besides the danger to windows and passers-by leads the police to stop that sport.

"One o' cat," as it is pronounced, has been the favorite game for the boys of Hebrew parentage, but this, too, has been generally suppressed on account of the accidents to showwindows and noncombatants. The sport is really a form of baseball, except that a piece of wood is used instead of a ball. It is some three or four inches long and an inch in diameter at the center, tapering to rather a dull point at either end. There are sides, as in baseball, but the total number of players is usually not larger than eight or ten. The piece of wood is laid on the ground, and the batsman touches the end lightly with his stick. It rises into the air two or three feet, and then he strikes it sharply. Sometimes it is sent half a block, and he makes the circuit of the bases before one of the fielders can return it to the home plate, where the catcher stands. If he cannot get beyond first or second base (the number of bases varies), he may be brought home by the next batsman. There is no need of a pitcher.

This for the children. The grown folk also reap benefits from the asphalt pavements. The children being on the street, there is more room on the sidewalk for their elders. Chairs are brought out on the sidewalk, and the curbstones furnish seats for many. With the old paving materials, the gutters were more or less unclean and noisome, but the asphalt makes the curbstone really an attractive place to sit.

When it is called to mind that a certain East Side block has 3,700 dwellers, it is easy to believe that these streets are crowded on summer evenings. And they are, even where the blocks have a much smaller population. Someone has said that there is not standing room at one time on these East Side streets for all the people that live in them. It is interesting to ride on the front platform of a car through one of these asphalted streets in the early evening, say at seven o'clock. You are in constant dread lest some of the children be run over. But the driver goes slowly and is constantly on the lookout.

The popularity of asphalt is attested in Avenue C. A line of cars runs through here, but on fair days and evenings children crowd the street, playing their various games. Avenue D has less traffic on it but, being paved with stones, has not nearly so many people, small and adult, upon it. The laying out of two new parks over there will keep many persons off the streets, but meanwhile the asphalt paving forms a fairly satisfactory substitute.

UNKNOWN PHOTOGRAPHER/HESTER STREET, UNDATED/LIBRARY OF CONGRESS

BYRON/ORCHARD STREET, 1898/THE BYRON COLLECTION, MUSEUM OF THE CITY OF NEW YORK

J. MORROW/STREET SCENE, c. 1900/COMMUNITY SERVICE SOCIETY, NEW YORK

UNKNOWN PHOTOGRAPHER/STREET SCENE, UNDATED/COMMUNITY SERVICE SOCIETY, NEW YORK

BYRON/STREET VENDORS, HESTER STREET, 1898/THE BYRON COLLECTION, MUSEUM OF THE CITY OF NEW YORK

UNKNOWN PHOTOGRAPHER/"I CASH CLOTHES," c. 1910/PICTURE COLLECTION, NEW YORK PUBLIC LIBRARY

LEWIS W. HINE/SOFT DRINK PEDDLER, c. 1910/GEORGE EASTMAN HOUSE

ALICE AUSTEN/SCISSORS GRINDER, c. 1895
ALICE AUSTEN COLLECTION,
STATEN ISLAND HISTORICAL SOCIETY

UNKNOWN PHOTOGRAPHER/TAKING MATZOS HOME, c. 1910/CULVER PICTURES, INC.

UNKNOWN PHOTOGRAPHER/BRINGING HOME THE MATZOS, c. 1925/UNDERWOOD & UNDERWOOD

LEWIS W. HINE/BOOTBLACKS PITCHING PENNIES, 1915/PHOTO LEAGUE ARCHIVE, NEW YORK PUBLIC LIBRARY

LEWIS W. HINE/NEWSBOYS, BROOKLYN BRIDGE, c. 1912/GEORGE EASTMAN HOUSE

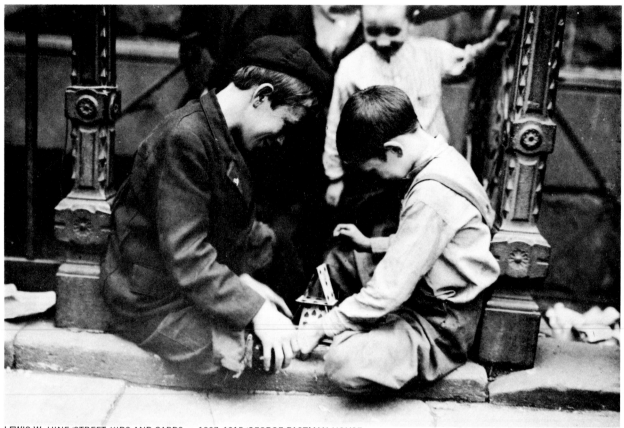

LEWIS W. HINE/STREET KIDS AND CARDS, c. 1907–1915/GEORGE EASTMAN HOUSE

JACOB A. RIIS/STREET ARABS, MULBERRY STREET, c. 1889/THE JACOB A. RIIS COLLECTION, MUSEUM OF THE CITY OF NEW YORK

JESSIE TARBOX BEALS/ITALIAN CHILDREN, c. 1915/COMMUNITY SERVICE SOCIETY, NEW YORK

LEWIS W. HINE/NEAR THE LUMBERYARDS, c. 1910
GEORGE EASTMAN HOUSE

JESSIE TARBOX BEALS/CHILDREN OF THE STREETS, c. 1915/COMMUNITY SERVICE SOCIETY, NEW YORK

JESSIE TARBOX BEALS/PLAYING IN THE STREET, c. 1915/COMMUNITY SERVICE SOCIETY, NEW YORK

JESSIE TARBOX BEALS/CHILDREN OF THE STREET, c. 1915/COMMUNITY SERVICE SOCIETY, NEW YORK

JESSIE TARBOX BEALS/STREET SPRINKLER, c. 1915/COMMUNITY SERVICE SOCIETY, NEW YORK

ALICE AUSTEN/BOOTBLACKS, CITY HALL PARK, 1896
PICTURE COLLECTION, NEW YORK PUBLIC LIBRARY

UNKNOWN PHOTOGRAPHER/BOYS SITTING IN MULBERRY STREET, c. 1897/THE BETTMANN ARCHIVE

ALICE AUSTEN/PUSHCARTS, 1896/PICTURE COLLECTION, NEW YORK PUBLIC LIBRARY

UNKNOWN PHOTOGRAPHER/MOVING PICTURE THEATER,
c. 1915/BROWN BROTHERS

ALICE AUSTEN/EGG BUYERS, HESTER STREET, 1895/ALICE AUSTEN COLLECTION, STATEN ISLAND HISTORICAL SOCIETY

UNKNOWN PHOTOGRAPHER/PUSHCART PEDDLER, UNDATED/PICTURE COLLECTION, NEW YORK PUBLIC LIBRARY

UNKNOWN PHOTOGRAPHER/FRANKFURTER MERCHANT, UNDATED/PICTURE COLLECTION, NEW YORK PUBLIC LIBRARY

UNKNOWN PHOTOGRAPHER/STREET PEDDLER, c. 1910/BROWN BROTHERS

ALICE AUSTEN/STREET PEDDLER, c. 1895
ALICE AUSTEN COLLECTION,
STATEN ISLAND HISTORICAL SOCIETY

ALICE AUSTEN/STREET PEDDLER, c. 1895/ALICE AUSTEN COLLECTION, STATEN ISLAND HISTORICAL SOCIETY

UNKNOWN PHOTOGRAPHER/STREET PEDDLER, c. 1905
BROWN BROTHERS

UNKNOWN PHOTOGRAPHER/MULBERRY STREET, UNDATED/LIBRARY OF CONGRESS

UNKNOWN PHOTOGRAPHER/STREET SCENE, c. 1900/CULVER PICTURES, INC.

UNKNOWN PHOTOGRAPHER/SILHOUETTE ARTIST, c. 1915/BROWN BROTHERS

ALICE AUSTEN/RAG MAN, c. 1896/ALICE AUSTEN COLLECTION, STATEN ISLAND HISTORICAL SOCIETY

ALICE AUSTEN/ORGAN GRINDER, c. 1895
ALICE AUSTEN COLLECTION,
STATEN ISLAND HISTORICAL SOCIETY

LEWIS W. HINE/POLICEMAN WITH CHILDREN, c. 1912/GEORGE EASTMAN HOUSE

UNKNOWN PHOTOGRAPHER/MAKING AN ARREST,
MULBERRY STREET, c. 1897/THE BETTMANN ARCHIVE

UNKNOWN PHOTOGRAPHER/POLICEMAN, UNDATED/BROWN BROTHERS

JACOB A. RIIS/BLIND BEGGAR, c. 1888/THE JACOB A. RIIS COLLECTION, MUSEUM OF THE CITY OF NEW YORK

דער יודישער

העניג ליער

THE JEWISH

KING LEAR

ARRANGED BY

H. A. RUSSOTTO.

Nº1. {KIDDUSCH
{AL TIRO AVDI JACOB.
.. 2. AUDE LO-EIL.

Nº3. COUPLET SCHAMAI.
.. 4. THE CHSIDIM DANCE.

Piano and Vocal 75 Cents

THE HEBREW PUBLISHING Cº

632 BROADWAY

NEW YORK

Copyright 1899 by Katzenelenbogen & Rabinowitz.

EVENING POST,
AUGUST 7, 1900

Rush to Be Naturalized

This is what is known as the "busy season" in naturalization work at the United States District Court. The busy season is an annual phenomenon. Especially manifest once in every four years, the present anniversary, according to the statements of the government officers at the federal building, shows every indication of being a "recordbreaker."

There is, of course, more or less naturalization business to be done throughout the year, but there seems to be a particular incentive to ambitious foreigners in the latter part of July and the early part of August. A ninety-day citizenship is required of all electors in the state before they are entitled to vote. In the case of the unnaturalized, this means that unless their papers are dated August 8, or earlier, they will not be permitted to participate in the Presidential and state elections this fall. As a matter of fact, unless the applications are signed by the Commissioner today, it will be impossible for the applicants to be sworn in by Judge Thomas tomorrow. To all intents and purposes, today is the latest period for naturalization of aliens who hope to vote this year. The applicants for citizenship have been, for the most part, perfectly well aware of that fact, for the numerous padrones and small politicians in both parties who cultivate the foreign vote had taken pains that they should not forget. Long before the Commissioner's court opened for business this morning, the line had begun to form. Those desirous of an early interview began to arrive at the Post Office building before seven o'clock. When Commissioner Alexander, who relieves the judges of the actual work of examining the candidates, made his appearance soon after nine, he found an interested and somewhat excited throng awaiting him. The deputy United States marshals had had their hands full for some time in attempting to arrange the crowd in an orderly array. They had formed them into two lines—one extended from Commissioner Alexander's room into the hall and to the rear of the Post Office building, and the other reached from the room of Commissioner York along the other side of the hall to the rear. When Commissioner York's applicants secured their papers, they were transferred to the tail of the line extending into Commissioner Alexander's rooms. Their eagerness, owing to the fact that no applicants would be received after today, was especially annoying to the deputy marshals. Latecomers resorted to any number of tricks to secure places near the head of the line; they were continually pushing and crowding and constantly disputed with one another for the right of precedence.

Both lines were made up, for the most part, of Russian Jews and Italians, though an occasional Irishman or German insisted upon his right to have an earlier hearing than an ordinary *dago*. At rare intervals still, an Englishman appeared to acknowledge his willingness to forswear his allegiance to the Queen. In one respect, the crowds were deceptive, for each applicant was accompanied by a witness to take the necessary oath as to the former's age, good character, and other qualifications for citizenship. Aside from the witnesses, however, the officers expected to prepare for naturalization today about 250 men, which, added to the 1,363 who have received their papers since July 18, gives a total of 1,613 for the "rush season" of 1900. The record for the same period in 1896 was 1,157.

None of the officers of the court could remember any time when they have had their hands so full in making citizens as they have had for about ten days. In the main, the present rush of foreigners for citizenship papers is attributed to the prosperity of the country. This is especially true, it was said today, in the case of the

Italians, whose chief interest in the country previously had seemed to be as a temporary abiding place—a place in which to make a "little pile" and then return to their fatherland. Their anxiety to escape the military conscription and the burdensome military taxes of the Italian government have inclined them to adopt the United States as their permanent home.

Most of the aliens who appeared before Commissioner Alexander today were fairly intelligent and orderly. They attacked his questions upon the Constitution of the United States and upon a few elementary facts in American history not only without trepidation, but with considerable eagerness. Just how far these replies, which were usually correct, displayed an intelligent grasp of the principles of American government, the officers do not say. There could be no doubt that the aliens had learned their lesson well; they had of course, been coached in their answers by their compatriots for some weeks. At any time in the course of recent weeks, visitors to the Italian or Jewish quarter would have found male members of a family who were of voting age poring over slips of paper prepared and distributed by the local leaders. Nearly all the candidates had these same slips with them, upon which their eyes were riveted up to the moment that the Commissioner took them in charge. A translation of these modest treatises upon the American Constitution —for they were all printed in the language with which the candidate is most familiar —would contain such bits of information as these:

Q: Who makes the laws of the United States? A: The Congress at Washington.
Q: Of how many houses is it composed? A: Two; the House of Representatives and the Senate.
Q: How many members of the House? A: According to population.
Q: How many members of the Senate? A: Two from each state.
Q: By whom is the President elected? A: By the electors.
Q: Who is the President now?

A: Mr. McKinley.
Q: Who was the first President? A: George Washington.
Q: How many Representatives from New York? A: Thirty-four.
Q: How long do they hold office? A: Two years.
Q: How many Senators? A: Two.
Q: How long do they hold office? A: Six years.

There are several other questions and answers upon the printed slips, but these are the principal ones. That the candidates learn them more or less in parrot fashion is evident when they begin to deluge the Commission with their learning. Few are so ignorant as to make Mr. McKinley the first President of the United States and General Washington the present executive, though this sometimes happens. Even today, an alien, in reply to the question as to the present President, gave the name of "William McCleveland." It is upon the fundamental principles of the Constitution, however, that they more frequently go astray. They are likely to confuse the senators and representatives, to give New York State thirty-four men in the more dignified chamber and only two congressmen. Neither can they understand why a senator should be elected for a six-year term and a representative for two, and they are likely to say that the former are chosen by the people and the latter by the legislatures. On one question, however, they seldom go astray:

"When was the Declaration of Independence signed?" asks the Commissioner.

"July 4, 1776," comes the proud reply in a loud tone.

"Who's the Governor of New York State?" he asks, quickly, jumping from past to present history.

The sudden transition is confusing; this is as intended. The candidate stammers and shifts from one foot to the other.

"Teodoro Rosevelta!" hisses a man at the end of the line, bursting with his own stock of information and with his desire to help out a fellow countryman in trouble. He is promptly pulled out of his place by the marshal and placed at the end of the procession as a punishment for furnishing surreptitious information.

With the exception of little incidents of this kind the examiners have little trouble, and they expressed today their satisfaction both with the intelligence and the good behavior of the candidates.

NEW YORK TRIBUNE,
AUGUST 16, 1903

Religious Life

"It is impossible to understand the Lower East Side," said Dr. David Blaustein, head of the Educational Alliance, speaking apropos of his recent statistical investigations of conditions in that section, "or the attitude of the people there toward American institutions without knowing the conditions from which these people came in Eastern Europe. For instance, the average Russian Jew of the Lower East Side will declare that there is more religious liberty in Russia than in America. He cannot understand the state's interfering with marriage and divorce, which in Russia are left entirely to the rabbi. He is especially puzzled by the state's attitude toward divorce. There are more divorces on the Lower East Side in proportion to the population than in any other part of the city, and far more than among the Jewish population of any other country on the globe.

"The reason is not far to seek. The man comes to this country first. Five years later, during which time he has lived as a single man, he sends for his wife. He finds her not five years behind him, but two centuries. He has acquired a new language, new clothes and customs, and a new country. He finds the union insupportable. In the old country all that was necessary was for the couple to go before the rabbi with a declaration of mutual consent, and he would divorce them. Some rabbis on the East Side continued to grant these divorces until recently, and a great deal of trouble was caused. Here in America, therefore, the immigrant finds the state interfering, according to his notion, with his private affairs, and he will claim there is no religious liberty in America.

"As a matter of fact, there is perfect liberty in Russia so far as the exercise of his religion is concerned. The Jew is never interfered with in his religious observances. He simply loses, on account of them, all civic and economic rights. He pays for his religious liberty with the latter. His church has infinitely greater power and importance in Russia than in America. The rabbi keeps all the vital statistics. The rabbi marries and divorces. The rabbi has charge of all education. He also acts as a court in both civil and criminal cases. Formerly, Jewish contestants in Russia were compelled by law to take their cases to the rabbi. In certain classes of cases they may now go before a general court. If they agree to take the case to the rabbi, they are required by law to abide by his decision.

"At every turn of the road the Jew's religion is recognized. He is taxed as a Jew, enlisted as a Jew. No matter how many Jews there may be in a city, or how many synagogues they may have, representing as many different shades of religious opinion, they are all lumped together as one congregation. One man represents this congregation to the government. He is responsible to the government for their taxes. The government will support him in any attitude he may take toward any individual in the matter of taxation. He is responsible for the number of soldiers required, fifty or one hundred, as the case may be. He can decide what young men shall be chosen.

"This representative to the government is elected by the Jews of the city. Their choice may be rejected by the government, but once it is confirmed, the people cannot change their representative. One can easily see in this method a fertile opportunity for tyranny and oppression.

Nevertheless it is a distinct and permanent recognition of the Jewish church.

"In fact, in Russia a man is first of all required to be a member of a church and next a citizen of Russia. The very passports so describe him. They begin, 'The Jew so-and-so is hereby authorized to travel,' or, 'The Christian so-and-so is hereby authorized to travel.' And 'the Christian' signifies a Greek Catholic. If he belongs to any other denomination it is so specified by 'The Lutheran,' or 'The Roman Catholic,' and so on. In theory, no man in Russia can be an atheist. In theory, no man is a freethinker. If he is born a Greek Catholic, he cannot change. There is imprisonment and often Siberia for life for a Greek Catholic who changes his religion. But if he is born a Jew, he is regarded strictly as a Jew and protected in the observance of his religion. Only, because he is not a Greek Catholic, he has no civil or economic rights.

"You can imagine the confusion in the immigrant's mind when he reaches America. He finds his church of no account whatever. No one cares what church he belongs to or whether he belongs to any church or not. The state delegates no rights or powers to the church. All that is asked is whether he is an American or not and whether he is loyal to his adopted country. No one cares anything about his loyalty to his church or regards his religious belief as a matter of any importance to anyone but himself. In place of finding the congregation all powerful and all embracing, he finds when he joins a congregation that he has simply joined a liberal society.

"There are 332 little congregations east of Broadway and south of Houston Street. They are founded not on differing shades of belief but merely on the fact that the members came from different towns or villages in Eastern Europe. Each congregation is a mutual benefit society. It has a sick benefit and in many cases free medical treatment. The rooms serve as a clubroom where the men meet to talk over old times, read letters from home, discuss politics and current events, or study the Talmud and other religious writings. Religious services are also held, with one of their number, not necessarily an ordained rabbi, acting as leader.

This is the puzzling and bewildering metamorphosis which the Jewish immigrant finds in America. The results are far-reaching. In Eastern Europe both educational life and social life center in the church. We have at the Educational Alliance one of the largest religious schools in America—thirty-two hundred pupils. Of these thirty-two hundred, only 15 per cent are boys. To understand this it is necessary to understand the position of woman in the church in Eastern Europe. The Jewish woman of Eastern Europe has no religious life. All that I have told you applies to men alone. All of the parochial schools there are for boys alone. Woman is disregarded so entirely that she is not even expected to attend religious services unless she chooses. Boys are confirmed; girls are not. Boys are called on to perform certain religious rites in the home; girls are not. When a boy reaches the age of thirteen, it is possible for him to occupy a position to which his mother can never aspire. The position of woman is such that when she ventures to offer an opinion in the presence of man—if she ever dares to do so—she will begin with an apology, 'Although I am a woman, yet it seems to me, and so on.' Even a mother addressing her little boy will do this because her womanly understanding is not supposed to be capable of grasping an idea as he would.

"The religion which we teach at the Educational Alliance, a religion without superstition or bigotry, is simply regarded by the people about us as no religion at all; therefore, it is good enough for the girls. Our school is free, but the people will not send their boys to it. They prefer to pay $5 a month to send them to the rabbinical schools. There are 279 such schools flourishing on the Lower East Side.

"The change in social life is as peculiar and puzzling to the immigrant as that in the religious life. In Eastern Europe the social life centers in the church and the home, and is pervaded by a devotional atmosphere. It is spontaneous. It flows from natural occasions. The social life to which we are accustomed—balls, receptions, banquets, class reunions—is not spontaneous; it is organized. All these affairs are arranged.

"For instance, it is the custom in the Jewish church to celebrate the eighth day after the birth of a son. This festival in Europe is always an occasion of much rejoicing. Suppose the day falls on a weekday, when there is work in the shop. The man goes to the shop, and the celebration is postponed until the following Sunday. Then the host knows and his guests know that it is not the right day. Their consciences smile then, and the occasion is one of secret sadness rather than rejoicing. They fall to mourning over the economic conditions which will not permit them to observe the old customs, rather than enjoying themselves.

"Always, before, the immigrant had room in which to entertain his friends. In the crowded condition of the quarter where he now lives, he cannot do this. The wedding is the pinnacle of Jewish social life. But on the Lower East Side the wedding must take place in a hall. The guest must pay at the door for his hat and coat check, and this at the very start takes away all the old feeling of openhanded hospitality. The hall wedding is a cold and comfortless function.

"So economic conditions prevent him from enjoying himself in his home with his family and his religion in the old way. If he seeks social enjoyment, he finds he must accommodate his time to that of others. A ball is to be held at a certain time. There is no special reason for it at that time, but the date has been fixed by a committee of arrangements, and he is asked to purchase a ticket. Remembering his good times in the old country, he goes, hoping to enjoy himself once more. He finds himself in a sea of strangers, with nothing as he has been used to. He goes

away weary and disheartened. It is the same in summer when he buys a ticket for one of the mammoth picnics. When he compares such a picnic with the harvest festival at home, a thing as happy and spontaneous as the play of children, his heart is sick. Often he says that America is no good and he would rather be back in the old country.

"As the woman in Eastern Europe has no religious life, so she has no social life. If you call at a house, you are received by the man of the house, not the woman. There are certain social feasts and celebrations of the church, but the men participate in them, not the women. If invitations are sent out to a wedding they are sent to the males of a family, not the women. At the wedding, the highest social function of Judaism, there are five men present to one woman.

"The woman is also a minor. She belongs to her father before her marriage, to her husband after. She cannot own property in her own name. Her testimony is not received in the ecclesiastical courts, although in the civil courts it has recently been admitted.

"Can you imagine what all this means to the immigrant? He goes to church here and finds women in the majority. He goes to the schools and finds women teaching most of them. He finds them behind every counter, beside him in every shop. What is the result? The result is that he loses all his respect for women."

Dr. Blaustein paused to let this declaration sink in and then went on to explain: "You may think," he said, "that from what I have said of the position of woman among the Jews of Eastern Europe that she is despised. On the contrary, she is an idolized being. She is adored. She is the queen of the home. The theory upon which she is excluded from all the things I have mentioned is not that she is not entitled to them, but that being busy with her household duties she is excused from them. She is excused from religious duties because something at home may require her attention. She is excused from education because more important duties await her. She is excused from looking after her own property. The men of her family will do that for her and protect all her rights. She is even excused from social duties," concluded Dr. Blaustein gravely.

"The immigrant sees woman in America excused from nothing. She bears the heat and burden of the day at his side. She has become his equal, and he supposes she is to be treated as an equal. He loses all respect for women and acts accordingly. Then he goes out into the American world and finds to his astonishment that women have privileges in America. He finds that there is a rule, 'ladies first.' It surprises him very much. He can't understand the apparent contradiction of things. It requires another mental readjustment.

"There is nothing that disturbs the Jew so much as to see his boy, and still more his girl, taking part in the athletics of the schools. The rage is something incomprehensible to him. He has cultivated his mind so long at the expense of his body that the American maxim 'a sound mind in a sound body' is something he cannot understand.

"All these things may explain to a slight degree the puzzled condition of the immigrant's mind, the difficulty he has in assimilating and adjusting himself to new conditions, his heavyheartedness oftentimes, and his frequent estrangement from his own children."

NEW YORK TRIBUNE,
NOVEMBER 12, 1899

A School for Hebrew

One of the schools of New York which is unknown beyond the Russian district has recently been enlarged and improved, and the building which it occupies, Nos. 225 and 227 East Broadway, has been changed into one of the most attractive structures in that part of the city. Many educational and charitable institutions in that neighborhood receive contributions from members of the Jewish community living in the upper part of the city, and some of these institutions could not exist without the support desired from that quarter. But the Machzikay Talmud Torah School depends for funds entirely on the Russian-Jewish population. This seems only natural when one knows that the school is maintained for the purpose of teaching the Hebrew language and Hebrew literature.

"The Reform Jews who live uptown," said a patriarch of the East Side, "know nothing about the Hebrew in their service. They still have a few words of the old language, but the young men and women who read and chant them, and even many of the older people, don't know their meaning unless they look at the printed translation. Another generation, and the little that they have now will pass away and the Hebrew will be forgotten. The beautiful poems in the holy books and the great writings of the Jewish philosophers cannot be translated, and we maintain this school so that our children may not grow up in ignorance of the language in which our fathers wrote."

The school was established about fifteen years ago, and has grown with the Jewish population from one class of twenty-five pupils to twenty-two classes having about eleven hundred pupils ranging in age from six to fifteen years. There are no charges for instruction, and besides being a free school in all that the term implies, needy children who attend are supplied with shoes and clothing. The money for maintaining the institution comes from the annual dues of the members, of whom there are about two thousand, and from contributions from Russian Jews who wish to pay more than the stipulated $3 a year. There is probably no schoolhouse in New York in which less money has been expended for interior decoration than this Hebrew school. The rooms are absolutely bare except for the plain benches and chairs and the desks of the instructors. The pupils are for the most part children of poor parents, and as a class would not bear close inspection for neatness, but they display an earnestness in their work which shows that they share, even in a childish way, the sentiments of their parents and regard the tasks set before them as more than ordinary school work. In order that the work required of them in the Hebrew school may not interfere with their regular school duties, the sessions are from four to seven o'clock on weekdays and from nine to one o'clock on Sunday. "We take no pupils," said Mr. Robison, the head of the school, "who do not attend the public schools, and the translations which the children make are from Hebrew into English."

On entering the building during the school session the stranger is likely to think that he has entered a place where boys are being instructed in chanting queer melodies. From all sides come wailing strains, sometimes uttered by a single voice and again in chorus. In the classroom the teacher stands at one end, directing not only the proper pronunciation of the words, but the intonation, and when a pupil has recited a line or passage, the rest of the class repeats it in concert. All sit with their hats or caps on, because according to the Jewish law—a relic of the Orient—no man may appear before God with his head uncovered. In the upper classes the Bible is the textbook, and the lessons are selected in keeping with the season of the year or the proximity of a holiday. In these classes the boys are also drilled in translation. In the lower classes the rudiments of the language and short words are taught, but even there the boys acquire the sing-song mode of recitation which seems to be a part of Hebrew. In speaking of this characteristic, one of the supporters of the school said: "The Hebrew prayers are chanted in a certain way. The sing-song which you consider queer and which our boys are learning is the same as has been used for thousands of years—not a note has been changed or modified. The music is not written, but it has outlived many compositions which were carefully put on paper. Our boys learn these chants here as we learned them from our fathers, and they will in turn hand them down to their children as we do.

"This all sounds queer to you, and so it does to the Reform Jews, but we hope to see it survive through many generations. That is why a school like this one is necessary. The boys learn to sing patriotic songs in the public schools, and then they come here to learn the sacred music." Some of the boys who are graduated from the Hebrew school go from there to the theological seminary and become rabbis, but that is only a small minority. Many of the graduates become East Side merchants, with the usual ambition toward a Broadway store and an uptown home. A fair percentage of the graduates have become practicing physicians and lawyers. Thirty of the graduates are now teachers in the public schools of New York.

"Why are there no girls in the school?" the visitor asked one of the teachers.

"The girls may learn at home," he answered, "and they do, but we have no place for them here."

This is also a remnant of Orientalism, like the custom by which these people compel the women to occupy a place apart from the men in the houses of worship.

EVENING POST,
SEPTEMBER 25, 1897

When the Shofar Blows

The ghetto is all bustle and hurry, preparing for the great season of song and prayer, which begins Monday. It is the Jewish New Year, the 5,658th anniversary of the creation of the world. Ushered in by the ten days of penance, the approaching holidays are to cover a period of more than three weeks, in the course of which the neighborhood will ring now with sobs of worshipers pleading for a happy new year, now with "Rejoicing of the Law." Many an hour will be spent in the synagogue, and every one tries to secure as good a seat in as fine a house of prayer as his means will allow. The qualities of the *chasan,* or cantor, and the size of his choir are primary considerations, for the average denizen of the ghetto is fond of music, and the most solemn part of the divine service is not devoid of a certain stage interest for him. To make up for this, he will exact from his actors some church song in their plays.

Some of the airs sung on the "Days of Penance" are traditional and trace their origin centuries back to the caves and woods of Spain, where the wandering people worshiped the God of their ancestors at the risk of their lives. The other parts of the service are left to the cantor's own devices and are, as a rule, intoned in melodies of his own composition—or plagiarism. At all events the *chasan* and his choir are the principal attractions, calculated to draw buyers of seats for the great festivals, and this accounts for the character of the placards and handbills, advertising the multitude of synagogues, which now flood the Jewish quarter. Following is a fair example: "The world-renowned cantor Rabbi Meyer Goldstein of the city of Ponevesh, recently arrived from the Old Country, will conduct the services at the Synagogue of the Men of Ponevesh. He will be assisted by a choir of five excellent men. The best singing in the city at the lowest prices. Make haste to secure a ticket, or the seats will all be sold."

Some of these show cards are emblazoned with the portrait of the man, others have only a conspicuous display of his name, but all of them contain a glowing eulogy of his powers. The net proceeds from the sale of seats are in many instances the main source of the congregation's income. Hence, the hiring of a good cantor is generally viewed in the light of an in-vestment. There are thousands upon thousands of Orthodox children of Israel who never see the inside of a "house of God" except during the great holidays, when they come to atone by "Penance, Prayer, and Charity" for the sins committed in the course of the whole wicked year—and it is for the patronage of these that the various synagogues are now competing. Few Orthodox congregations are large enough to afford a separate building for a house of worship. Most of them are small societies made up of fellow townsmen and bearing the name of their native place. Almost every town within the Pale of Jewish settlement in Russia, Austria, or Rumania is represented here by a synagogue. Accordingly, the average congregation must be content with a room and bedroom on the top floor of some overcrowded tenement house, the smaller room usually being set aside for the female worshipers, who follow the *chasan* through the portieres. Most of these struggling societies sublet their rooms for weekdays to *melamdim,* or instructors in the *Bible* and the *Talmud,* who teach their scholars in the afternoon, when they come from the public schools. As a rule, each synagogue is also a kind of clubhouse, the more devout of the members coming to spend their leisure moments there, reading Psalms, swapping news of the old home, or exchanging notes upon the adopted country.

In addition to the permanent congregations, of which there are several hundred in the Jewish quarter, at least as many temporary ones spring into existence for the great holidays. To accommodate these, every dancing hall and assembly room and many a sweatshop are transformed into synagogues, and every tailor or teacher of Hebrew who lays any claim to musical gifts enters the lists in competition for the place of cantor or chorister. The two large Jewish theaters of this city, the Windsor and the Thalia, are announced as houses of worship for the coming festivals, with some of the leading Jewish actors for *chasans.*

Some celebrities are paid for the four principal services of the Days of Awe as much as $1,000 but, such virtuosos apart, $200 would be a fair average of the cantor's fee. The humbler congregations cannot afford to pay more than $50 for the season. The wealthier synagogues engage their *chasans* by contract on a monthly salary and often import them from some large city in Russia or Galicia. The Hebrew communities of those countries are said to have been drained of their best religious singers by their brethren of the New York ghetto, who are by far the highest bidders in the world's cantor market.

Sometimes a man who shaves his beard, who does not exclude pork from his bill of fare, and who is otherwise unmindful of the laws of Moses takes it into his head to earn a few dollars by officiating in some synagogue during the Days of Awe. To do this, if otherwise qualified, he must assume an Orthodox appearance, growing a full beard and sidelocks and donning a high hat and a long frock coat —the insignia of sacerdotal dignity—into the bargain. The number of applicants exceeds by far the number of vacancies, and as a consequence, competition is extremely bitter. But by now the probationary service to which the many rivals have been subjected is over, selections have been made, and those who have been lucky enough to procure an engagement contribute the harmonies of their rehearsing choirs to the general hubbub of the quarter. Scarcely a large tenement house in that region fails to shelter some proud *chasan* and is in the evening filled with the plaintive strains of penance-days music. If you pass through the ghetto these days, you will be likely now and then to come across some pious-looking individual humming an air as, curling his sidelocks, he proceeds on his way, or stands, gazing at the window display of a Hebrew bookstore. This is a *chasan;* it is not hard to tell from his manner and from the spirit of his tune whether he has procured a job or not.

However, the cantors and their choirs are not the only ones to be busy rehearsing for the holidays. There is a kind of instrumental music which resounds in the synagogue on both New Year's days—the only kind allowed between the walls of an Orthodox house of prayer, outside of the unimportant Feast of Dedication, when a full-fledged orchestra may be a feature of the service. It is performed on the shofar, a ram's horn, and is suggestive of the clarinet or, more frequently, of the bleating of a goat. The blowing of the horn is perhaps the most important part of the New Year service. Each sound is believed to carry an angel-advocate to heaven to plead for the whole congregation. Even the housemaid who stays home minding the babies cannot taste her breakfast before she has attended the performance, if only through her window. Accordingly, the horn blower bestows great care upon his task, and he will spend some time before the holidays practicing the prescribed notes which he is expected to sound under the dictation of some venerable old man.

The Days of Penance are followed after an interval of four days by the Feast of Tabernacles, when in the course of a week the faithful take their meals in booths, covered with fir trees, which are constructed for the purpose in the courtyards of the Jewish quarter. Palm branches and citrons are then used by the worshipers as an accessory of the morning prayer. The Rejoicing of the Law is the last of the great holidays. It is so called because on that day the reading of the scrolls of the "Five Books of Moses," which are divided into weekly sections to be read on Saturdays, is concluded and commenced over again; it is considered a good deed to make it an occasion for great merriment. This accounts for the frequency with which people are under the influence of liquor on that day in the Jewish neighborhood, where such a spectacle is generally a rare occurrence.

This is also the season of the Hebrew book trade. Thousands of Orthodox people are forgetful of their prayer books during the year and let them get lost; now they find themselves in need of new ones. Also, many of those who can afford it will want to appear in the synagogue in a new praying shawl. The book dealers, as a rule, sell these things and palm branches and citrons, as well as all sorts of religious publications. Nor are the clothier, the hatter, the shoe dealer, and the jeweler left out of consideration; no one who is not out of work will fail to invest in a new suit, or a hat, or a pair of shoes, or a watch and chain for the greatest of holidays. The butcher and the grocer, too, await the advent of the holiday season with impatience. However poor one's fare may be during the year, on New Year's and particularly during the Feast of the Tabernacles (when one's dinner is exposed to the view of the other occupants of the booth), every housewife is sure to exhaust her culinary resources to produce a dish worthy of the day and her name. Take it all in all, it is a money-making season as well as a money-spending one, at once the most solemn and the most cheerful part of the Jewish year.

EVENING POST,
JUNE 26, 1897

Killing for Kosher Meat

Do we use the Jewish method of killing here, the *shechitah?*" said the manager of an East Side slaughterhouse. "Yes. We reserve from fifteen to eighteen hundred head of cattle a week for *kosher* meat, although about 70 per cent of that number only prove available. The rest are condemned, not so much because they fail to meet certain physiological requirements, as because some one of the five rules that make the *shechitah* unlawful have been transgressed in the killing.

"Come up to one of our refrigerated compartments," he added, "and I will show you a supply of chucks. A chuck is the forequarter of the steer, the only part that is lawfully used by the Orthodox Jew. The fifth rib is the dividing line. The porterhouse steaks, filets, tenderloin, and all of the hindquarter, so much prized by the Gentiles, are never eaten by the Israelites. The forequarter is strictly *kosher* and really contains the most nutritious, life-sustaining elements of the animal. The meat of the forequarter requires long and skillful cooking to make it at its best. When properly prepared, it is incomparably finer than the cuts and joints usually thought so much of that sell for a far higher price."

Admitted to the big refrigerator floor, the visitor is surprised that anything as prosaic as dressed beef can be made into so pleasing a picture. The compartment is so cold, 36 degrees, that you have to put on a wrap to stand the change of temperature, but the rows of regularly hung "sides" stretching off in succession down the long enclosure with barely walking room between them are a sight to see. There are a hundred great halves of animals neck downward, each from its own hook, suspended with such orderly precision that scarcely a variation of outline appears.

"This is *kosher,*" says the manager, pausing before a specimen. "Isn't that a beauty? The fat shows up like marble, and the pink meat is of clear and wholesome tone. See, there is the tag," pointing to a label attached to the forequarter by a wire.

"This Hebrew inscription testifies to the date of the killing and the fact that the *shechitah* in the case of this bullock was lawful. The signature is that of Dr. Kline, chief assistant of Rabbi Joseph, who is the authority for Jewish law in this respect for the whole United States. Rabbi Joseph is an invalid now, but he has efficient deputies."

Each hanging beef around this *kosher* specimen has tags and labels signifying the lot it belonged to, the inspection of government officials, and the mark of the butcher whose shop it is destined for, but the *kosher* label is unique and appended only to the chosen few. "We select only the finest, heaviest steers for *kosher,*" says the manager. "We get a half cent a pound more for the chucks, and the prime hind-quarters of the *shechitah*—slaughtered animals bring us a good price. The steers reserved for *kosher* chucks that prove to be unlawful, according to religious tenets, are of excellent quality of meat, the meat being called *terefa*. *Terefa* may be excellent, but such flesh is not for the Israelite to partake of. We do not make much money on our *kosher* meat, but the demand for it must be supplied and as the largest finest wastes and cuts are always wanted by the Gentile butcher, and those three-rib roasts, weighing fifteen pounds or so, have to be cut off large heavy animals, the two demands work in together. The *kosher* meat would bring us in more but for the fact that it is only used from those portions generally considered inferior and selling in the ordinary market for less. Another thing: no matter how fine or in what good condition a *kosher* chuck may be, if the animal has been killed over seventy-two hours it is unsalable as *kosher* and has to go at the usual price to people who don't care whether it was killed by one method or another."

The big, rough-walled enclosure where the actual process of killing goes forward is full of pictures. There is continually the sound of scrambling hoofs behind the heavy barred partition, telling of the tussle that inevitably ensues when any powerful creature gives up its life. From under the bottom of this partitioned-off apartment oozes a never ceasing flow of blood that levels itself all over the surrounding floor. "They are killing *kosher* meat this morning," explains the manager. "There is our *shochet*. He has been here seven years. He is a learned man. The rabbi, there on the bench, is also a scholar. See him examine the knife."

The rabbi looks like a scholar. He is spare and pale, with spectacled eyes and a black skull cap pushed back from his forehead. He runs his finger critically over the broad shining blade of the *shochet's* knife. If it is satisfactory, he returns it to the *shochet,* who withdraws into the boarded enclosure where his skillful and religious act must be performed. There are fresh scrambling and tussling behind those boards. Another steer dies. The *shochet* again brings his blade to the rabbi for inspection, but this time it must be sharpened; so another gleaming scimitar is brought to him. Far more archaic and Oriental looking is the long bearded Jew of great stature, but of delicate touch and perception, who stands at the long table examining into the condition of the slaughtered animals. He is removing a tissue from the suspected lungs. He leads his long fingers repeatedly over the membrane and finally dislodges it. Then he examines the under part by pouring warm water on it to find out if a hole has been made in the lung by the separation of the tissue from it. If a hole has been made, the meat of that animal will be *terefa* and not *kosher*. If the warm water leaks through, the animal has had at sometime inflammation of the lung, and is condemned. The *shochet* performed his functions carefully and correctly, the steer was apparently in splendid condition, but Israelites may not eat of its flesh.

"If, in the act of killing, the *shochet* separated the windpipe or gullet by pressing on them with the knife, or if he killed with a knife that has a notch, or if he put the knife underneath the windpipe or gullet, or if he tore loose the windpipe or the gullet, or if the *shochet's* hands trembled when performing the *shechitah* (the Jewish killing), Israelites may not eat of the flesh of the animal," says the rabbi. "The skillful operation in the act of *shechitah* depends on two conditions—the fitness of the *shochet* and the fitness of the knife. The *shochet* must be careful, active, and brisk. A *shochet* must, first of all, be strong, that his hands may not tremble and cause undue suffering; then he must be well versed in the laws of *shechitah* and be expert in examining the inner structure of the animal. He must also be a believer in the Mosaic and Israelite law. If he breaks the Sabbath, he is no longer called a *shochet,* but his name is *nabal,* a miscreant. An animal, no matter how wholesome its condition, if killed by such a man, is called *nevelah,* or dead of itself. The second condition of a good *shechitah* is a good knife; that is, one of the required length, sharp and smooth, without the least indentation, in order to cut with it the windpipe and esophagus in the middle of the throat without stopping and without pressing down the knife in the least. In this way the two bodies of the animal, the exterior body, containing the brain, and the interior body, containing the heart, are separated from one another in the easiest and best manner.

"In our ancient writings the most painful and the most painless kinds of death are described. In the most painful death, the soul is said to depart from the body with the same difficulty that wool is taken out from thorns. In the easiest kind of death, body and soul part with the same ease that a hair is drawn out from milk. We maintain that the *shechitah* or the Jewish method of killing, although slower, is easier and less painful than that caused by blows inflicted on the head.

"One thing is certain," continued the manager. "The flesh of an animal killed by the Jewish method looks more inviting than that killed in the usual way, because the breast has bled freely. Sometimes co-agulated blood is found on the ribs of an animal killed by blows on the head, on the inside near the spine, and the clots of blood cannot be removed by washing. The flesh of an animal killed by blows is heavier than the flesh of one killed by *shechitah,* because the blood has been absorbed by the members. The blood is the soul, and is forbidden to the Orthodox Jew. 'Only be sure that thou eat not the blood, for the blood is the life,' it is written in Deuteronomy, and we believe that if a man eat blood, he partakes of its properties and transmits those qualities to his children after him."

"What is the matter with that beef?" the visitor asks, seeing the examiner shake his head dubiously over a part of the lacy-looking membrane he held and then confer with the *shochet.*

"A nail had penetrated the lining of the stomach," is the answer. "It had not injured the creature. The flaw was healed, but still it existed; so the meat is not *kosher.* How does a steer get hold of a nail? Oh, we frequently find needles and all sorts of foreign substances in the stomach. Of course not so much in the range cattle that are grass fed, but the large proportion of *kosher* meat must come from cattle that are stall fed. The Western buyers get them, thin and in poor condition on the range, and then fatten them up in the stable."

What is true of the care exercised with regard to *kosher* beef is equally true of poultry killing. There are hundreds of poultry dealers on the populous East Side and in the uptown districts where prosperous Jews live who have only *shechitah*-killed geese, ducks, fowls, and turkeys for their customers. Some few of these slaughterers have establishments of their own, keeping in their employ a *shochet* and a rabbi or examiner authorized to affix the seal guaranteeing that the ceremony of killing has been lawful. By far the most general custom, however, is for the individual poultry dealer to buy a coop of live fowls and lodge them at the big slaughterhouse where they can be killed at a cent a head after the lawful and prescribed manner.

The slaughterhouse at Gouverneur Slip has tier upon tier of padlocked wire cages on the various floors rented out to the individual poultry dealers, much as Post Office boxes are leased to patrons. Fifteen thousand head of poultry a day are killed after the Jewish method at this house. Eighteen *shochets* are kept regularly employed, and average $15 a week each. The feathered candidate for killing is swung by the legs, which are tied together, from a hook overhanging a trough. The windpipe and gullet are cut, exactly as in the case of beef. The knives are kept steeped up to the handles in a preparation of lime in order that they may not rust. Even after the *shechitah* has been properly performed, there is a variety of reasons why the flesh of that particular duck, turkey or goose may be *terefa* and not *kosher*. If there is an enlargement of the crop, if a wing or leg be injured, or if anything the least abnormal has befallen the interior body, the fowl is condemned. If killed properly, the fowl is taken to a cunningly contrived machine where, in a twinkling the Hebrew seal signifying approval is affixed to the legs. In the winter season from 6,000 to 7,000 geese are sealed in a single week.

Up to ten years ago there was no public official charged with the care of this department of domestic and religious well-being. The increase of Jewish population, however, prompted the importation of Rabbi Joseph, who is of Russian birth and training. Before his coming, each slaughter-house that catered to Jewish trade employed its private *shochet*, but there was no affixing of official seals. There are numerous butcher shops having mystical letters in the windows, signifying *kosher* meat, but the initiated say that not all of these are to be trusted. They have customers because the customers are ignorant that the lawful ceremonies have been dispensed with.

NEW YORK TRIBUNE,
APRIL 20, 1902

The Passover Bread

The Jewish Passover will begin tomorrow, and for one week from the date the people who adhere to the ancient customs of the Jews will eat no leavened bread and will abstain from many articles of food which at other times of the year are looked upon as necessary. Among the Reform Jews, the season is of importance only in so far as they have religious services at their houses of worship on the first and last days of the week and have the unleavened bread on their table at mealtimes, more as a reminder of the ancient custom than as a part of the meal. But among the Orthodox Jews great preparations are made for the proper celebration of the feast. The habitations, no matter whether they are large or small, a dark apartment in a double-decker tenement house or a pretentious private house, are thoroughly cleansed, and every kitchen utensil which is used in the rest of the year is put away to make room for the *Pesach* kitchenware. An Orthodox Jewish household must be extremely poor where there are not special kitchen utensils and tableware for the Passover.

On the first evening of the feast the members of the family gather about the table, which is laid as elaborately as the householder's purse will allow, and then the story of the Passover is read by the head of the family and the origin of the feast is explained to the children, who take part in the quaint ceremony by responses and songs. No matter how poor the family may be, there is always a vacant chair at the table when this ceremony, known as the *Seder,* takes place, to typify hospitality. The *Seder* is the chief religious ceremony of the week, and is observed to some extent even among Reform Jews, who have modernized the ceremony, however, by reading the story in English instead of using the original Hebrew.

The amount of unleavened bread consumed in the course of the week following the *Seder* may be estimated from the fact that about thirty thousand barrels of flour are used to furnish the supply for this city. Several bakeries make the unleavened bread, called *matzo,* all the year. Some of the product is sold out of season, but the greater part is delivered within a few weeks of the Passover. Besides the large concerns, there are many small baking establishments on the East Side where work is carried on for two or three months in anticipation of the Passover rush. The product of the small East Side concerns goes for the most part to the ultra-Orthodox Jews for whom the regular factory-made *matzos* are too modern. This bread, which resembles large crackers, is made entirely from flour and water. In the large concerns the mass is mixed and kneaded by machinery, but in the smaller establishments this work is done by hand. The dough is passed between metal rollers and then cut into square or round pieces. A venerable man who stood watching the men at work in one of the basement bakeries in Clinton Street explained why only square *matzos* were made there. He said: "According to the Mosaic law the *matzos* must be in the oven within eighteen minutes after the dough is mixed. This can be done very easily when all the material is cut into squares. But when you have to gather up the pieces that fall between the disks, roll them out and cut them up, more time is consumed and the mass is liable to leaven. That's the reason we have our Passover bread square."

There are several grades of *matzos* on the market, ranging in price from 1 to 10 cents a pound, and these are delivered in bulk or packed in dry-goods boxes, in paper packages, or in fancy boxes.

"Of course," said one East Side baker, "our customers are for the most part Jews who buy the *matzos* because they wish to keep the Passover, but we have many customers also who are not Jews, who prefer the unleavened bread to crackers, and our list of such customers is becoming larger every year."

NEW YORK TRIBUNE,
OCTOBER 15, 1905

Orthodox Inconvenient

A careful student of East Side conditions, a Hebrew himself, recently declared that not more than 40 per cent of American-born Jews observed the dietary laws and religious ceremonies prescribed by the Mosaic law.

"Convenience," said this Jewish student of his race, "convenience and the customs of the society about him—write that down as the explanation of the irreligion of the American-born Jew. No intellectual protest against the traditions of his race moves this class of apostate. The public school; the business world, adjusted to the observation of the Christian, not the Jewish Sabbath; the Saturday night dance; and the complete ignoring of all Jewish holidays by the mass of people surrounding him—these, and a score of similar reasons, explain the situation. The Jew of the second generation does not become a Christian. He is as far from any such conversion as his father, but he finds that to live in a business world adjusted to a Christian calendar is hopelessly inconvenient, if not practically impossible, if he clings to his racial religious observances.

"So long as the boy is in school and lives with his parents, he more or less willingly submits to the parental training, but when he goes out to work and becomes self-supporting, then conditions change. He finds that to keep his job he must work on Saturday, the Jewish Sabbath, and rest on Sunday, the Christian holiday. Similarly, he learns to surrender his celebration of other religious days for business reasons. Thus, little by little, the Jewish boy is transformed into a workaday member of the American business community. Natural as such a result is, it brings with it endless unhappiness to Jewish homes on the East Side. The father, with bewildered sorrow, sees his child steadily becoming estranged from him, not merely in education and in the ordinary things of American life, but even in the observance of rites and laws peculiar to his race through countless centuries. Moreover, since every Jewish ceremony is more or less patriarchal in character and comprehends the whole family in its festivities, sacred days, such as the approaching Day of Atonement, are fraught with extreme sadness, because, from their observation, the second generation will in countless instances be absent. Even in homes where both generations are together, the chasm between Asia and America will not infrequently separate father and son sitting at the same table."

Apart from matters of religion the gulf between father and son on the East Side is broad. Students of local conditions have declared that the vast majority of Jewish immigrants live and die obeying the laws and following the customs of their native land. American language and ways alike remain unintelligible to them, and they depend with almost pathetic helplessness on their children for association with the world about them.

"He is an American—born American— not a 'greenhorn' like me." This is the fashion in which the average Jewish immigrant describes his child. From the very start, this child unconsciously acquires a contempt for the un-American habits and characteristics of his father. The American public school and associations with business life do the rest. The average Jewish boy of fifteen lives the life of New York, contemporaneous to the minute; his father still slumbers in the existence of Kishinev, Lemberg, or Jassy. The separation in habits of religion follows as a natural sequence that earlier separation in all the common phases of life. The laissez-faire spirit of our national life seems in many cases to accomplish what the persecution of ages has failed to bring about—namely, the alienating of the Jewish child from the strict observance of his racial religious rites.

NEW YORK TRIBUNE,
SEPTEMBER 30, 1900

Shadchens Find Business Bad

This has been a hard year for the Cupids of the Ghetto, as the matrimonial agents of the Jewish quarter might be called. To the Jews he is known as the *shadchen,* but unless the marriage business picks up, the broker is going to drop out of sight. Already he is branching out into other ways of making a living. He writes letters for the illiterate, acts as interpreter in business transactions, or does odd jobs around the synagogues. Marriage brokerage used to be one of the best-paying businesses on the East Side, but that day has passed, and the *shadchens* think it will never return.

When the Jews began to come to this city in large numbers and to crowd the Germans out of the East Side district, they brought the marriage broker with them. They had always been accustomed to having a professional matchmaker arrange their marriages, and at that time they did not know how to get along without it. The young men were bashful and were more than willing to give up 10 percent of the girl's dowry if some one else would put the question. Besides, they made sure of getting a wife in this way. They would go to the broker, or *shadchen,* and outline their ideal of a wife, not forgetting to mention the amount of dowry they expected. The *shadchen* would take note of all of the young man's advantages— personal appearance, education, and money–making ability. Then he would go among the young women of his extended acquaintance and speedily find someone who was willing to wed on the terms which the broker had to offer.

The *shadchen's* fee was paid as soon as the engagement was announced. It usually amounted to 10 per cent of the dowry, but in some cases a stipulated fee was charged where the girl was very pretty and her people unable to give a large marriage portion. Sometimes the *shadchen* had trouble collecting his fee; in those cases he evened things up by breaking off the match. There were many ways of doing this. If the man was at fault, the *shadchen* would get the girl a more desirable match. As love had not entered into the first engagement, it was speedily broken, leaving the man sadder but wiser. If the *shadchen* discovered that the girl objected to paying the fee he found a prettier girl for the man.

This was the way it used to be done. Let the oldest *shadchen* in the colony tell why it is that his services are no longer in great demand. He is to be found in Hester Street, and the sign outside his door asserts that he writes letters, makes translations, and teaches Hebrew or English.

"I would starve to death in a month if I depended on matchmaking for a living," he said bitterly. "Once I lived on the fat of the land, and most of the marriageable young men and women in the quarter depended on me to make them happy for life. Now they believe in love and all that rot. They are making their own marriages, and many of them will be unhappy. Several things combined to bring about the change. In the first place there are too many girls in the Jewish quarter. There are six or seven girls after every man. This makes the young fellows hard to deal with. They can marry into almost any family in the block just for the asking. Some of the women still come to me, but it is hard to find mates for them.

"They learned how to start their own love affairs from the Americans, and it is one of the worst things they have picked up. How can a Jewish couple expect to be happy in a marriage of their own making when it has been the custom of their fathers and mothers for ages not to see each other until after marriage? The love which they have learned to put so much faith in dribbles out in trips to Coney and walks around the parks before marriage. In a month they are figuring out ways of getting rid of each other. In the old way every month of married life made the young people more attached to each other. They may come back to the old way of doing things, and for their own sake, I hope they do."

NEW YORK TRIBUNE,
JANUARY 9, 1898

Going Under the Chupah

Uniting people in wedlock according to the old Jewish customs and with the pomp and display which indicates their Oriental origin is one of the industries which always flourishes in the New York ghetto and which is affected by none of the mercantile or political disturbances that frequently influence ordinary business. East Side weddings come under the head of business because they give employment to many people, and these and the many public halls where most of the weddings take place could not exist if the business fell off.

Such a thing as a strictly quiet wedding, with no witnesses except the immediate members of the family, is almost unknown in the Jewish quarter. When the wedding contract has been signed and the *shadchen's* work completed, there is usually an engagement party at which the parents of the bride-elect make public announcement of the engagement of their daughter and break a glass in the presence of their guests to indicate that the contract is not fragile, like the works of man, and cannot be broken like them. All those who come to the engagement party are usually asked to the wedding ceremony, and receive invitations which are printed on fancy embossed cards in English and Yiddish, and sometimes in German also. These invitations are worded nearly like the ordinary wedding invitation, but in every instance a line follows the address where the ceremony will take place, which tells the bride's residence.

The people who are the least blessed with worldly goods have the ceremony performed at the home of the bride; those who have more hire the synagogue for the occasion, and those who are of the highest circle in the ghetto have the ceremony performed in the synagogue and hire a hall for the wedding dance and dinner. But the largest number of weddings takes place in the halls which are arranged for the purpose. These halls usually contain a women's reception room, a dining room, and a ballroom, and are rented for evening weddings and balls for from $5 to $10. This does not include what is known as the "hatbox," where the wardrobe of the guests is left. The proprietor of the hall usually charges from 10 to 30 cents a couple for taking care of hats and wraps.

"When people are very swell," said the proprietor of one of these halls, "they hire the hatbox, and their guests don't have to pay for hatchecks."

The invitations usually give five or six o'clock as the hour for the ceremony, and at the time named the bride and bridegroom arrive with their respective kinspeople. The bride is attired in white satin and long veil, and has many flowers; the man is in evening clothes. They take stations in different rooms, and as the guests arrive the ceremony of *Kabolath-ponim*, or presenting, takes place. This lasts until the guests have all arrived—generally an hour or two later than the time named on the invitation cards—and then, if it is a large company, the young people have a dance or two. This over, the bridegroom takes his place under the *chupah*, or canopy, in the large hall, and there awaits the coming of his bride, who is brought to him by her father. The *chupah*, or canopy, has been an important feature in the Jewish wedding ceremonial ever since there has been any record. One of the East Side rabbis said that a verse of the Bible refers plainly to the "joyous voice of the bridegroom from under the *chupah*."

The canopy is made of velvet and may be of any color, although it is usually purple or deep red; it is trimmed with gold lace, and has the Star of David embroidered in gold on one end. Under this canopy, which symbolizes the future home of the family, the bride is taken by her parents, and the rabbi performs the marriage ceremony. When the couple have taken wine from the same glass to show that they will be partners in joy, and the ring has been placed on the bride's finger, a glass is again broken, which ceremony the rabbi explained thus:

"At no joyous occasion should the Jew forget that the glory of the Jewish nation is broken. The broken glass reminds him of that. It also reminds the young people that sooner or later all must return to dust, and, even like the beautiful glass, be shattered and destroyed."

The ceremony over, everybody congratulates his neighbor as well as the bridal couple, and then, under the leadership of the chief actors, the whole party goes to the dining room, where luncheon is served. Since early in the morning the kitchen has been in charge of a *kochfrau*, under whose direction a luncheon as well as a supper, which is served later in the evening, has been prepared. The luncheon lasts only a short time, and then the dancing begins and lasts until supper is served at about 11 o'clock.

The synagogue wedding, when the *chupah* is reared in the sanctuary, is more expensive than the hall wedding, because, aside from the fee paid to the rabbi and the hall rent, there is an expense of $5 for the use of the synagogue. There are several Jewish houses of worship on the East Side which are particularly popular, and the one at No. 38 Henry Street rarely has less than two and frequently as many as four weddings on a Sunday. There is a hall in East Broadway where many of these weddings and wedding balls take place which is used on two nights every week as a dancing school. The sanctuary, containing the sacred scroll behind embroidered curtains, is at one end. The little sign on the wall with the words "No refusals" seems to clash, until one is told that "No refusals" is posted for the benefit of fastidious East Side maidens, who are warned in that way not to bring about any unpleasantness in the dancing class by refusing to dance with any "gent." At two points in the hall there are automatic machines, where a cent in the slot brings forth a dash of perfume, and a dumbwaiter communicates with the bar, which is in the basement.

Buying
a Doctor

The choice of the son of the family may be poor and of inferior connections, and there will be nothing worse than disappointment, but should the daughter look beneath her, there are storms and entreaties and even curses. So great is the desire for sons-in-law above the rank of the family that extraordinary measures are taken to secure a desirable specimen. The son-in-law for whom the soul of every East Sider pines is a professional man—a doctor preferably. Now, there are not so many physicians to be had, and there is only a slight chance that one of the number will look kindly on any given girl; so the affair cannot be left to chance. An ambitious youth is "caught young," his fancy fired with pictures of social and professional glory; financial help is promised him, and then, like a pill in jelly, is tucked the condition "marry my daughter afterward." This practice is so common that there has arisen a saying, used when any girl marries a physician, "Her father bought a doctor for her." The young men do not seem to object. Indeed, at the age of seventeen the prospect of marriage is little worthy of consideration to a boy. If repentance comes after, he manages to keep it to himself and to live up to the bargain.

The case of one young man, recently married, will serve to illustrate the practice. At the age of eighteen the father of a girl a year or two his senior made a contract with him, the one promising a medical education and the other side marriage and social elevation. The boy agreed, went through the medical school, and duly announced his engagement. The girl's father furnished his office and living rooms, paying the rent and promising support until the young man's practice should pay. They have put their daughter a rung higher up the social ladder; they shine with reflected glory. Henceforth, their conversation will be peppered and salted with "my son-in-law, Dr. So-and-so" and "my son-in-law—he's a doctor, you know." Should he be present when neighbors visit, his title will be hurled at their heads at least once a minute.

Still more extraordinary is the case of a girl doing the purchasing of a doctor quite without assistance. Some ambitious maidens, others, having their parents lacking in social ambition or failing parents altogether, have negotiated the whole affair alone. These cases are kept quiet, naturally, but the neighbors usually find out and spread the news that such a one "is buying a doctor." But it amuses them, it excites them, and perhaps the game is worth the candle after all.

Keeping
in Style

As Broadway is to upper New York, so is Grand Street to the Lower East Side. Here and in the streets immediately adjoining, one sees what lower Manhattan considers "the glass of fashion and the mould of form." Of "form" there may be something lacking, but fashion is there in full force. Grand Street out-Broadways Broadway. Here one sees all the styles ever devised by the brain of man—sees them in all their glory, having their fullest scope, allowed to expand at their own sweet will. Does Broadway wear a feather? Grand Street dons two, without loss of time. Are trailing skirts seen in Fifth Avenue? Grand Street trails its yards with a dignity all its own. Are daring color effects sent over from Paris? The rainbow hides its diminished head before Grand Street on a Sunday afternoon. Grand Street is Broadway plus Fifth Avenue, only very much more so. Its wide sidewalks show more fashion to the square foot on a Sunday than any other part of the city.

In Grand Street the East Side buys its dresses, coats, and a thousand and one other things. For its hats it goes to Division Street, which begins its picturesque career at Chatham Square and runs along to Clinton Street. From Chatham Square, for the length of a couple of blocks or so, the neighborhood christens the street "Millinery Lane" for good and obvious reasons. Let no unwary traveler, unversed in the ways of the East Side shopkeeper, set foot in this spot, under pain of being forced to buy the most marvelous creations of the modiste's brain that were ever designed to assist Cupid in subjugating the heart of man (East Side man). There are fully twenty millinery stores in the "lane," and each store has one or more "sidewalk ladies" to "pull in." The term "puller-in" is not wrongly applied. They smile seductively as they ask, "Anything in a stylish hat, ma'am?" If the fascination does not work properly, the puller-in gently but firmly takes hold of the arm of the passer-by and proceeds to argue the question. These enterprising ladies devise the hat fashions for the Lower East Side. The system is simple. Whatever a hat may lack in quality, there is never anything to be desired in the matter of quantity. The East Side, though poor enough in all truth, is ever-generous. So far as the people can afford, there is no stint in hospitality or charity, and the same rule is applied to hats.

It is not easy for an unpracticed eye to judge the quantity of chiffon or silk used on an ordinary summer hat, but on one recently seen in Millinery Lane there was a bulwark certainly no less than ten inches high all around the huge brim of the creation. And it cost only $4—all that chiffon for $4—not to mention the handful of flowers and fruit which grew in the center! Purple and yellow is a favorite combination, and may truthfully be said to give more show for the money than any other effect. Black, except in large black velvet hats with feathers, is not popular. When a black straw is used, a microscope is needed to distinguish it at the bottom of a pyramid of peacock colors. The average East Side girl who earns a few dollars every week and is not in destitute circumstances buys every winter a hat with feathers. It is always a large one, and sometimes it groans beneath the weight of nearly or quite a dozen plumes which may once have called an ostrich their parent, although it is certain that the bird would disown her offspring at sight could she again see them.

It is to hats that the young girl's fancy lightly turns not only in spring, but in autumn also. She cares for dress, but it would be impossible to maintain throughout the high standard of elegance set by the headgear. Nevertheless she does very well in this respect. The "habit back" flourished on the East Side from the first moment of its arrival from Paris. If skirts are long, no self-respecting girl would be seen in any costume that did not sweep a yard or two behind. If sleeves are tight, she would consider it a disgrace to be able to raise her arms above her head. She ties her neck scarf as low on the waist of her dress as it is shown in Paris fashions—and just a little lower—at the same minute that Fifth Avenue adopts the same style. If overskirts are worn, there is nothing else to be seen in Grand Street. But in the matter of dresses, it is natural that the East Side should be strictly up-to-date, for does it not furnish clothes for the rest of the town? If my lady wears a velvet gown, put together for her in an East Side sweatshop, may not the girl whose tired fingers fashioned it rejoice her soul by astonishing Grand Street with a copy of it on the next Sunday? My lady's is in velvet, and the East Side girl's is in the cheapest of cloth, but it's the style that counts.

The artistic taste of the East Side men is also highly developed, but the cruel hand of fashion has shut to them the door to its full enjoyment. Only in the matter of collars, neckties, and socks can their fancy display itself. But if the field is restricted, it is worked with energy. There are "sports" and "hot sports" and "stiffs." The "sport" is known by his necktie or his socks. The point is to combine on the small space allowed as many colors as possible. Purple and lavender, green and red, dark and light blue make contrasts which, as the wearers say, are "not to be beat." A "hot sport" is the common or garden "sport" in the superlative. A "stiff" is known by his collar. There are many gilded youths on the East Side who would never be guilty of wearing a "standup" collar when "high turndowns" were in fashion.

There need not be any evil to choose, however, as many East Side girls realize. Not all overdress, by any means. The uptown world is always underestimating the amount of refinement to be found in the tenements of lower Manhattan. Many girls dress neatly, stylishly, and tastefully, and the mystery of their toilets is often amusingly explained. One story will illustrate. The writer recently had occasion to go out of town on a Sunday in company with a girl whose family is in genuine poverty. People of less indomitable pride, of less intense self-respect, would long ago have applied for help instead of eating bread and water day after day. At the appointed hour the girl appeared, dressed not only well, but stylishly. She had a good figure, and she was positively stunning. One who did not know East Side girls would have said, uncharitably, that the heartless young woman was spending on clothes the money needed to buy bread for her old mother and small sisters. But a few friendly words turned the conversation to the subject of dress, and the mystery was explained. The waist, thin and charmingly cool-looking, she had made herself, buying the material from a Hester pushcart for 20 cents. Its style came from the really handsome neck arrangement, which she had made herself; she worked at neckwear, and the boss had allowed her to take the

odds and ends from which she had fashioned the pretty thing. The skirt, her brother-in-law, who "works at skirts," had made for her at odd times, and it cost, getting the material at wholesale, $2.50. Her hat, her chum made at an expense of 60 cents. To the uninitiated the costume represented an outlay of $20, at least, although she had achieved it at an expense of $3.30, and was able to go abroad without proclaiming to the world the dire poverty at home. Her cleverness and the kindness of others had saved the proud old mother a severe humiliation. There are many such on the East Side.

But although such girls are not rare, the other kind forms the great majority. It is apparently a part of the process of becoming Americanized. The girl whose Russian mother knew but the wig of the religious Jewess and a soft shawl, the girl who, had she remained in bright Italy, would have kept but one kerchief for weekdays and another for Sunday—these girls feel vastly fine in a "three-story hat" which might well vie with the historic coat of Joseph. In the land of equality shall not one wear what another wears? Shall not Fifth Avenue and Grand Street walk hand in hand—the lion and the lamb lie down together? It would be rank heresy to insinuate that there is anything faulty in the process of Americanizing as it goes on on the East Side.

NEW YORK TRIBUNE,
JULY 3, 1898

New Names for East Siders

The directory makers are experiencing less difficulty every year with the names of the Russian and Polish Jews on the East Side of New York. The names with which they are burdened when they come to this country are made pronounceable by the children or the teachers when the second generation goes to school, and while in some instances the new names sound like the original, they are written differently, and in most cases, bear no resemblance to the roots from which they were taken. This is true not only of family names but of the "front" names, too. A long-bearded pushcart man was asked in court recently, "What is your name?"

"Yaikef Rabinowski," he answered.

The magistrate evidently thought that was the man's family name and asked, "What's your Christian name?"

The man became indignant at being suspected of having anything "Christian" about him, and "front name" has been the proper expression at that seat of justice ever since.

Yitzchok, the Hebrew of Jacob, has been made Hitchcock, and an old man whose neighbors know him as Cheskel has assumed the more euphonious name of Elwell. There are many similar cases of evolution, but there are more American, English, and even French names among the dwellers in the ghetto are the result of accident as much as anything else. Children are sent to school, and their names are placed on the records by the teacher, who does the best he can with the unpronounceable thing. After the children have been in school a short time, they and their parents become known by the name given to them by the teacher.

An example of this kind was mentioned recently by a young woman who had been a teacher in a school where many Russian children were pupils. "A man came in one day," she said, "with two boys who could not say a word in English. Their names were impossible except for those who had acquired the East Side jargon. When the man was gone, I made one understand that his name would be John and the other that he would have to answer to the name William, and in some way or other their family name which was full of twists and turns, and ended with a 'witch,' became Holz. Within a few weeks John and William Holz made themselves understood in fair English, and within a year they were star pupils. One day the father called at the school to see me about his boys and introduced himself as Mr. Holz! He seemed to be as much at home with the name as though he had been born with it, and so there are hundreds in our district."

In many instances a sign bought at a bargain has caused men to assume a new name, and the changes are made without the least feeling in the matter. One East Side patriarch said, "We honor our fathers just as much, even if we drop their names. Nothing good ever came to us while we bore them; possibly we'll have more luck with the new names."

But there are cases where men changed their names because they wanted to obliterate their foreign origin. Thus a family came to New York with the name of Neuberger. Presently the name became Newburger; then it was changed to Newburg, and now the two remaining brothers are known, one as Mr. New and the other as Mr. Berg.

The merchant on the East Side who rejoices in the name Karzenellenbogen and his neighbor Leworosinski continue to do business despite the numerous syllables in their names, but not so Mr. Bochlowitz. His son changed his name to Buckley, and even this was too long for the second son, who cut it down a peg and made it Buck. The father and son, it is said, are in business under the firm name of Bochlowitz & Buckley, and they send checks signed that way to the young Buck, who is still at school.

"It does some people good to change their names," said an East Side observer, "and I doubt whether Mr. Gladstone would ever have been the great man he was if his ancestors had not dropped the name Freudenstein for Gladstone or whether other German names would have been as well received as their Americanized substitutes." The man could not be convinced that Gladstone was not originally Freudenstein.

One group of names on the East Side is always recognized by the knowing ones as Bohemian. To this class belong the names Yelteles, Abeles, Karpeles, Kakeles, and a number of other names ending in "les." When the owners of some of these names outgrow the East Side and move uptown they drop one of the "e's" in their name and then blossom forth as Karpels, Kakels, etc. One Bohemian said that his countrymen were proud of the "les" names, because they show that Aristotles, Sophocles, Pericles, and Hercules were all Bohemians.

NEW YORK TRIBUNE,
SEPTEMBER 2, 1900

The East Side Boy

I think," said the East Side boy to his friend, the practical sociologist, "that most people have very queer ideas about the East Side boy." These two were on exceedingly good terms, and it was understood that differences of age, social training, and the like should be forgotten when the East Side boy came up to the sociologist's den and discoursed while that worthy smoked his pipe. This had been going on for three or four years to the edification of each. The two had met when the boy was just an ordinary, bright East Side youngster, and mutual curiosity mingled with growing affection had done the rest. Now the youth had developed a taste for study, and the pair read Latin together, while the boy and his parents saved up money to send him to college. Yet the boy remained an East Side boy, loyal to his part of the city, even though he knew well the formerly unexplored country above Fourteenth Street. As for the sociologist, he was merely a philosopher who spelled life with a capital L. He was interested in humanity, rich or poor, and reflected with satisfaction that on one occasion he had attended the anarchist ball on one evening and a gorgeous Fifth Avenue function the next . . . which shows what manner of man the sociologist was.

"Most of the popular ideas on any subject are queer, my young friend," said he to the boy, yet pleased with the prospect of conversation from that sometimes taciturn youth. "But you'd think," persisted the boy, "that the East Side children were a special brand. Now, I was an ordinary boy, in all conscience, and I'm sure I wasn't very wicked or very unhappy. I think I was, in the main, remarkably like a West Side boy or any other kind of boy. I don't think the East Side boy has any more temptations to commit a crime than the richer ones, not so many, perhaps. You hear so much about 'gangs' and crap playing and cigarette smoking. Well, we do have all that, but it isn't as bad as it's painted."

"How about the gangs?" inquired the sociologist. "Did you ever belong to one?"

"Did I? Why, of course. But, then, there are at least three kinds of gangs. First, there's the really tough gang. The boys who belong to this kind of gang meet at corners to make trouble. They fight, and sometimes they hold up other boys and make them give up money. There used to be lots of these fellows around Cherry and Water Streets, but they've been suppressed now. Some of the gangs were pretty hard to break up, and there may be a few fellows of this kind still hanging around, but not many. Of course, these were bad boys, and the police used to get after them. But this kind of gang didn't form the majority, by any means, and they were only around the docks and other places that are tough anyway.

"Then, there was another kind, and I think that most of the gangs they have now belong to this class. These boys hang around a corner and flirt with girls and amuse themselves with people who pass by. I call these the flirty gangs, because that is really what they do. The boys who belong to these gangs may be bad, but most of them are all right, I think. They wouldn't hurt anybody, unless under unusual circumstances.

"The third kind of gang, the kind I used to belong to, was just a social gang, formed chiefly for the purpose of playing games and especially baseball. We used to joke and have fun, but we never did anything worse than mischief, and we used to let the girls alone. Some of the boys were not as good as they might have been, but most of them were decent enough. Most of them worked, and none of them have turned out badly at all. We didn't have any organization, except that we all looked up to the one who was strongest and who played ball best. This is the only way in which any of the decent gangs have a leader, but the gangs that used to fight had recognized leaders.

"There used to be a good deal of crap playing around Henry Street, where most of the richer boys lived, and part of East Broadway. I don't think the crap playing was any worse among our boys than gambling among uptown boys. Some of our boys who had well-to-do parents, or who had good places, used to lose as much as $2 or $3 on a Sunday, sometimes more. Then, around Essex Street there used to be a crap club of men—expressmen and peddlers who were not good men at all. They used to play on the street or in yards with some one to look out for the policeman. I don't think that there is as much crap playing as there used to be. All these gangs, except the tough gangs, are likely at any time to form a club, and if they get into one of the institutions they may turn into a fine organization. Even outside of institutions, there are clubs which may last a long time.

"The smoking isn't general, except among the tough gangs. There were only three or four in our gang who ever smoked. I don't want to make out the gang to be too good. They used a good deal of bad language, because they think it is smart, but they outgrew this, and I don't think the East Side boys are any worse than others in this respect after they get to be sixteen or so.

"When I belonged to a gang, there was no place for a playground on the East Side. In fact, there isn't really any place now where we can play baseball. There is always Central Park, but a small boy can't afford much carfare. We used to play in the street whenever the policeman wasn't around, and even when he was, we would play prisoner's base and pussy cat. If people don't want gangs they will have to give us something else and make it very attractive, too, for the gangs have a good time. I don't see why the city can't make a place for baseball and that sort of thing.

"Then, when people talk about the East Side boy, they don't speak enough about the studious boy. Although I liked to play ball and go around with the gang, I didn't shirk school, and I tried to read books. It is hard for a boy who has just come over here to start right. I was ten when I came, and I had to sell papers when I didn't know more of English than was enough to call out the name of the paper, and more arithmetic than to make the right change. You'd smile if I told you what a time I had to get hold of the books I wanted. The gang wasn't a literary set, by any means, though. I joined a gang because I was fond of games, and that was my only chance for playing. At first I was the only member of the crowd who belonged to a library, but more joined later on.

I was a poor boy, and hadn't any money to spend, but I don't think any boy was ever happier than I was. I had to stay in the city all summer and run errands for my mother when I wanted to play, and I used even to have to scrub the floor, but I was a very happy boy most of the time."

"I agree with you," observed the sociologist, "that the East Side boy receives a good deal of undeserved pity."

"Well," returned the boy, "he doesn't want pity—he wants a place to play and a little sensible companionship. He makes the best of circumstances, but the circumstances could be improved. But nobody will ever do anything for the East Side boy who isn't willing to make a friend and companion of him. People who meet and talk always get on the wrong track. Why, it stands to reason that the small boy on the street can tell them more in three minutes than all their uptown speech-makers."

"Oh," suggested his friend, "some good does come out of the Upper West Side once in a while."

"Yes," wound up the boy, "but if people would spend less money and give more companionship there would be less trouble with the East Side boy. He's all right, if you give him half a chance."

And the sociologist looked at the bright face of one who had had his "half a chance" and decided that the boy was correct.

NEW YORK TRIBUNE,
SEPTEMBER 18, 1898

East Side Love of Learning

The people of the East Side are again confronted with the problem of how to educate their children, and the limited capacity of the city schools, which is evident again this fall, is once more a cause for keen disappointment and unfulfilled hopes. Those who do not know the inner life of the tenement-house dwellers can hardly realize the general extent of this disappointment or the acute suffering which it entails for parents and children alike.

There were several cases brought to public notice last fall where boys who had been denied school advantages committed suicide. In other cases similar disappointments resulted in insanity. Such facts can only occasion surprise to those who are unfamiliar with the intense craving for knowledge which prevails in that part of New York where "the other half" lives. It will astonish many people to learn that the average small boy of the ghetto has none of the commercial instinct which is ordinarily taken as a sign and heritage of his race. There, boys want to become doctors and lawyers—some look forward to a political career—and social questions fill their young lives with restless longing. It is a peculiar fact, too, that the fathers of these boys, who spend their days in the ill-smelling fish market of Hester Street or live their lives haggling over the price of pushcart wares, encourage the younger generation in their desire for knowledge.

"It is enough that I am a merchant," said a long-gabardined peddler yesterday. "What is such a life? What can I do for my people or myself? My boy shall be a lawyer, learned and respected of men. And it is for that that I stand here, sometimes when my feet ache so that I would gladly go and rest. My boy shall have knowledge. He shall go to college."

College! That is the aim and ambition of hundreds of them. The father, bent beneath the load of coats he is carrying to the factory or trudging along with his push-cart, dreams of a better life than his own for the boy or girl who is so dear to his heart. When evening comes and the day's work is over, he sits in the little tenement, at the doorstoop or on the sidewalk, and instills into his children's minds the necessity for knowledge. He points to his own life—how meager, sordid, and poor it is—and he tells them that to avoid it they must study hard and learn much.

The book of daily prayer and the *Talmud*, often the only books in the house, are brought out and eagerly studied. It is by no means unusual for a boy of nine years to be able to recite the *Talmud* from memory. The rapidity with which these children acquire knowledge is a constant cause of surprise when they enter the public schools. Those who come in contact with them are continually amazed at the evidences of precocity which they display. There are many who have no fathers to bear the family burden while they pursue their studies. To them day school is a luxury not to be thought of, but after the work in the sweatshop is over they repair to the Educational Alliance, Cooper Union, or other places of a similar character, where the lectures supply, in a measure, satisfaction for their craving for knowledge. The lecture is often supplemented with books rescued from a second-hand shop at the sacrifice of breakfast or dinner. These are carried to the poor lodgings where they are pored over until the coming of the first ray of morning tells the student that he must snatch an hour's rest before the working day begins. It is no uncommon thing for the East Side student to live on $3 a month while he is struggling for his education. In the ghetto, such a thing is possible.

The 'sweater' with a large family can always find room on the floor for one more, and the boarder gets a corner where he may sleep or study as he sees fit. In the morning he has a cup of weak tea or coffee with the family, and once a month, possibly, he is allowed to share the Friday evening dinner of dried fish.

EVENING POST,
JANUARY 10, 1903

Citizens in the Making

The training of future citizens is the first duty of the public schools, and the work in that congested quarter of this city on the Lower East Side, which reflects more of the foreign than the American coloring in its population, its language, and its outdoor religious observances, presents features unique in many respects. In this quarter the schools are focal points of civilization, as well as centers of the intellectual life of the neighborhood.

In the streets, even in the playgrounds of the schools, Yiddish east of the Bowery and Italian west of the Bowery often join with the latest slang to form the ordinary language of the youngest pupils. Upstairs in the classrooms, all day long, the teachers are struggling to overcome these habits of expression, and, considering that the child hears English for only five hours out of the twenty-four, the results at the end of the fifth and sixth years of school life are wonderful. But these schools are centers of thought life in more ways than one. The children who attend them are often the teachers of their parents, and hundreds of Italian and Russian adults in this foreign quarter are being taught daily the rudiments of English through the medium of their children.

This gives some slight idea of the influence of these institutions, but were we to stop there possibly the best work of the school would be lost. The principal and teachers, supported at present by the Health Officer, must deal with the question of cleanliness, not as a mere matter of appearance, but rather as an absolute necessity for the good health of the children. This is sometimes the most difficult task of all. Only by insisting—doubly insisting—on clean hands and faces can the teacher lay the foundation for habits of cleanliness. The next step is to insist on combed hair, then on cleaned shoes or boots, and it is not a rare sight in some schools to see a monitor or teacher placed at the entrance to the assembly room as Inspector-General of faces, hair, and shoes. In no other respect does the influence of the school tell more strongly than in this matter of cleanliness. Visitors who are taken to low primary classes first and then immediately afterwards to the highest grammar grades are astonished at the difference. While in the lowest grades a glance shows how necessary is the eternal vigilance of the teacher, in the higher grades one can see the effect of training and habit. Both boys and girls are equal in appearance—especially the girls— to the pupils of similar grades in any quarter of the city. Of course, many of them were from the beginning carefully attended to at home, but many others, whose mothers and fathers possibly went out to daily work as the youngsters were getting up for the day, acquired their habits through compulsion and insistence.

There are many children in these schools whose parents are really wealthy, conducting good paying businesses and owning the great tenements in the neighborhood. These children are not only finely but even expensively dressed, and in most cases have their private tutors after 3:00 P.M. in music and foreign languages. Even the children of much poorer parents to a great extent take private lessons in instrumental music, the piano for girls, the violin and mandolin among the Italians for boys.

First in interest in this citizenship training is the work in civics and the history of the United States. In addition to the regular class work in these subjects this training includes the recitation of patriotic pieces at the morning assemblies, the singing of patriotic songs, and the daily salute to the flag. As one of the best means of rousing the patriotic sentiment, the principal of one school endeavors to make the special exercise in honor of national holidays the red-letter days of school life. During the last five years the speakers at these exercises have been such men as Major General Howard, General Albert D. Shaw, National Commander of G. A. R., the Reverend Father McLoughlin, General George B. Loed, General Henry E. Tremain, Colonel Jospeh A. Gouiden, and Colonel A. P. Ketchum. On the occasion of General Shaw's visit to the school, after delivering the address on Washington, he was so moved by the flag salute and singing that he wrote in the visitors' book: "I have been greatly impressed by all I have seen, and the happy and neat appearance of the boys and girls touch me deeply. Such schools as these are the nurseries of the nation and the safeguards of our civilization."

In the work in civics it is interesting to note the practical knowledge of politics the children have. Three out of four pupils in the higher grades know the names of the assemblyman, alderman, and senator of the district, not to forget the district leader. They usually speak of these men by their first names. They know about the primary fights for leadership, and it is amusing to hear the heated arguments that take place between the partisans around election time.

On one occasion, the principal was visited by a parent before promotion time. The parent was very anxious about his son's promotion, and the teacher was asked to furnish the boy's record for the term. The record being good the parent was informed that his boy would probably be promoted. The father then handed a sealed envelope to the principal and after profuse thankings started to leave the school. On opening the envelope a two-dollar bill was found inside. When the parent was called back and informed that such action was wrong, he took the bill and seemed greatly surprised. In broken English he informed the principal that this was the first time in New York he had ever asked a favor without expecting to pay for it. From a case like this we can see the value of sending out from a school in this neighborhood the true principles of civic virtue, the duties of citizens, and the responsibilities of the city's officers.

As to work in manual training, No. 23 was one of the first schools in this city selected for the experiment. In a very short time the pupils had become expert in the new subjects, and the school was visited by distinguished educators from all parts of the country looking for information as to the results of this training. Ten years ago President Gilman of Johns Hopkins, after a day spent in the classrooms inspecting this work, wrote to the superintendent in charge: "The trustees of the John F. Slater Fund desire me to thank you especially for taking them through ward school No. 23, where one of the most interesting experiments is in progress in respect to the eye and hand under very disadvantageous circumstances. Not one of us will fail to remember the extraordinary progress shown by the boys of that school." The visitors on that occasion included two university presidents and an ex-President of the United States, Rutherford B. Hayes. Since that time manual training work has grown to be one of the most important considerations in elementary education. In No. 23 every branch of the work is represented and it does serve in many instances as a direct preparation for the future life work of the children. But the training has a practical value even during the school life of the pupils. The boys make many necessary and ornamental articles in woodwork for their homes, such as bookracks, shelves, and china closets, while many of the girls in the upper grades learn to prepare the family dinner or attend to the home sewing. In this way the parents are led directly to appreciate the value of school training.

As for the English work in this quarter, the struggle for the teacher is never ending with the vast majority of the pupils up to the sixth and seventh years. There must be constant drill on enunciation and pronunciation all through the school. The class libraries must be made popular, and, by the way, No. 23 has one of the largest school libraries of the city schools. This is because of the consolidation into one grammar department of four grammar schools of the old Sixth Ward, thereby consolidating four school libraries into one. The books in the class libraries amount to a total of 900, and the circulation of these books for October was 2,519. The children, especially the Jewish children, make use of the public circulating libraries in the vicinity, of which there are several. The use of libraries naturally increases the knowledge of the pupils and develops a liking for good reading, but it does not materially affect the natural mistakes in expression. These must be corrected in school by the teacher. One means especially useful here is found in memorizing selections for class drill. This is followed by recitations at the morning assemblies, usually of patriotic pieces. The speakers at these assemblies are supposed to set models of good English before their fellow pupils and are marked by the principal. The best compete twice a year for medals, and the excellence of the speaking on these occasions is remarkable.

Of the graduates of No. 23, some go to high school or to the City College. The great number are forced to end their scholastic work with elementary school, except for the further training that many of them get in evening high school. Of those boys and girls from this and other East Side schools who are able to complete their courses in the City College or the Normal College, the city may well be proud. Of all the vast sums spent by the municipality none is better expended than that required for the training of those bright, studious, and patriotic graduates of the free colleges who represent the schools of the foreign quarter of this city. And they often, as lawyers, doctors, and teachers in that same locality, give back to the city in useful citizenship all the city has done for them.

NEW YORK TRIBUNE, SEPTEMBER 16, 1906

The Largest Public School in the World

Public School No. 188 is the largest public school in the world. In the great play yard in the central court the children were romping about so noisily that the two men had to cease talking. They could not hear each other. Then, of a sudden a gong sounded, and the hubbub was hushed. The boys on one side of the yard, the girls on the other, fell into lines, each representing a class and slowly and noiselessly, save for the shuffling of feet, they marched away to their classrooms. "You won't believe it, perhaps, but that little army you have just seen contained five thousand children, or as many as attend all the schools in the entire State of Nevada. Under this roof there are a quarter of a thousand more pupils than in all Columbia University. Indeed, there are seats enough for the students of Yale, Brown, Amherst, and Bowdoin combined."

Following the boys upstairs, the two

men met Mr. Mandel, the principal, whose face brightened as soon as he was asked if they might visit the classrooms. "I guess you won't have time to go into all of them," he said, as he led the way. "You see there are ninety-six altogether." Turning through a door the visitors found themselves confronted by forty lads poring over a history lesson. In the teacher's chair a boy had been left in charge. "A small-sized republic," remarked the principal. "You see how well they can govern themselves. They have elected this president to administer affairs in the interim."

"They do maintain good decorum to be sure," said the writer, "although there must be some tough rowdies among them. They doubtless go to school because they have to, and so when they get through the slums will swallow them up again. I suppose there is hardly one of them who has in view any definite vocation."

"I'd be glad to take a census of the class to find out," said Mr. Mandel, and, turning to the teacher, who had just returned, he asked him to call the roll. Of the thirty-nine present, only one was undecided as to his life work. Eleven wanted to take up various business careers. Nine intended to be lawyers, six civil engineers, three dentists, three doctors, two teachers, and one each for the various callings of mechanic, engraver, designer of clothes, and electrical engineer. Of the thirty-nine, the majority were Jewish. On inquiry the teacher found that the reason why six had chosen civil engineering was because they had watched the construction of the Williamsburg Bridge. The engineers who directed the work, who "bossed the *dagoes*," as one Irish boy put it, had made many of the youth of the neighborhood ambitious to rise to a like position of wisdom and authority. The average age of the boys of this class was fourteen. They will be graduated next February.

Across the hall the visitors found a class hard at work at English composition. It was made up of pupils who contrasted strongly with those they had just left. They were four or five years younger and showed more clearly the influence of their home life. Their faces were dirtier, their hair more snarled, and their clothes more ragged.

"We haven't had as much opportunity to bring out what is best in these little fellows," Mr. Mandel explained.

The subject of the essays was, "My Vacation." And when they were handed in they showed that nearly all of the class had spent the summer in East Side streets. One spoke of an "outing" in Central Park, and another had gone "camping" in the Bronx. A third devoted his whole composition to a baseball game. It, to him, was the most important happening in the last two months. The teacher read it aloud as It was to be played at 6th Street dock for $2. The game started and it was the follows: "During vacation our team and another team arranged a game of baseball. ending of the fifth inning. The score was in favor of the other side, 7 to 0 when the pitcher went to pieces and we hit him for ten runs and won out by 10 to 7."

A hand was waving wildly in the rear of the room, and as soon as its possessor was recognized by the teacher a voice resounded shrilly, "I tell youse about dat game. I wuz on the side dat lost. Each side put up a dollar. We wuz beat cuz dey bribed our pitcher."

The writer of the composition hotly denounced this as a falsehood, and words would have led to blows had not the teacher interposed. Meanwhile the sociologist nodded his head thoughtfully and to his friend muttered, "No wonder our politics and commercial methods are corrupt. Ah, ha, I'll put this in my book."

"No city in the world spends as much as New York for education. Even London takes second rank," was the response. "With 2,000,000 more inhabitants London appropriates several million dollars less a year for schools than we do. In 1900 that city spent for 500,000 pupils $16,988,000, or a little more than two-thirds New York's appropriation for an enrollment of 555,-000." Mr. Mandel brought the conversation to a close by leading the visitors into another classroom. "This is the foreign class of boys," he explained. "Here we take them almost out of the steamships. When we have sifted this class thoroughly, we will leave not one who can speak the English language." As it happened, the teacher had just asked all those who could speak English to stand up. Only two rose to their feet. One, a bright-eyed, black-haired lad of fourteen, said he had just arrived from Jerusalem but that he had studied English there in an institution called the Zionist Normal Polytechnic Kindergarten College. He said he could also speak German, Hebrew, Spanish, and Arabic. The second pupil said he had picked up enough English to understand most Americans because of having lived two months in London. He was a Jew boy also, and was born in Russia. The two lads were told that they would be assigned to other classes, and then the lesson proceeded. The teacher was endeavoring to make her pupils understand the words "open" and "shut." She would go to the door and, swinging it back, say, "I open the door." Closing it she would say, "I shut the door." Then, retreating to her chair, she would point to some pupil and give the command, "You, open the door." This done, she would address another boy with, "You, shut the door." After the class had apparently caught the meaning of the new words, the teacher put it to another test. Nodding to a little Hungarian and closing the door at the same time, she asked, "Now what do I do?" In his reply the lad showed that he had already imbibed a little English from his East Side playmates, for he shouted at the top of his voice, "You shut up. You shut up."

Mr. Mandel accordingly turned the visitors over to his assistant, Mr. Radik, as guide, who, as he led the way, chanced to say: "I suppose you have inspected our carpenter shop. We are quite proud of it."

"No, we haven't seen that," replied the author. "Who works in it, the janitor?"

Mr. Radik was so taken back by this utterance that he grasped the first door knob he came to as if for support. Then he explained that the carpenter shop was a regular classroom, where all the students had instruction the last two years of their course. Opening the door, he disclosed to view a score of boys each at a bench and at work making tabourets. "The finished product will adorn many an East Side parlor," said Mr. Radik. "Some of them show an unusually high degree of skill. Each student works from an original design. There is no opportunity for one to copy from another."

The class of foreign girls was hard at work learning such words as "head," "hand," and "foot" when the visitors arrived. After this drill the teacher took a crayon and, holding it up, said slowly, "I have a piece of chalk." Pupil after pupil took the chalk and repeated the same words. "Now," said the teacher, "I am going back to our old lesson," and patting the head of a little girl, she asked her what part of the body it was. With a serious, almost sad, look the child faced the class, and tapping her curly locks she said, "Dis ist my piece of head." But her classmates never showed the slightest trace of a smile. Even if any of them noticed the mistake, the language was all too foreign and too strange to contain any humor.

All of the thirty-three girls were Hebrews. Twenty were born in Russia, seven in Hungary, and six in Austria. Half had arrived in New York in the last six months and had fled from Russia to escape the torch and the saber. Several of the girls were thirteen or fourteen years old, and, according to their teachers, they were proficient in arithmetic and Russian literature. "But do they appreciate the opportunities of this country?" asked the author. "Ask that little one whom you call Rosie how she regards America." In Yiddish the teacher asked the question, and Rosie's answer, translated, was, "I love sweet America. They are kind to me here."

East Side Women Stone Schoolhouses

Rioting women and children by the thousand, swept into a senseless panic by an absurd story that children's throats were being cut by physicians in various East Side schools, swarmed down on those buildings all over the Lower East Side in great mobs yesterday, intent on rescuing their children and companions. Excitable, ignorant Jews, fearing Russian massacres here, knowing nothing of American sanitary ideas and the supervision exercised over school children by the Health Board, outdid all previous resistance to vaccination. They stoned the schoolhouses, smashing windows and door panes, and, except for the timely intervention of the police reserves from several precincts, would without doubt have done serious injury to the frightened women teachers.

The excitement lasted all afternoon, however. Three or four patrolmen were kept on duty at each schoolhouse in the East Side, and the doors and windows of each building were closed. These guards adopted summary methods for quelling what excitement was left. Almost every one armed himself with a long supple slat from one of the numerous new buildings all through that section, and when voluble Yiddish women of luxuriant flesh or chattering young Hebrews formed a group before the schoolhouses, they were persuaded to depart by vigorous application of the slats to the most convenient section of the nearest "Yiddisher."

"There's goin' to be no spoilin' of these children," explained a patrolman who was engaged in this unusual occupation to a passer-by. "We're not sparin' the rod any. They want riot over here all the time— bread riots, meat riots, coal riots—and now the wimmin and childer is havin' one for themselves. "They'll git it," he declared grimly, as he set about hastening the departure of some half-grown boys who had become obstreperous. They got it, soundly.

The panic grew out of minor operations by Health Board physicians on several of the children and a great deal of vaccination among the children in preparation for the usual summer disease epidemic. Such vaccination is always accomplished only by force in the Lower East Side. Last week Miss A. E. Simpson, principal of Public School 100 at Broome and Cannon Streets, found that many of the children were suffering from adenoids, a fungus growth at the back of the mouth and nasal passages which can be removed by a simple operation. The consent of parents is necessary before physicians may perform such an operation. Miss Simpson weeded out the cases and explained the situation, telling the parents that, if possible, their children should go to private physicians or hospitals, but, if not, the Board of Health physicians would do the work. Most of the parents probably misunderstood, but last Thursday public physicians operated on many of the children.

The trouble came to a head in half an hour yesterday. The mobs of women descended on the schools crying out that their children were being murdered and buried in the school yards. The riot belt extended from Rivington Street to Grand and from the Bowery to the East River. In the more easterly section the violence was greatest. In almost every case the windows of the schoolhouses were riddled with stones. And then, as suddenly as it had risen, the trouble lost its serious aspect. The teachers had learned its reason, and line after line of children began marching out of the buildings. The screaming, fighting mothers caught their own progeny and hurried home, helped along by indignant police reserves whose sleep had been spoiled. Commencement exercises in many schools were postponed. No fatalities were reported, but the East Side lost all interest in the discussion of *kosher* "wurst" to gossip over this "near massacre."

ADAPTATION/1

Jew Babes
at the Library

Lines of children reaching down two flights of stairs and into the street may not infrequently be seen at the Chatham Square branch of the Public Library when school closes at three o'clock in the afternoon. On the newsstands round about only Yiddish and Italian newspapers are sold. These are read by the grown-up people. Meanwhile, the children are drawing books in English at the rate of 1,000 a day. Little wonder the branch is waiting anxiously for the completion of its new quarters, the second Carnegie building at Nos. 31 and 33 East Broadway, which would have been ready now had it not been for the strike in the building trades. Opened four years ago, the branch has 15,000 members. It stands third in the number of its circulation and since its opening has ranked first in the proportion of history and science taken out. It is almost wholly used by Jews. A few Italians from Mulberry Street, a handful of Chinese from Mott and Doyer, and a scanty representation from other races come there occasionally.

There is probably no other circulating library where the *Bible* goes out like the last new novel. The Chatham branch has a shelfful of *Bibles,* which, with books of *Bible* stories, are a favorite "call" for Friday night. It is probably the only library where copies of the *Bible* go out to fashionably dressed young women. The children are also devoted to all the various juvenile compilations of *Bible* stories which have appeared in recent years.

Probably the most popular book in the whole library is a history for young people entitled *The Story of the Chosen People,* the many copies of which are always traveling raggedly to the bindery. Rivaling it, however, is *Uncle Tom's Cabin.* As the story of an oppressed race it strikes a responsive chord in the Jewish child. Sue's *The Wandering Jew* is another prime favorite, and *The Merchant of Venice* has no more passionate admirers than among the patrons of the Chatham branch. This strong race bias in their reading vents itself in the opposite direction occasionally. Not long ago, the library put on its shelves a set of art and literature primers, beautiful little books exquisitely illustrated with reproductions of classic art. There is not a Madonna or Christ Child left undisfigured in those primers now. The faces have been marked with derisive crosses, blackened with stubby lead pencil points wet in contumelious little mouths, or eliminated entirely by scissors and penknives. The library has a bulletin board for the news of the day. One day an item concerning the death of a prominent church dignitary appeared among the others. Every boy of twelve or fourteen who stopped to read the notice deliberately spat upon it in the coolest and most matter-of-fact manner.

The librarians are a constant source of astonishment to the children. A peculiarly cordial spirit pervades the building. Every assistant is interested in her work, for those who are not interested do not stay. In return the children love them all, write them fervid letters of adoration, make them presents, and run their errands. And that the objects of so much sincere admiration should be Christians puzzles their small heads.

"Dast you write on the Sabbath?" they ask wonderingly, as they see the assistants writing on Saturday.

"Dast you tear paper?"

"Dast you hold money?"

All these occupations are against the tenets of that strictly Orthodox neighborhood. Some of the girls who are fond of working about the library have been promoted to the rank of unofficial helpers. They replace books on the shelves on Saturday, but will not remove soiled covers as this necessitates tearing paper. They sometimes bring in letters from home received on Saturday with the request from their parents that the "teachers" kindly open them, to obviate the necessity of tearing paper on that day. Those who have been used to running errands for a penny will not do so on Saturday as that means "holding money."

The letters written to the librarians by the children display all the luxuriance of an Oriental imagination. "I send you as many kisses as there are stars in the sky." "I send you as many kisses as there are fishes in the sea"—such phrases roll from their pencil tips while they are still the merest children. "My dear, sweet Miss Sheerin, only God knows how much I love you. I send you as many kisses as there are pennies in the world," wrote one fanatical little adorer.

The Jewish child has more than an eagerness for mental food; it is an intellectual mania. He wants to learn everything in the library and everything the librarians know. He is interested not only in knowledge that will be of practical benefit, but in knowledge for its own sake. Girls and boys under twelve will stand before the library shelves so much absorbed in looking up a new book that they do not hear when spoken to. No people reads so large a proportion of solid reading. In fact, the librarians say that no other race reads so much fiction as the American.

There is a fourteen-year-old Sicilian boy who frequents the Chatham branch. He is learning the goldsmith's trade, and he goes to the reference room to read biographical sketches of artists in the *Encyclopedia Britannica*. He takes out books on art and music, but never fiction. One of the assistants tried to tempt him one day with Crawford's Italian stories, but he replied indifferently that he did not care for them.

There is one little table at the rear of the ground floor, the only place in the building where one can sit and study. Many boys and girls have graduated from that little table into universities having accomplished there the study necessary to pass their examinations. Several of the boys have entered Cornell and New York University. One girl graduated from the table into a scholarship at Barnard, where she took sophomore honors this year. Jewish boys seldom turn to engineering, electricity, mechanics, or anything implying manual labor. Their tastes are all for abstract science, sociology, business, or professional life. The girls turn naturally to teaching and bookkeeping.

Sidelights on English as she is spoken among the New York foreign-born may be heard among the children at Chatham. "Dasent" is used in more ways than an American would ever think of. "Those things dasent be touched," they will say. "He's a murder," will succinctly describe a disagreeable person, and "I have a mad on her" sufficiently depicts a slight difference of opinion. "He's come to be joined into the library" is the accepted form of introduction for a new friend. The installment plan seems graven in the nature of these infants. They wish to pay their fines a penny a day even when they have the whole amount in their pockets. "I might as well be getting the interest on this as you," said one boy frankly of a three-cent fine. Excuses for maltreated books give glimpses of home life. "The baby dropped it in the herring" is the favorite explanation for a soiled cover.

THE NEW YORK TIMES,
NOVEMBER 25, 1900

The University Settlement's Work

One of the leading factors working for the betterment of conditions on the Lower East Side, especially as it relates to the problem of social life, is the University Settlement, now housed in commodious quarters on the corner of Eldridge and Rivington Streets. From the six-story building of colonial style that stands as a sentinel over the clustering tenements radiates much of that scientific social work that in time is to do for the crowded districts thereabout all that its earnest workers have been striving for. Like the Educational Alliance, the University Settlement deprecates the patronizing spirit. In all its work, both social and educational, and particularly in the former, the settlement is following the principles of cooperation rather than of control.

"We seek to be intelligent promoters of every kind of social reform," says Mr. Reynolds, head worker of the settlement, "and we find that what we have to offer is so greatly appreciated that already, in our enlarged quarters, we are unable to supply the demand made upon us to provide meeting places for clubs and organizations. To the extent of our capacity, however, we gladly receive all organizations having reputable aims, and our relationship to them becomes that of advisers and coadjutors in the accomplishment of these aims.

"This club idea is carried out in all its various forms by the settlement, and the members of the various organizations that meet within our walls are undertaking the work for their own districts and for their own community, having been led thereto by the cooperation of the workers and residents in the settlement. Some have become teachers; some, while still in City College, have taken charge of other lines of social work.

"We feel sure," says Mr. Reynolds again, "that the young people who have already shown qualifications for these lines of work will manifest the same qualities and the same interest in the welfare of their fellow men as they pass into mature life and so justify to the fullest extent the efforts made in their behalf."

The work of the settlement, outside of that done by the club members themselves, is carried on by James B. Reynolds, the head worker and Franklin L. Talbert, his assistant, who are the only salaried officers; by the workers, of whom there are several scores, both men and women; and by the residents. These latter are a distinctive feature of settlement life. They are university men who have made special studies of various branches of sociology or education. They live in the settlement house, paying for their accommodation there, and act as advisers to the various clubs of younger men and give instruction to the various classes. The residents at present are Willard E. Hotchkiss, who was at the head of the George Junior Republic, Walter Scott Andrews, Reverend M. Baxter, Frederick A. King, William A. Dunn, Frank Simonds, Durand Drake, Mr. Reynolds, and Mr. Talbert. The affairs of the settlement are administered by a council of which Seth Low is president and which numbers among its members some of the best-known men of affairs in New York.

In carrying on the campaign for social reform through the workers and residents, the settlement illustrates the practical application of the scientific method to the problem of social life and the insistence upon scientific training as a necessary qualification for social workers. "The man who comes to the settlement as a resident comes not only as a worker but as a student," says Mr. Reynolds. "He comes to study the conditions and people of our quarter; to investigate and analyze the controlling forces of its life; to learn through the detail of its family, social, and commercial relations what the forces are that make for righteousness and what for unrighteousness and how these forces are conditioned. In short, we impress upon the man who comes to us that it is necessary for him to know conditions before he attempts to alter them."

Careful and scientific analysis of conditions, however, is recognized as only the first step toward social betterment. When there is found the hopeless and despairing surrender to forces that have been too much for the body and mind, weakened by tenement house conditions, the worker seeks to reawaken ambition, to give encouragement in time of depression, to indicate the way, and to help clear the way to better things. The keynote of the work is struck by Mr. Reynolds when he says, "In all these efforts our aim is to work with the people rather than to work for the people. Not for ourselves, but for others, is the motto."

The work of the settlement through the medium of clubs and classes goes on right through the week. There are a number of finely fitted up clubrooms which are given for the use of the various clubs at a purely nominal sum as rental. This is made from about half of the club dues and the dues themselves range from three to five cents a week. The clubs are for girls and boys and for young men and young women. They are entirely independent organizations, and supervision is exercised only over the clubs composed of young children, the worker appearing even here only in the guise of adviser. The Outward Club, for instance, is a club of men with a large membership which interests itself in the general affairs of the neighborhood. There are discussions and a "smoker" at the monthly meeting. The Neighborhood Civic Club is composed of young men over eighteen years of age. It interests itself in social and civic questions and meets every Friday evening. The S.E.I. Club is also for young men of the same age and has for its object the social and educational improvement of its members.

Among the other clubs and classes are one on cooking for young girls; a dramatic class; a Thread and Needle Club, where young girls learn systematic sewing and simple garment making; a boys' and girls' dancing class; mothers' meetings for the mothers of the kindergarten children; the People's Orchestra and the Seidl Orchestra, the members of which are residents of the neighborhood with musical tastes and education; a Whist Club, in which twenty-five young men and women meet every week to play and study whist; a Penny Provident Bank, where children can start an account with one cent and where they learn the habits of frugality and economy; innumerable history and literature classes; a splendidly equipped gymnasium, under the charge of a competent instructor; a roof garden for use in the summer, which is widely patronized; and baths where every requisite is furnished at a nominal price.

NEW YORK TRIBUNE, APRIL 22, 1900

The Candy Store— A New Social Center

Benjamin Reich, in the annual report of the University Settlement, which has just been published, tells about the candy store as a factor in East Side life: "To the boy home from work in the office or factory and to the schoolboy with nothing to do in the evening, the candy store serves as a clubhouse where he can meet old friends and make new ones, as well as a haven of refuge and a safe retreat from the persecution of the corner policeman. Here he finds what is lacking in his stuffy little home of two or three rooms—boys whose friendship he desires to cultivate because he sees in them traits which appear to him to be in keeping with his own notions of American ideas and ideals. Altogether, he finds in the candy store an agreeable change from his usual surroundings during the day. Not only are the candy stores used by individuals or groups but likewise, the members of some social or pleasure club meeting in a little room above a dance hall once a week, discuss or wrangle over club business, the remainder of the week, play cards in some favorite candy store nightly, smoke cigarettes, and manage to pass a pleasant evening."

The entire East Side is pretty well dotted with these stores. A careful census of the Tenth Ward alone, shows the existence of fully fifty of them, nearly all of which have more or less of a clientele of these youngsters. Quite a number of these stores—some, true enough, not literally candy stores (they may be cigar stores or small lunch rooms)—are used as meeting places for clubs.

The candy stores, however, are the true social centers. A counter along the length of the store decked with cheap candles and perhaps with cigars, some shelving behind filled with cigar and cigarette boxes, and invariably a soda water fountain make up the entire furniture of the store, if we except a few cigarette pictures on the wall. Usually the proprietor lives with his family in the rear of the store. Some stores, making a pretense to stylishness, have partitioned off a little room from the store to which they give the elegant name of "ice cream parlor," a sign over the door to that effect apprising you of its existence. One or two bare tables and a few chairs furnish the "ice cream parlor." But this little room is very useful as a meeting place for a small club for boys or as a general lounging room. Occasionally a dozen or more youngsters are entertained here by a team of aspiring amateur comedians of the ages of sixteen or seventeen, whose sole ambition is to shine on the stage of some Bowery theater. The comedian or comedians will try their new "hits" on their critical audiences (and a more critical one cannot be found), dance, jig, and tell the jokes heard by them in the continuous performances at vaudeville theaters. It must be borne in mind, however, that the privileges accorded the boys are not given out of the goodness of the proprietor's heart. He exacts a small sum for the use of his cards, and if they play for money (as they often do) he must come in for his share of the winnings; the boys must also liberally patronize his goods and stand all the curses and kicks he chooses to inflict upon them. He is practically the tyrant of the place, and woe betide the person who gains his displeasure. It is no more than fair to state, however, that many candy store proprietors do not seek the patronage of the class of boys here referred to, for they must be constantly on guard that no mischief is done.

From the above somewhat short and meager description the candy store may not appear to be an evil, but there is no question that it has in a large number of cases led to evil effects. The boys who congregate in these stores are of an age to be susceptible to either good or evil influences. They are under no restraining or uplifting influence whatever; as a matter of fact, the proprietors, in many instances, if not indifferent to what is going on in their presence, encourage extravagance and viciousness so long as it does not interfere with their trade and custom. Unless there are some outside factors at work to counteract the preponderating evil that the candy store exerts, the boy is bound to succumb to it. As he grows older and earns more money, the candy store ceases to fascinate him, it loses its attraction, and, to use his own words, he finds it "too slow." The invitation of the barker of the Bowery concert hall to "come right in, a free show's going on" meets with a ready response. He is enchanted with the cheerfulness and brightness about him, and with his friends he finds the show more pleasing over a glass of beer than was ever the amateur performance over a glass of soda. He commences to frequent poolrooms and other more or less questionable resorts, stays out all night, and in the end makes the beer saloon or the poolroom his nightly headquarters. Of course, it would be hardly fair to say that the candy stores are entirely responsible for this condition, but there is no doubt in the writer's mind that if the boys were given better and healthier moral surroundings and better places to meet in than are afforded by the candy stores, much of the evil would disappear. It is a fact to the writer's own knowledge that the work of the settlement and kindred institutions in this direction and the extension of the evening school and lecture system by the Board of Education have perceptibly diminished the use of the candy stores for the purposes mentioned in this paper.

In the East Side Cafés

At this season the subject of politics claims the chief attention of every one, but one kind of politics, which is certainly as interesting if not as important as many, is invariably overlooked. Newspapers keep us informed of the doings of the great parties; writers of fiction have made so-called "saloon politics" an open book; the spellbinder receives attention; the wizard of the stump is exploited, and so on. But few people know of the sort of thing that goes on in the Russian quarter of the city.

There must be some clubs, for the gregarious instinct is strong there as everywhere, and the need is well supplied by the Russian cafés. These people want no saloons. When they drink liquor, they drink at home in a properly well-bred fashion. But their tea, they take in public and over it discuss the questions of the day for hours at a time. In these cafés there is much political work done, much earnest and clever talk on the problems of government. They are in a sense intellectual centers.

Not every Russian café reaches this level. There are many which exist for the purpose of dispensing food and for that alone. Four or five, however, make this only a part of their business. At most hours of the day and night, until three o'clock in the morning, these places are filled with men who have come there to sip Russian tea out of tumblers, meet their friends, and discuss everything under heaven. They are the intellectual aristocracy of the East Side, although aristocracy is a word tabooed among them, for they are almost all socialists or dreamy and peaceable anarchists. The socialistic feeling is widespread on the East Side,

and in these cafés most of it is fostered.

The literary men, the newspaper writers, the actors, the professional men form the clientele of the cafés. Not all of them are interested in the socialist movement, but nearly all are of radical opinions. The air of the East Side is unfavorable to conservatism. Too much is remembered of the old Russian home across the water, and while nobody would apply here the rules that hold good in the Czar's dominion, the habit of being "ag'in the government," once formed, is not easily broken.

One of the cafés on the East Side is the official meeting place for the socialists of the district. Another, higher up, serves as a Tammany stronghold, but the latter is not typically East Side, like the other. The other cafés are Russian, pure and simple. As one steps into them, he has taken a journey into another world. At the little bare tables there are groups of men, with here and there a woman, all of them bearing the stamp of intelligence and earnestness on faces which testify only too plainly to the life of unnatural confinement led by most of them.

"She must have just come over," remarked an habitué of the cafés the other evening of a girl sitting near, "she looks so fat and healthy." The characteristic face is pale, sharp-featured, intensely eager, and earnest—the face of one who thinks too much and breathes the air of heaven too little. They drink their tea slowly, biting off bits of the sugar, in true Russian style, instead of dropping it into the glass. It is not the most healthful occupation in the world, after a long day's work to sit and sip tea until long after midnight, but it makes an interesting sight for spectators. These people do not give their overwrought brains much time to rest. Life is a struggle for a livelihood part of the time and a feverish search after knowledge for another part. Not all are poor, of course—there are many prosperous-looking men and women among the groups in these places—but the pale-faced, overworked type prevails.

There is a general air of cheerfulness, however. The East Side loves a joke, and many go the rounds. There is always fun of some sort in the Russian cafés, together with the earnest discussion which characterizes the places. Games of one sort or another are frequently played. A group of men will gather in a corner and crowd together in such earnest conference that a timid visitor might suppose that they were plotting the destruction of society, while in reality they are only watching a game of chess and discussing the good or bad points of the play. Being Russians, they are all chess players, and intellectual strain marks even their recreation. One might think that for overnervous people there might be a better prescription, but it seems the nature of these folk to live at high pressure.

Anyone who knows the East Side well will easily recognize a fair proportion of the men in any of the well-known cafés on any evening after eleven o'clock. At that time the intellectual East Side sets forth to enjoy itself. The humdrum worker is asleep, but these men cannot exist without companionship, and this is the time to find it. When the theaters are closed and the meetings ended, the cafés begin to fill. If there has been a great socialist gathering, the talk is of that. If the brilliant playwright who gives the Jewish stage plays considerably stronger than those produced in English has just brought out a new work, that is the general theme.

Among the tables moves the proprietor. He is not a man who stands behind a counter or who holds himself aloof from his guests. He is a true host, and in more than one café he is the chief attraction. The proprietors of these cafés are social powers in the neighborhood. They are clever, well-informed men who can talk well on any subject with their guests. Most of the clever men on the East Side patronize some one café in particular, and the choice is frequently decided according to their personal liking for the proprietor. He must need be a bright man, for his visitors are men of education and ability. Here,

one sees the editor of some socialist paper; there, is a musician of more than local reputation. Another man is a physician of high repute on the East Side and one of its best educated men. Yet another—and with what respect is he regarded!—is the same playwright who thrills the East Side with productions worthy of any stage in the city. Another is the actor who makes the East Side laugh, and with him may be the actress who makes it cry.

Everybody is clever-looking; everybody knows everybody else; all is sociability and bright talk. The earnest groups who are talking politics retire to the corners, if there is not a special meeting in some room in the rear. Any one who wishes is at liberty to join in the talk. It is Bohemia; a socialist as well as a literary free missionary prevails. Introductions are not necessary, beyond that of a smile and an appropriate remark.

To those who know it, this life is fascinating in the extreme. It is a phase which is little known, for few not born in it can lay aside preconceived notions so far as to permit themselves to recognize in the habitués of these places their intellectual equals or superiors. If students and sociologists and workers in the political field would turn their attention to these happy hunting grounds of radical thinkers, they would find out how limited is their knowledge of conditions in this great city.

HUTCHINS HAPGOOD,
THE SPIRIT OF THE GHETTO

Yiddish Theater

In the three Yiddish theaters on the Bowery is expressed the world of the ghetto—that New York City of Russian Jews, large, complex, with a full life and civilization. In the midst of the frivolous Bowery, devoted to tinsel variety shows, "dive" music halls, fake museums, trivial amusement booths of all sorts, cheap lodginghouses, ten-cent shops, and Irish-American tough saloons, the theaters of the chosen people alone present the serious as well as the trivial interests of an entire community. Into these three buildings crowd Jews of all ghetto classes—the sweatshop woman with her baby, the day laborer, the small Hester Street shopkeeper, the Russian-Jewish anarchist and socialist, the ghetto rabbi and scholar, the poet, the journalist. The poor and ignorant are in the great majority, but the learned, the intellectual, and the progressive are also represented, and here, as elsewhere, exert a more than numerically proportionate influence on the character of the theatrical productions, which, nevertheless, remain essentially popular. The socialists and the literati create the demand that forces into the mass of vaudeville, light opera, and historical and melodramatic plays a more serious art element, a simple transcript from life, or the theatrical presentation of a ghetto problem. But this more serious element is so saturated with the simple manners, humor, and pathos of the life of the poor Jew that it is seldom above the heartfelt understanding of the crowd.

The audiences vary in character from night to night rather more than in an uptown theater. On the evenings of the first four weekdays the theater is let to a guild or club, many hundred of which exist among the working people of the East Side. Many are labor organizations representing the different trades, many are purely social, and others are in the nature of secret societies. Some of these clubs are formed on the basis of a common home in Russia. Then, too, the anarchists have a society; there are many socialist orders; the newspapers of the ghetto have their constituency, which sometimes hires the theater. Two or three hundred dollars is paid to the theater by the guild, which then sells tickets among the faithful for a good price. Every member of the society is forced to buy, whether he wants to see the play or not, and the money made over and above the expenses of hiring the theater is for the benefit of the guild. These performances are therefore called "benefits." The widespread existence of such a custom is a striking indication of the growing sense of corporate interests among the laboring classes of the Jewish East Side.

On Friday, Saturday, and Sunday nights the theater is not let, for these are the Jewish holidays, and the house is always completely sold out, although prices range from twenty-five cents to a dollar. Friday night is, properly speaking, the gala occasion of the week. That is the legitimate Jewish holiday, the night before the Sabbath. Orthodox Jews, as well as others, may then amuse themselves. Saturday, although the day of worship, also has a holiday character in the ghetto. This is due to Christian influences to which the Jews are more and more sensitive. Through economic necessity Jewish workingmen are compelled to work on Saturday, and, like other workingmen, look upon Saturday night as a holiday, in spite of the frown of the Orthodox. Into Sunday, too, they extend their freedom, and so in the ghetto there are now three popularly recognized nights on which to go with all the world to the theater.

On those nights the theater presents a peculiarly picturesque sight. Poor workingmen and women with their babies of all ages fill the theater. Great enthusiasm is manifested; sincere laughter and tears accompany the sincere acting on the stage. Peddlers of soda water, candy, and fantastic gewgaws of many kinds mix freely with the audience between the acts. Conversation during the play is received with strenuous hisses, but the falling of the curtain is the signal for groups of friends to get together and gossip about the play or the affairs of the week. Introductions are not necessary, and the Yiddish community can then be seen and approached with great freedom. On the stage curtain are advertisements of the programmes, and circulars distributed in the audience are sometimes amusing announcements of coming attractions or lyric praise of the "stars."

BYRON/AUTOMATIC ONE CENT VAUDEVILLE, FOURTEENTH STREET, c. 1900/THE BYRON COLLECTION, MUSEUM OF THE CITY OF NEW YORK

BYRON/AUTOMATIC ONE CENT VAUDEVILLE, INTERIOR, c. 1900/THE BYRON COLLECTION, MUSEUM OF THE CITY OF
NEW YORK

UNKNOWN PHOTOGRAPHER/MOVING PICTURE THEATER, 1912/CULVER PICTURES, INC.

BYRON/THE GRAND THEATER, c. 1900/THE BYRON COLLECTION, MUSEUM OF THE CITY OF NEW YORK

UNKNOWN PHOTOGRAPHER/THALIA THEATER, c. 1900
PICTURE COLLECTION, NEW YORK PUBLIC LIBRARY   ADAPTATION/144

BYRON/JACOB P. ADLER AND CAST OF *THE BROKEN HEARTS*, c. 1900/THE BYRON COLLECTION, MUSEUM OF THE CITY OF NEW YORK

JACOB A. RIIS/ESSEX MARKET SCHOOL, c. 1889
THE JACOB A. RIIS COLLECTION,
MUSEUM OF THE CITY OF NEW YORK

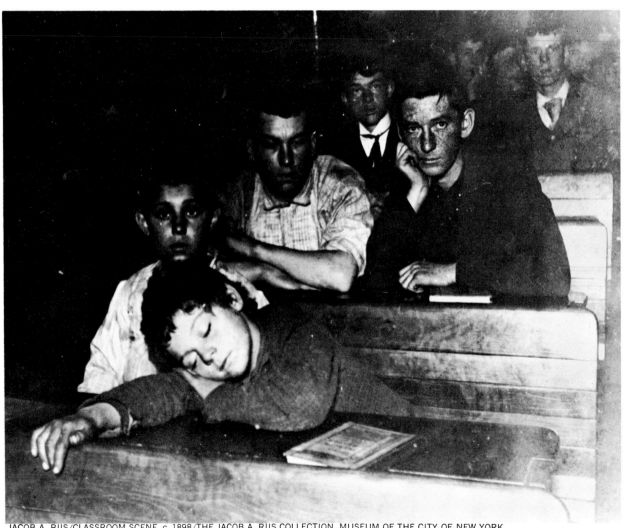

JACOB A. RIIS/CLASSROOM SCENE, c. 1898/THE JACOB A. RIIS COLLECTION, MUSEUM OF THE CITY OF NEW YORK

JACOB A. RIIS/ESSEX MARKET SCHOOL, c. 1890/THE JACOB A. RIIS COLLECTION, MUSEUM OF THE CITY OF NEW YORK

JACOB A. RIIS/MANUAL TRAINING CLASS, c. 1890/THE JACOB A. RIIS COLLECTION,
MUSEUM OF THE CITY OF NEW YORK

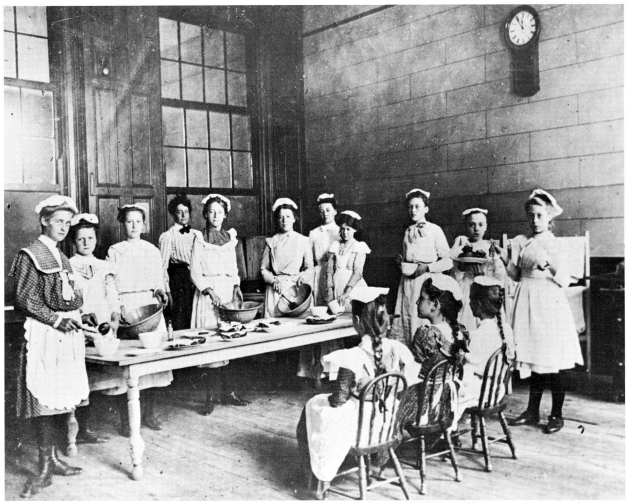

JACOB A. RIIS/HOME ECONOMICS CLASS, c. 1890/THE JACOB A. RIIS COLLECTION,
MUSEUM OF THE CITY OF NEW YORK

LEWIS W. HINE/MILLINERY CLASS IN PUBLIC SCHOOL,
c. 1912/PHOTO LEAGUE ARCHIVE,
NEW YORK PUBLIC LIBRARY

UNKNOWN PHOTOGRAPHER/LIBRARY, EDUCATIONAL ALLIANCE, c. 1898/PICTURE COLLECTION, NEW YORK
PUBLIC LIBRARY

LEWIS W. HINE/LONDON BRIDGE, c. 1915/PICTURE COLLECTION, NEW YORK PUBLIC LIBRARY

JACOB A. RIIS/ROOF PLAYGROUND, PUBLIC SCHOOL, c. 1898/THE JACOB A. RIIS COLLECTION, MUSEUM OF THE CITY
OF NEW YORK

JACOB A. RIIS/PUBLIC BATHS, EAST RIVER, c. 1898/THE JACOB A. RIIS COLLECTION, MUSEUM OF THE CITY
OF NEW YORK

JACOB A. RIIS/HENRY STREET SETTLEMENT, c. 1898/THE JACOB A. RIIS COLLECTION, MUSEUM OF THE CITY OF NEW YORK

UNKNOWN PHOTOGRAPHER
CHILDREN DOING CALISTHENICS,
c. 1904/THE GRANGER COLLECTION

JACOB A. RIIS/TALMUD SCHOOL, HESTER STREET, c. 1889/THE JACOB A. RIIS COLLECTION, MUSEUM OF THE CITY OF NEW YORK

UNKNOWN PHOTOGRAPHER/SYNAGOGUE, CHRYSTIE STREET, 1911/THIS BUILDING WAS THE LOCATION OF TEMPLE
EMANU-EL (1848–1854), CONGREGATION BETH ISRAEL BIKUR CHOLIM (1855–1886), AND CONGREGATION MISHKAN
ISRAEL SUVALK (1886–1901)/THE NEW YORK HISTORICAL SOCIETY

"MAMENIU"!

Including an Elegy to the Triangle
Fire Victims

Words by
A. SCHORR

HEBREW PUBLISHING CO.
50 ELDRIDGE ST. NEW YORK
COPYRIGHT 1911

MUSIC BY
J. M. RUMSHISKY

Piano 50¢

Violin 30¢

NEW YORK TRIBUNE,
JUNE 18, 1897

Sweatshop Girl Tailors

The girl tailor of the New York sweatshop has a grievance and she proposes airing it in every little meeting hall on East Broadway, Delancey, and Canal Streets, though her mother and sisters have their serious doubts about the propriety of doing any such thing and though she herself has little hope of accomplishing much thereby. She wonders why the sweating system is not legislated out of existence, why factory inspectors' eyes are so poor, and why Jewish bosses do not join hands with the bosses of other nationalities and buy the city. All of this goes to show that a diet of black bread and pickles does not kill the thinking apparatus after all, nor do eighteen hours work a day do as much harm as some of the labor agitators say it does. She thinks sometimes that two additional hours are needed to create perfect machines, "but," she adds, "of what use is a machine that thinks?"

Miss Minnie Rosen, who is a young woman of the thinking kind, says that all the girls demand are living wages and fifty-nine hours work a week instead of the present system of one hundred eight hours work weekly on salaries ranging from $3 to $6 weekly, according to the size and age of the worker. Miss Rosen is a finisher and lives in a three-room flat on the top floor of No. 248 Monroe Street where she is assisted in providing the family living by a sister and two brothers, who make cigars and peddle around the tenement district. She speaks Yiddish with the usual gurgling sound and speaks English with her tongue, two most expressive hands, and a cultured shrug of the shoulders that says volumes and must eventually straighten the shoulders, now slightly rounded by the sewing machine. She says "vell" in a way that no linguist on earth can properly translate. If she says it about the contractor, it may mean anything; if she speaks of "the boss," it implies all manner of things; and if applied to herself, it means that there is no one like unto her in woe.

Miss Rosen does not work now. Even the worm will turn, and after vainly trying to obtain justice from her employer, she gave up her place. Instantly six others tried to obtain it, and that is all the turning of the worm effected. She was seen a few evenings ago surrounded by some of the most stolid-looking unimpressionable-faced women ever looked upon, women who were as incapable of meeting an issue and acting upon it as so many babes and whose faces showed a lack of stability of character, but a great deal of indecision and indifference. They listened to all she had to say. When she became enthusiastic, they looked calmly at her, and when she spoke quietly and distinctly of the wrongs done the Jewish girl, they looked helplessly at each other.

Here and there were a few exceptions, among them Eleonora Reilly, whose name and religion do not interfere with her fellowship, Rose Stone, a finisher on coats, and a few others with names that can only be pronounced by their own people. Miss Reilly is forewoman of a shirt factory uptown and is not a personal sufferer, but Miss Stone has lost her place and speaks strongly against what she terms "hell upon earth."

"I worked twelve hours a day for $6 a week," she said, "and at last, when I could obtain no redress nor a raise in pay, I complained to the factory inspector that we were all working overtime, that many minors were employed, and that the sweating system was in full progress. He looked curiously at me, and I suppose spoke to the boss because he told me next morning that there were some 'kickers' who ought to be dead, but I told him that if they worked in his shop a little while longer they would be too dead to kick. This kicker-destroying shop, by the way, is Mr. Shadlowsky's, No. 17 Catharine Street, and Mr. Shadlowsky evidently attended the Lexow investigation and picked up some valuable points because he declared he was a big fellow, had a pull with every government on the earth, and did not care two cents for the factory laws."

Miss Stone wanted to prove this so she decided to work nine hours a day and received only $5 salary at the end of the week. She stormed and threatened and pointed to the minors and the law and a lot of other things, but Mr. Shadlowsky laughed at her and got another girl in her place. And now Miss Stone is supported by her sister in a little dingy furnished room at No. 180 Madison Street for which they pay $5 a month. Her sister is a peddler.

"She will have many rivals soon," said one of the girls, "because boss peddlers have not sprung into existence yet, so that in selling pretzels and shoelaces we need not support the contractor and the other go-betweens, as we have to do now."

THE NEW YORK TIMES,
MAY 2, 1897

Socialists Parade on May Day

May Day was celebrated last evening by the socialist trade and labor unions of the city with a grand parade and demonstration. Notwithstanding the threatening weather, the socialists turned out in force with music, Chinese lanterns, banners, and transparencies. When paraders and curiosity-seekers assembled in front of the cottage in Union Square, there were between 6,000 and 7,000 persons.

A feature of the parade was the presence of about 200 young women and girls, many of whom carried Chinese lanterns. They belonged to the Workingwomen's Educational Club of the Socialist Ladies'

Society. All wore their best clothes, and were commanded by Miss Jessie Bennett and Miss Gertrude Fredrickson.

The parade consisted of five divisions. The first formed in East Fourth Street, off Third Avenue, and included the two female societies above mentioned, the socialist turners, the New York Section of the Socialist Labor Party, and several bricklayers' and carpenters' unions. The second division formed one block higher up and embraced the architectural iron workers, machinists, tailors, upholsterers, brewers, cap and hat makers, and celluloid and plush box makers. The third division formed in Sixth Street and included cigar-makers, packers, furriers, waiters, bakers, and piano makers. The fourth was one of the largest divisions and took in several of the Jewish clothing trades and the Jewish section of the Socialist Labor Party. In the fifth division marched socialist sections of Brooklyn and Jersey City.

The fourth division did most of the marching from Henry Street and Rutgers Square. Going through several East Side streets to Second Avenue and Fourth Street, it fell in line with the rest of the parade, which went up Second Avenue to Tenth Street, to Third Avenue, to Nineteenth Street and Fourth Avenue, and from there to Union Square.

The paraders presented a pretty spectacle as they marched past the cottage. First came a company of police, and then the American flag was borne between two socialist blood-red flags, a distinction that has not heretofore been granted by socialists to the Stars and Stripes. Another large green flag bore the novel inscription, "Socialist Labor Party of Ireland. Founded 1896." This was followed by the blacksmiths who carried large hammers across their shoulders and bore a socialist flag with an American flag on either side. The socialist boys' fife and drum corps played as loudly as the arms and lungs of its members allowed. There were numerous transparencies that bore Socialist mottoes such as, "Workingmen of All Countries, Unite!" "Poverty Still Exists! Strike at the

Ballot!" "Wages for Slaves! Prosperity for Masters!"

Lucien Sanial was the chairman at the cottage, and there were three other stands in other parts of the square for German, Jewish, and Italian speakers. Mr. Sanial started by proposing three cheers for the Socialist Labor Party, and these were given with a will. After explaining that May Day parades had been instituted to demand fewer hours of labor, he said that the present demonstrations were no longer made to ask concessions from capitalists, but for the purpose of "abolishing the robber band" that despoiled the workingman. The socialists, he continued, had made enormous gains in France. A few years ago, they polled 60,000 votes. Last fall they polled 140,000 votes in Austria, and they had made tremendous gains in England. Alexander Jonas, Daniel De Leon, and Theodore Cuno also made addresses. Resolutions were adopted denouncing capitalists and the old political parties. All were urged to vote the socialist ticket.

JOHN R. COMMONS,
U. S. INDUSTRIAL COMMISSION,
REPORTS, 1901

Contractor at Center of the Sweating System

The term "sweating," or "sweating system," originally denoted a system of subcontract, wherein the work is let out to contractors to be done in small shops or homes. "In practice," says the report of the Illinois Bureau of Labor Statistics, "sweating consists of the farming out by competing manufacturers to competing contractors of the material for garments, which in turn is distributed among competing men and women to be made up." The system to be contrasted with the sweating system is the "factory system," wherein the manufacturer employs his own workmen, under the management of his own foreman or superintendent, in his own building, with steam, electric, or water power. In the sweating system the foreman becomes a contractor, with his own small shop and foot-power machine. In the factory system the workmen are congregated where they can be seen by the factory inspectors and where they can organize or develop a common understanding. In the sweating system they are isolated and unknown.

The position of the contractor or sweater now in the business in American cities is peculiarly that of an organizer and employer of immigrants. The man best fitted to be a contractor is the man who is well-acquainted with his neighbors, who is able to speak the languages of several classes of immigrants, who can easily persuade his neighbors or their wives and children to work for him, and who in this way can obtain the cheapest help. During the busy season, when the work doubles, the number of people employed increases in the same proportion. All the contractors are agents and go around among the people. Housewives, who formerly worked at the trade and abandoned it after marriage, are called into service for an increased price of a dollar or two a week. Men who have engaged in other occupations, such as small business and peddling, but who are out of business most of the year, are marshaled into service by the contractor, who knows all of them and can easily look them up and put them in as competitors by offering them a dollar or two a week more than they are getting elsewhere. Usually when work comes to the contractor from the manufacturer and is offered to his employees for a smaller price than has previously been paid, the help will remonstrate and ask to be paid the full price. Then the contractor tells them, "I have nothing to do with the price. The price is made for me by the manufacturer. I have very little to say about the price." That is, he cuts himself completely loose from any responsibility to his employees as to how much they are to get for their labor. The help do not know the manufacturer. They cannot register their complaint with the man who made the price for their labor. The contractor, who did not make the price for their labor, claims that it is of no use to complain to him. So that however much the price for labor goes down, there is no one responsible for it.

There is always cutthroat competition among contractors. A contractor feels more dependent than any of his employees. He is always speculating on the idea of making a fortune by getting more work from the manufacturer than his neighbor and by having it made cheaper. Usually when he applies for work in the inside shop he comes in, hat in hand, very much like a beggar. He seems to feel the utter uselessness of his calling. Oftentimes the contractor is forced to send work back because he cannot make it under the conditions on which he took it; yet he does not dare to refuse an offer for fear the manufacturer will not give him more of his work. So he tries to figure it down by every device, and yet, perhaps, in the end is forced to send it back.

The futility of directing the energies of reform solely against the contractor may be seen in New York in one branch of the clothing trade, that of ladies' ready-made garments, including cloaks and so-called "tailor-made suits." Already in this line of manufacture fully 75 per cent of the product has passed out of the hands of contractors into those of manufacturers. Ten years ago probably 90 per cent of women's clothing was made by people who worked for contractors, while now only about 25 per cent of the trade are working for contractors. But so far as the people employed in the business are concerned there has not been any material change for the better, since these small manufacturers retain all the abuses of long hours, small pay, and unsanitary shops. The way in which this new class of manufacturer has arisen in the clothing trade and has driven out of business the large manufacturer on Broadway who sent his work out to contractors is one of the remarkable developments of this remarkable trade. These former large manufacturers who have abandoned the ready-made business have gone into the retail or custom trade, and have set up model "inside" factories on Broadway, where they cater to the more well-to-do purchasers. Small manufacturers on Division and other streets have absorbed the former wholesale trade.

EDWIN MARKHAM,
COSMOPOLITAN MAGAZINE,
JANUARY, 1907

60,000 Children in Sweatshops

Long before Hannah made a coat for little Samuel, women sat in the home at garmentmaking. The sweated sewing in the tenement home today is only a belated following of this custom of the ages. But the leisurely sewing of the old times was far away from the nerve-racking work of our hurried age. The slow ways are gone. In unaired rooms, mothers and fathers sew by day and by night. Those in the home sweatshop must work cheaper than those in the factory sweatshops if they would drain work from the factory, which has already skinned the wage down to a miserable pittance. And the children are called in from play to drive and drudge beside their elders. The load falls upon the ones least able to bear it—upon the backs of the little children at the base of the labor pyramid.

All the year in New York and in other cities you may watch children radiating to and from such pitiful homes. Nearly any hour on the East Side of New York City you can see them—pallid boy or spindling girl—their faces dulled, their backs bent under a heavy load of garments piled on head and shoulders, the muscles of the whole frame in a long strain. The boy always has bowlegs and walks with feet wide apart and wobbling. Here, obviously, is a hoe man in the making. Once at home with the sewing, the little worker sits close to the inadequate window, struggling with the snarls of thread or shoving the needle through unwielding cloth. Even if by happy chance the small worker goes to school, the sewing which he puts down at the last moment in the morning waits for his return.

Never again should one complain of buttons hanging by a thread, for tiny, tortured fingers have doubtless done their little ineffectual best. And for his lifting of burdens, this giving of youth and strength, this sacrifice of all that should make childhood radiant, a child may add to the family purse from 50 cents to $1.50 a week. In the rush times of the year, preparing for the changes of seasons or for the great "white sales," there are no idle fingers in the sweatshops. A little child of "seven times one" can be very useful in threading needles, in cutting the loose threads at the ends of seams, and in pulling out bastings. To be sure, the sewer is docked for any threads left on or for any stitch broken by the little bungling fingers. The light is not good, but baby eyes must "look sharp."

Besides work at sewing, there is another industry for little girls in the grim tenements. The mother must be busy at her sewing, or, perhaps, she is away from dark to dark at office cleaning. A little daughter, therefore, must assume the work and care of the family. She becomes the "little mother," washing, scrubbing, cooking. In New York City alone, 60,000 children are shut up in the home sweatshops. This is a conservative estimate, based upon a recent investigation of the Lower East Side of Manhattan Island, south of 14th Street and east of the Bowery. Many of this immense host will never sit on a school bench. Is it not a cruel civilization that allows little hearts and little shoulders to strain under these grown-up responsibilities, while in the same city a pet cur is jeweled and pampered and aired on a fine lady's velvet lap on the beautiful boulevards?

Governor Roosevelt Visits Sweatshops

Governor Roosevelt, accompanied by James B. Reynolds, a member of the Tenement House Commission, and Jacob A. Riis, made a personal tour of the East Side tenement district south of Houston Street yesterday in order to investigate for himself the complaints which have been made that the factory law, so far as it applies to sweatshops, has not been enforced properly by the authorities. The governor has taken much interest in this subject, and last winter he requested Mr. Reynolds and Mr. Riis to look into the matter and make a report to him. A few days ago he arranged to make a personal inspection and made an appointment with his special commissioners for a tour of the East Side.

The party met yesterday morning at the Union League Club and proceeded to the branch office of the Factory Inspector at 1 Madison Avenue in order to invite some one of the inspector's staff to accompany them and answer any questions as to the conditions found. None of the officials was present at the time of the governor's call, and the party went to the offices of the Consumers' League in the United Charities Building. The league has done much work in the direction of tenement-house reform, and it was the desire of the governor to have some officer of the league go with them. Finding the offices closed, the governor and his two companions proceeded unaccompanied. About twenty tenements were visited altogether. The law says that every room in which manufacturing is carried on must be licensed, and, as the governor had been informed that there were many violations, he determined to give the matter his personal attention.

The party went first to Elizabeth

Street, where many tenements were visited. At 206 Elizabeth Street, which is tenanted exclusively by Italians, they found that two families, and in one case three, occupied a flat in which manufacturing was going on in violation of the rules and regulations, which provide that a license shall not be issued to manufacture in any apartment containing more than one family. Licenses were hanging on the walls of these places although a subsequent examination of the books of the Factory Inspector showed that no licenses had been issued. The house was also found to be in a filthy condition in violation of another section of the law. The house is a big double-decker, with four flats of three rooms each on a floor. Mr. Riis informed the governor that while conditions were not as could be desired, there had been some improvements in the house, which he had visited last winter, when he found four families in an apartment. At 234 Elizabeth Street the governor found a woman working in the basement contrary to law. At 147 and 151 Elizabeth Street they found that conditions were far from good while 145 Elizabeth Street, which had been reported as being very dirty, was in good condition for a house of that kind. At 90 Elizabeth Street, two women were at work in the basement. The place was clean, however, and the governor remarked that there was not much to complain of. At 44 Elizabeth Street, a sweatshop in which three men were at work was found to be running without a license.

Reports had been received by the governor that some of the houses in Mulberry Street were in bad condition, and the party visited 89, 123, 125, and 171, but the governor said that the conditions which he found in those houses were much better than had been represented to him. It had been reported that a woman was working without a license, but the governor ascertained that she had a license. Many illegal conditions were found to exist at 141 Hester Street, and at 163 on the same street an unlicensed sweatshop was in operation with several employees. It was said that the place had been running for two months.

The next place visited was at Bayard and Division Streets, where conditions were found to be the worst possible. One woman was working with a license and one without, and the halls and rooms were extremely filthy. The governor expressed the opinion that licenses should be refused for such places. A sweatshop was found running in the rear of 23 Allen Street in a shanty. A license had been refused by the Factory Inspector for this place six months ago, but the proprietor had paid no attention to the refusal and has been carrying on his business without a license. The last place visited was 1 Forsyth Street about which many complaints had been made. This was found to be in fairly good shape.

The party then went to a well-known Bowery restaurant where they had luncheon. The governor received a cordial greeting from the habitués of the place as he frequently took his meals there when he was President of the Board of Police Commissioners. After luncheon a second call was made at the office of the Factory Inspector, and Deputy Inspector O'Brien, who was in charge, noted the governor's comments. The governor told him that while conditions were better than they were a year ago, still there was plenty of room for improvement. He told Mr. O'Brien that perhaps the inspectors did not understand what he meant when he said he wanted the law enforced. He did not want it made as easy as possible for the manufacturer but wanted licenses refused to applicants in all cases where the houses did not come up to the required standard. He said that licenses should not have been granted to houses such as 23 Allen Street and 62 and 64 Division Street. Under conditions existing at 206 Elizabeth Street, he said, no license should have been issued, as the buildings were faulty and overcrowded.

The governor said that hereafter, in granting applications for licenses, the construction of the buildings and the hygienic surroundings should be more strictly regarded. He wished to have the department make owners of buildings understand that badly constructed and unclean buildings should not be used for manufacturing purposes and that only those places which met the requirements of the law should receive licenses. This would do more, in the Governor's opinion, to bring about reform than anything else which could be devised. The governor said that he wished the inspector to keep a special book and enter all complaints. Each complaint should be sent to the Department of Health, and the latter's attention should be called every day to instances of filth, overcrowding, and all defects in the tenement-house district. He also urged a better system of keeping records and said that an inspector should be held strictly accountable for his districts and that if evils exist which the inspector fails to find, he should be dismissed for a second offense. He advised the department to keep in touch with the Tenement House Commission and the Consumers' League and suggested that it would be a wise plan for some employee of the department, preferably Inspector O'Leary, to accompany Mr. Reynolds to Boston and study the system in vogue in that city. Mr. Riis said that this was the first time that a governor of this state had ever made a tour of this kind. The governor's visit attracted much attention in the neighborhoods which he visited.

THE NEW YORK TIMES,
JULY 29, 1895

13,000 Tailors on Strike

The great strike threatened by the Brotherhood of Tailors and said to involve nearly 13,000 men, women, and girls began yesterday. It is the largest strike in this branch of the trade that has taken place, and the members of the brotherhood responded to the order to strike with unanimity. There are some 630 shops represented in the brotherhood, and of these, 610 immediately obeyed the order to strike. By ten o'clock yesterday morning about 10,000 workers had left their employment, and two hours later 3,000 more joined the ranks of the strikers. Walhalla Hall in Orchard Street was made the headquarters for the strikers and their executive board. That place and the street in front were soon packed with crowds of excited people. Messengers had been hurriedly sent to all the shops to order the people out, and as the workers went trooping along to the rallying place, they were greeted with cheers by those who were already there.

The order to strike was issued very early in the day, and read as follows: "To all members of the United Brotherhood of Tailors. Stop Working at Once. By order of all locals." Then followed the signatures of the members of the general executive board of the brotherhood. Before sunrise over 100 tailors had assembled in Walhalla Hall. These were hurriedly sent out as committees of two and three to the shops in Suffolk Street and Rutgers Place and vicinity to call out the tailors. Meyer Schoenfeld, who is regarded as the manager of the brotherhood, formed a kind of central committee of some of the first comers, and this committee organized the other committees with orders to the shops to strike. These committees began their work in Attorney Street and, after dividing the territory among themselves, worked their way westward to the Bowery visiting every shop. The working people who had been prepared for the strike quit work as soon as the committee appeared. These were principally operators, basters, finishers, and pressers.

About ten o'clock in the morning the first general meeting of the day was held in Walhalla Hall. Meyer Schoenfeld made a brief address advising the strikers to be calm and orderly. At noon there was another meeting, and at one o'clock addresses were made to a packed house. The people, although excited, were orderly. B. Schweitzer said that the contractors did not believe that the workers would go out. They kept increasing the day's task of every man until his condition was reduced to worse than slavery, for if he could not complete his task one day, he had to finish it on the day following. These remarks were received with cries of, "No task work! Down with the sweating system!"

Schoenfeld continued that the manufacturers themselves had spoken very fairly to the men. "Then," he said, "we found out that they wanted to get seven weeks work out of us. They would have kept us working night and day, and in the beginning of September they would have have had an enormous quantity of made-up goods in stock. Then, they would not have cared whether we struck or not."

The principal cause of the strike was the refusal of the Contractors' Association to sign an agreement prepared by the brotherhood to date from September 15. This agreement provides that the contractors are to employ only union members in good standing and that the brotherhood shall give the contractors all the hands they need. Fifty-nine hours shall constitute a week's work, ten hours a day for the first five working days, from 7:00 A.M. to 6:00 P.M., with one hour for dinner, and nine hours on the sixth day, from 7:00 A.M. to 5:00 P.M., with one hour for dinner. No overtime is to be permitted. The minimum rates of wages demanded in the agreement are: basters $13 per week and upward, finishers $9 per week. The tenement-house sweating system is to be abolished.

The contractors met at 200 East Broadway, and Secretary B. Witkowsky said, "It is not true that the contractors have forced the strike by violating the agreement of last year. We are willing to grant a continuance of the weekly wage system on a ten-hour workday basis, but we claim the right to judge for ourselves as to who earn the wages and who do not. If the workers were educated to a basis of common sense, we might fix a settled scale. On the whole, we believe that the piecework system is the best, for under it, the best man makes the best wages."

Police Club Strikers

Strikers or their sympathizers wrecked the bakeshop of Philip Federman at No. 183 Orchard Street early last night amid scenes of the most tumultuous excitement. Policemen smashed heads right and left with their nightsticks after two of their number had been roughly dealt with by the mob. Two men were arrested and charged with inciting to riot, assault, and disorderly conduct. Bricks and bottles were thrown down on the heads of the policemen from houses in the neighborhood. The reserves of the Eldridge Street station had their hands more than full coping with the maddened crowd.

Word was passed to the headquarters of the strikers in Great Central Palace at No. 90 Clinton Street shortly after seven o'clock that there was a "roughhouse" in Federman's bakery in Orchard Street between Rivington and Stanton Streets, one of the most densely populated sections of the East Side. It had been rumored that Federman, who usually had eight bakers in his employ, had set three men to work in the places of the strikers. Shouting "scabs," accompanied with unintelligible maledictions on them, the crowd in the Central Palace rushed pellmell to Federman's. There they found the street filled with a howling mob which swayed back and forth from sidewalk to sidewalk shouting and beating each other. Half a hundred of the first of the new arrivals piled on top of Isidor Bernstein of No. 11 King Street, a watchman for Federman, and bore down his burly form in spite of the vigorous way he played on their heads and shoulders with his club. Four of the crowd forced their way to the basement bakery where Federman and his three assistants cowered in one corner. Dough filled the great mixing troughs and furnished fine ammunition for the insurgent quartet. They threw it at the boss and his three men and, when tired of that, slashed it about the floor and walls of the rooms. They tried to destroy every implement they could lay hands on, and by the time their energy was somewhat exhausted there was not a pane of glass in the windows or any value left in the material in the place.

Attempting vainly to follow the crowd that streamed from the Palace at the word of the doings at Federman's, Patrolman Finley of the Eldridge Street station fought his way through the mob to the head of the steps leading to the basement where he found Bernstein, the watchman, almost done for. Finley had sent in a call for the reserves when he saw the threatening nature of the crowd. When he got to Bernstein's side, the crowd immediately attacked him. He is a giant. All of his efforts to ward off the crowd without recourse to violence were of no avail. A well-directed brick sent him to the street. Then when he got to his feet he used his nightstick with telling effect. Many of the people must have suffered severely from the blows of the policemen's clubs; yet they fought like tigers. So great was the press of the crowd that the patrol wagon bearing the reserves could not force a way through the densely packed bodies. The horses' bridles were grabbed in spite of their rearing and plunging, and forward progress was stopped. Detectives Landers and Galligan, sitting with their feet hanging out of the tail of the wagon were pulled out into the street by their heels. Then the other policemen in the wagon leaped out and charged the crowd, striking right and left, forward and back with their nightsticks.

Howls of pain rose higher than the shouts against the police. The police tore the crowd apart and plunged into the basement of the bakery where the trouble originated. They pulled out two men, Louis Mandesiever of No. 249 Broome Street and Max Siegel of No. 55 Norfolk Street, both almost unrecognizable from the dough that smeared their clothes and faces and both bleeding from gashes in their heads.

It was impossible to get the patrol wagon started when the two prisoners had been bundled into it. Then the bricks and bottles began to descend from the windows. Patrolmen Hart and Sweeney forced their way into the houses and searched for the throwers high and low, but in vain. The mob finally gave way under repeated charges by the police and permitted the patrol wagon to pass. Patrolman Finley was bruised and cut and his uniform ruined from his being rolled in the mud. Bernstein was so badly beaten that he was sent home in care of a physician. The mob gave way only bit by bit under the repeated charges of the police to clear the street; it then retreated into the nearest doorways from which it hooted and jeered police and bosses alike.

Previous to the outbreak of the trouble and the deserting of headquarters, it had been announced that a request had been sent to the International Union in Chicago to call out the journeymen and the English-speaking bakers. It was not expected that there would be any word received from Chicago until today.

Reports that the bosses were attempting to man their shops with nonunion labor led to the sending out of pickets from strike headquarters in bunches of ten and twelve. They not only permeated the East Side but also penetrated to Harlem and the Bronx, with orders to stop all work. Riots all over the East Side were the chief characteristic of the strike yesterday. "Strong–arm men," the employers say, have been brought here from outside by the strikers to start the riots. The strikers assert that thugs have been engaged by the employers.

Meantime, the *kosher* bread famine had become acute. Lunchrooms lay idle, and the Hebrew grocers could not get any bread to sell, as it was unsafe to receive any. The strike leaders' evident intention was to starve out the people in the hope of bringing matters to a climax. The bread famine was principally confined to the district between Hester and Houston Streets as far as Avenue C. Rye bread, which was selling before the strike at two and one-half cents a pound, was eight cents a pound and hard to get at the money. At Pyocken Polski's union restaurant at No. 87 Attorney Street, there was no bread, and there was no business done all day. Groceries were in the same plight, and biscuits which were on the shelves for months went off like hot cakes. The most serious riot of the afternoon took place at the bakery of Joseph Bock, No. 138 Orchard Street. Bock, who is treasurer of the boss bakers' association, was away at the time, and his assistants barricaded the place. Forty strikers tried to storm the cellars in order to get the employees on strike, but Patrolman Sofsky of the Eldridge Street station came along on a run and captured a ringleader, using his club freely.

By this time the street was blocked with people, among whom were a number of women. Sofsky had to fight his way to the station, and once was borne down by the crowd. A number of reserves then arrived under Captain Murtha, wielding their clubs, and a furious fight took place before the crowd was dispersed. Patrolman Benjamin Stern received an ugly cut on the head from a flying piece of rock. Three men in all were arrested and discharged with a reprimand in Essex Market Court later, Magistrate Moss considering the evidence not sufficient to justify a fine.

Another fight took place at Abraham Waidstricken's bakery, No. 150 Allen Street, where a number of strikers dragged out barrels of flour and scattered their contents in the street. An attempt was made by the Jersey Model Bakery of Hoboken to deliver bread at a shop in Clinton Street. When two wagons filled with the bread appeared, a crowd seemed to rise out of the ground, assailing the wagons with bricks and other missiles. A number of police charged the crowd and took the wagons to the police station. Israel Reisler, a grocer, of No. 103 Clinton Street, had his place besieged with an angry throng of strikers when an attempt was made to deliver *kosher* bread to him. The place is nearly opposite Great Central Palace, the headquarters of the strikers, out of which the strikers poured in hundreds. They cut the harness of the horses, but reserves from the Union Market and Delancey Street stations appeared and scattered the rioters.

There was a disposition on the part of the strikers to get women into the mobs, with the object of working public sentiment if women were clubbed. The police, seeing this, were careful not to make too indiscriminate a use of their sticks. Five women upset a pushcart loaded with bread at Orchard and Stanton Streets, trampling the loaves into the mud. A number of women also snatched a basket from a man who was delivering bread at Stanton and Ridge Streets.

The strikers sent committees around on every pretext. One committee was sent to Philadelphia to prevent *kosher* bread from being sent from that city to New York. Another committee was sent to Jersey City and Hoboken with the same object. A meeting of the Hebrew boss bakers' association, which has been formed since the strike began, was held yesterday afternoon at No. 252 Broome Street, and the boss bakers had a noisy time. The meeting was behind closed doors, but the wrangling could be heard outside. A schedule of demands from the strikers had been submitted, based on recognition of the union. After the meeting the following statement was made:

"We are ready to pay the wages demanded, but will on no account recognize the union or sign any agreement. Further, we can consider no negotiations with walking delegates or the strike leader, Samuel Kurtz. Our bakeries are closed. We can get men, but they are afraid to go to work, and we are not asking our men who did not strike to work for fear of provoking riots."

The employers also said that Kurtz came from Providence and never appeared except when there was a strike. They made a number of vague charges against strike leaders but were not willing to give their names as making the charges. On the invitation of Secretary Emery of the Citizen's Industrial Association, Kurtz, the strike leader, called at its headquarters in the St. James Building, 26th Street and Broadway, and presented a list of their demands and complaints. The employers will give their side to the association today. A committee of three headed by Kurtz called on Acting Mayor Fornes and said that the strikers, now 2,500 strong, wanted to go to the mayor's office to ask for protection from the police. Mr. Fornes said that it would be better for a committee of twenty-five or thirty to go instead, but he said that he did not see what good it could do as the trouble was between the strikers and their employers. The strikers later decided to abandon the parade, and will send a committee of thirty to the mayor at one o'clock tomorrow.

The strikers decided last night to hold a mass meeting tomorrow night either at Hamilton Fish Park or Rutgers Square. They reported that John Heintz, international secretary of the bakers, would be here today to take charge of the strike. At a secret meeting of delegates from Locals No. 23, 40, 305, 163, and 4 in Great Central Hall yesterday, a formal agreement which the bosses will be required to sign was drawn up. Its fourteen sections include agreement for a ten-hour day and the wages which the bosses said on Tuesday that they would grant, as well as many minor details as to the relations between employers and employees. Section 1 of this agreement requires the bosses to employ only union men in good standing. Section 2, about the only one in which the unions agree to do anything on their part, provides that the unions will provide sufficient journeymen bakers for the employers. Section 3 requires a ten-hour day, including thirty minutes for luncheon. It also requires that no work shall be done on

Friday, not even sponging or arranging and delivering flour.

Representatives of the union, Section 7 requires, must be permitted access to all bakeries under the agreement at any time in or after working hours. Section 10 defines the wages to be insisted upon by the strikers. These are oven hands $20 and up a week; bench hands $16 and up a week; jobbers on oven work, $4 a day and up; jobbers on bench work, $3.50 a day and up. In this section it is further agreed that wages shall be paid in full on the Jewish holiday weeks. Section 13 requires the employers to deposit $25 each as security for strictly complying with the provisions of the agreement. Upon the first violation of the agreement this $25 is to be forfeited to the union. Section 13 also requires the bakers to buy union labels at $3 a 1,000. Section 14 makes the life of the agreement one year, beginning on October 1 or whenever may be agreed upon by the different unions.

ERNEST POOLE,
THE OUTLOOK,
NOVEMBER 21, 1903

Task Work Bowing to Factory System

Go tonight at nine or even ten o'clock down through the ghetto. You will find scores of small coat shops still lighted. These are nonunion shops, and a glimpse into one of them reveals the task system running at full speed. The room is low and crowded. The air is close, impure, and alive with the ceaseless whir of machines. The operator bends close over his machine —his foot on the treadle in swift, ceaseless motion; the baster stands just behind, at the table; the finisher works close between them. On the table is a pile of twenty coats. This is their "task"—the day's work, which most teams never accomplish. Of the three teams here, the swiftest can finish their task in fourteen hours' labor. The other two seem forever behind and striving to catch up. Five tasks a week is their average. They need no overseer, no rules, no regular hours. They drive themselves. This is the secret of the system, for three men seldom feel sick or dull or exhausted at the same moment. If the operator slackens his pace, the baster calls for more coats. If at six o'clock the baster gives out, the finisher spurs him on through the evening.

The positions are tense, their eyes strained, their movements quick and nervous. Most of them smoke cigarettes while they work; beer and cheap whisky are brought in several times a day by a peddler. Some sing Yiddish songs—while they race. The women chat and laugh sometimes—while they race. For these are not yet dumb slaves, but intensely human beings—young, and straining every ounce of youth's vitality. Among operators twenty years is an active lifetime. Forty-five is old age. They make but half a living.

This is but the rough underside of the system. Widen the focus, include employers, then employers of employers, and the whole is a live human picture of cutthroat competition. At the top the great New York manufacturers of clothing compete fiercely for half the country's trade—a trade of sudden changes, new styles, rush seasons. When, three years back, the raglan overcoat came suddenly into favor, at once this chance was seized by a score of rivals, each striving to make the coat cheapest and place it first on the market. Each summoned his contractors and set them in turn competing for orders. He knew them all and knew how desperately dependent they were upon his trade. Slowly the prices were hammered down and down until the lowest possible bids had been forced. Then enormous rush orders were given.

This system is now hard pushed by a swifter rival, and is falling behind in the race. In these days of machine invention, a process to live must not only be swift and cheap; it must be able, by saving labor, to grow forever swifter and cheaper.

This the task system can no longer do. The factory system, so long delayed by the desperate driving of the task, began in 1896. In New York today, 70 per cent of the coats are made by the factory. The small shops—on task or week wages—are mere survivals of the past.

Endless saving, dividing, narrowing labor—this is the factory. Down either side of the long factory table forty operators bend over machines, and each one sews the twentieth part of a coat. One man makes hundreds of pockets. On sewing pockets his whole working life is narrowed. To this intensity he is helped and forced and stimulated at every possible point. His strength is no longer wasted on pushing a treadle; the machine is run by other power. The coat passes down the long bench, then through the hands of a dozen pressers and basters and finishers—each doing one minute part swiftly, with exact precision. Through thirty hands it comes out at last fourteen minutes quicker, four cents cheaper; the factory has beaten the task shop.

And the human cost—is it, too, reduced? Is the worker better off here than he was in the sweatshop? To consider this fairly we must compare the nonunion factory with the nonunion sweatshop. Wages by the week for the most skilled workers are slightly higher in the factory than they were in the sweatshop. They are lower for the unskilled majority. This majority must slowly increase, for the factory system progresses by transferring skill to machinery. Hours are shorter; work is less irregular; the shop is sanitary; the air is more wholesome—but the pocketmaker is often as exhausted at 6:00 P.M. as the coatmaker was at 10:00 P.M., for his work is more minute, more intense, more monotonous. This concentration, too, is growing.

Still, the workers have gained most decidedly. The factory is a help to the union. Through the past twenty years labor unions were formed again and again, only to be broken by new waves of ignorant immigrants. In the system of small scattered shops the unions had no chance. The free American workman bargained alone, with a contractor who said, "I have no power," and a manufacturer who said, "I have no workmen." All this is ended. Contractor and manufacturer are slowly becoming one. The bargain is direct, and the workmen are learning to strike it together.

NEW YORK WORLD,
MARCH 26, 1911

The Triangle Fire

At 4:35 o'clock yesterday afternoon, fire, springing from a source that may never be positively identified, was discovered in the rear of the eighth floor of the ten-story building at the northwest corner of Washington Place and Greene Street, the first of three floors occupied as a factory by the Triangle Waist Company. At two o'clock this morning Chief Croker estimated the total dead as 154. More than a third of those who lost their lives did so in jumping from windows. The firemen who answered the first of the four alarms turned in found thirty bodies on the pavements of Washington Place and Greene Street.

It was the most appalling horror since the Slocum disaster and the Iroquois Theater fire in Chicago. Every available ambulance in Manhattan was called upon to cart the dead to the morgue—bodies charred to unrecognizable blackness or reddened to a sickly hue—as was to be seen by shoulders or limbs protruding through flame-eaten clothing. Men and women, boys and girls were of the dead that littered the street; that is actually the condition—the streets were littered.

The fire began in the eighth story. The flames licked and shot their way up through the other two stories. All three floors were occupied by the Triangle Waist Company. The estimate of the number of employees at work is made by Chief Croker at about 1,000. The proprietors of the company say 700 men and girls were in their place. Before smoke or flame gave signs from the windows, the loss of life was fully under way. The first signs that persons in the street knew that these three top stories had turned into red furnaces in which human creatures were being caught and incinerated was when screaming men and women and boys and girls crowded out on the many window ledges and threw themselves into the streets far below. They jumped with their clothing ablaze. The hair of some of the girls streamed up aflame as they leaped. Thud after thud sounded on the pavements. It is a ghastly fact that on both the Greene Street and Washington Place sides of the building there grew mounds of the dead and dying. And the worst horror of all was that in this heap of the dead now and then there stirred a limb or sounded a moan.

Within the three flaming floors it was as frightful. There flames enveloped many so that they died instantly. When Fire Chief Croker could make his way into these three floors, he found sights that utterly staggered him, that sent him, a man used to viewing horrors, back and down into the street with quivering lips. The floors were black with smoke. And then he saw as the smoke drifted away bodies burned to bare bones. There were skeletons bending over sewing machines.

The elevator boys saved hundreds. They each made twenty trips from the time of the alarm until twenty minutes later when they could do no more. Fire was streaming into the shaft, flames biting at the cables. They fled for their own lives. Some, about seventy, chose a successful avenue of escape. They clambered up a ladder to the roof. A few remembered the fire escape. Many may have thought of it but only as they uttered cries of dismay.

Wretchedly inadequate was this fire escape—a lone ladder running down to a rear narrow court, which was smoke filled as the fire raged, one narrow door giving access to the ladder. By the score they fought and struggled and breathed fire and died trying to make that needle-eye road to self-preservation.

Shivering at the chasm below them, scorched by the fire behind, there were some that still held positions on the window sills when the first squad of firemen arrived. The nets were spread below with all promptness. Citizens were commandeered into service, as the firemen necessarily gave their attention to the one engine and hose of the force that first arrived. The catapult force that the bodies gathered in the long plunges made the nets utterly without avail. Screaming girls and men, as they fell, tore the nets from the grasp of the holders, and the bodies struck the sidewalks and lay just as they fell. Some of the bodies ripped big holes through the life nets.

Concentrated, the fire burned within. The flames caught all the flimsy lace stuff and linens that go into the making of spring and summer shirtwaists and fed eagerly upon the rolls of silk. The cutting room was laden with the stuff on long tables. The employees were toiling over such material at the rows and rows of machines. Sinisterly the spring day gave aid to the fire. Many of the window panes facing south and east were drawn down. Draughts had full play. The experts say that the three floors must each have become a whirlpool of fire. Whichever way the entrapped creatures fled they met a curving sweep of flame. Many swooned and died. Others fought their way to the windows or the elevator or fell fighting for a chance at the fire escape, the single fire escape leading into the blind court that was to be reached from the upper floors by clambering over a window sill! On all of the three floors, at a narrow window, a crowd met death trying to get out to that one slender fire escape ladder.

It was a fireproof building in which this enormous tragedy occurred. Save for the three stories of blackened windows at the top, you would scarcely have been able to tell where the fire had happened. The walls stood firmly. A thin tongue of flame now and then licked around a window sash. On the ledge of a ninth-story window two girls stood silently watching the arrival of the first fire apparatus. Twice one of the girls made a move to jump. The other restrained her, tottering in her foothold as she did so. They watched firemen rig the ladders up against the wall. They saw the last ladder lifted and pushed into place. They saw that it reached only the seventh floor. For the third time, the more frightened girl tried to leap. The bells of arriving fire wagons must have risen to them. The other girl gesticulated in the direction of the sounds. But she talked to ears that could no longer hear. Scarcely turning, her companion dived head first into the street. The other girl drew herself erect. The crowds in the street were stretching their arms up at her shouting and imploring her not to leap. She made a steady gesture, looking down as if to assure them she would remain brave. But a thin flame shot out of the window at her back and touched her hair. In an instant her head was aflame. She tore at her burning hair, lost her balance, and came shooting down upon the mound of bodies below. From opposite windows spectators saw again and again pitiable companionships formed in the instant of death—girls who placed their arms around each other as they leaped. In many cases their clothing was flaming or their hair flaring as they fell.

By eight o'clock the available supply of coffins had been exhausted, and those that had already been used began to come back from the morgue. By that time bodies were lowered at the rate of one a minute, and the number of patrol wagons became inadequate, so that four, sometimes six, coffins were loaded upon each. At intervals throughout the night the very horror of their task overcame the most experienced of the policemen and morgue attendants at work under the moving finger of the searchlight. The crews were completely changed no less than three times.

UNKNOWN PHOTOGRAPHER/DELIVERING GARMENTS, UNDATED/AMALGAMATED CLOTHING WORKERS OF AMERICA

LEWIS W. HINE/CARRYING KINDLING, 1910/GEORGE EASTMAN HOUSE

UNKNOWN PHOTOGRAPHER/CARRYING WORK HOME, c. 1910/BROWN BROTHERS

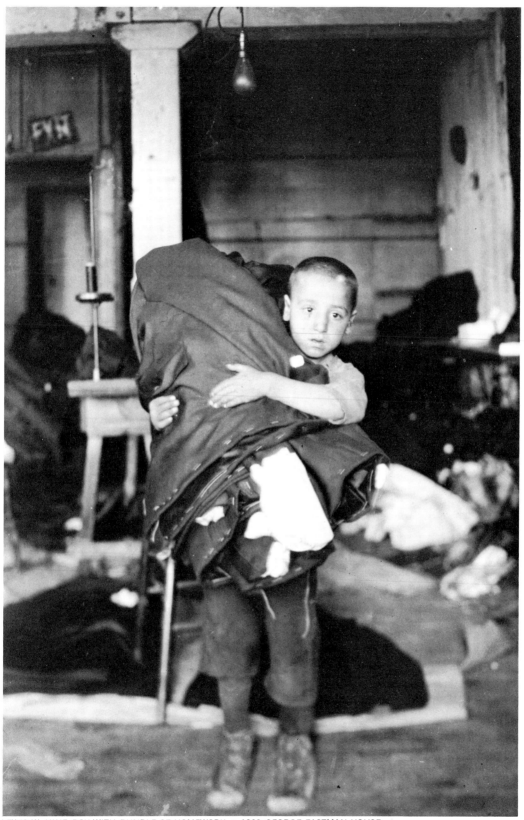

LEWIS W. HINE/BOY WITH BUNDLE OF HOMEWORK, c. 1909/GEORGE EASTMAN HOUSE

LEWIS W. HINE/CARRYING BOXES, c. 1910/NATIONAL COMMITTEE ON EMPLOYMENT OF YOUTH

LEWIS W. HINE/CARRYING WORK HOME, c. 1910
NATIONAL COMMITTEE ON EMPLOYMENT OF YOUTH

LEWIS W. HINE/CARRYING WORK HOME, c. 1910/NATIONAL COMMITTEE ON EMPLOYMENT OF YOUTH

LEWIS W. HINE/CARRYING RAGS, c. 1907–1915/GEORGE EASTMAN HOUSE

UNKNOWN PHOTOGRAPHER/DELIVERY BOY, c. 1910/BROWN BROTHERS

UNKNOWN PHOTOGRAPHER/DELIVERING GARMENTS, UNDATED/AMALGAMATED CLOTHING WORKERS OF AMERICA

LEWIS W. HINE/HOMEWORK–CLOTHING, c. 1910/NATIONAL COMMITTEE ON EMPLOYMENT OF YOUTH

LEWIS W. HINE/HOME WORK, c. 1910/GEORGE EASTMAN HOUSE

LEWIS W. HINE/SWEATSHOP—GARMENT WORKER, c. 1909–1913/GEORGE EASTMAN HOUSE

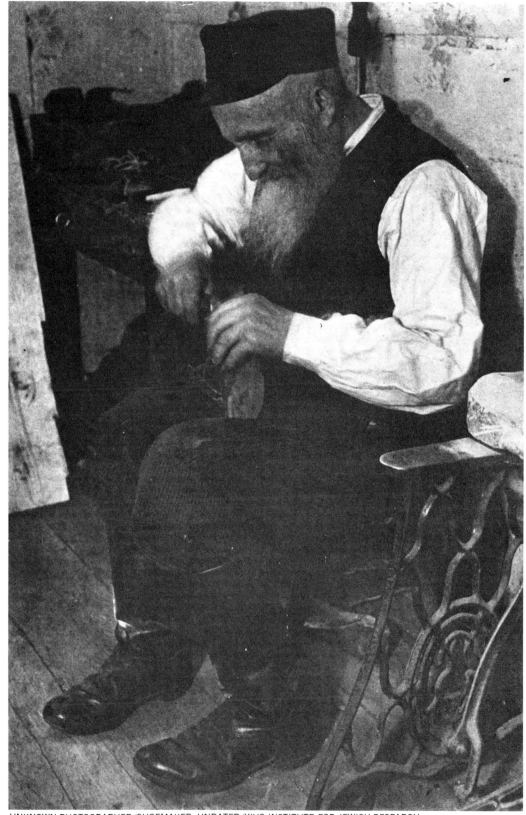

UNKNOWN PHOTOGRAPHER/SHOEMAKER, UNDATED/YIVO INSTITUTE FOR JEWISH RESEARCH

LEWIS W. HINE/HOMEWORK–CLOTHING, c. 1910/NATIONAL COMMITTEE ON EMPLOYMENT OF YOUTH

LEWIS W. HINE/HOMEWORK–GARTERS, c. 1910/GEORGE EASTMAN HOUSE

LEWIS W. HINE/HOMEWORK–CRACKING NUTS, c. 1910/PICTURE COLLECTION, NEW YORK PUBLIC LIBRARY

LEWIS W. HINE/HOME WORK, c. 1910/NATIONAL COMMITTEE ON EMPLOYMENT OF YOUTH

JACOB A. RIIS/BOHEMIAN CIGARMAKERS WORKING IN A TENEMENT, c. 1890/THE JACOB A. RIIS COLLECTION,
MUSEUM OF THE CITY OF NEW YORK

LEWIS W. HINE/SORTING RAGS, c. 1915
GEORGE EASTMAN HOUSE

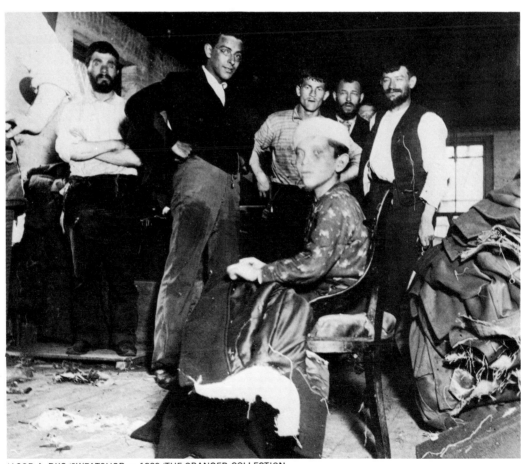

JACOB A. RIIS/SWEATSHOP, c. 1889/THE GRANGER COLLECTION

UNKNOWN PHOTOGRAPHER/HOME WORK, UNDATED/CULVER PICTURES, INC.

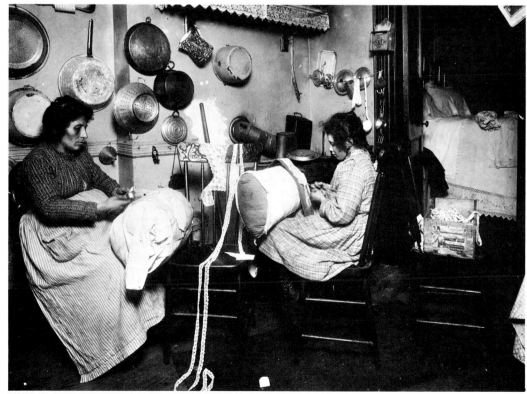

LEWIS W. HINE/HOMEWORK–LACE, c. 1910/NATIONAL COMMITTEE ON EMPLOYMENT OF YOUTH

BYRON/THE SHOP—MOE LEVY & CO., c. 1912/THE BYRON COLLECTION, MUSEUM OF THE CITY OF NEW YORK

BYRON/THE STORE—MOE LEVY & CO., 1908/THE BYRON COLLECTION, MUSEUM OF THE CITY OF NEW YORK

LEWIS W. HINE/SWEATSHOP, c. 1909–1914/GEORGE EASTMAN HOUSE

UNKNOWN PHOTOGRAPHER/SWEATSHOP, c. 1910/INTERNATIONAL LADIES' GARMENT WORKERS' UNION

LEWIS W. HINE/SWEATSHOP OF MR. GOLDSTEIN, 1910
GEORGE EASTMAN HOUSE

LEWIS W. HINE/BAKING BREAD, c. 1915/PICTURE COLLECTION, NEW YORK PUBLIC LIBRARY

UNKNOWN PHOTOGRAPHER/BAKING ROLLS, c. 1920/THE BETTMANN ARCHIVE

UNKNOWN PHOTOGRAPHER/CLOTHING WORKERS' STRIKE, UNDATED/BROWN BROTHERS

UNKNOWN PHOTOGRAPHER/LAST MEETING OF THE GARMENT WORKERS' STRIKE, 1913/AMALGAMATED CLOTHING
WORKERS OF AMERICA

UNKNOWN PHOTOGRAPHER/SAMUEL GOMPERS ADDRESSING SHIRT WAIST STRIKE MEETING IN COOPER UNION HALL, 1909/BROWN BROTHERS

UNKNOWN PHOTOGRAPHER/POLLING PLACE FOR STRIKE VOTE, c. 1915/INTERNATIONAL LADIES' GARMENT WORKERS' UNION

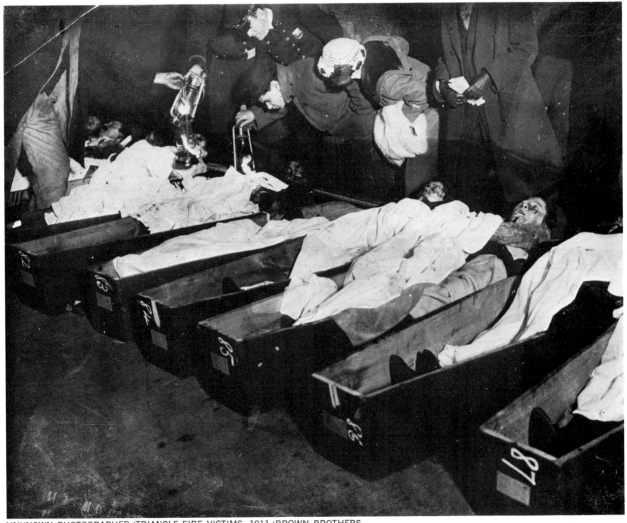

UNKNOWN PHOTOGRAPHER/TRIANGLE FIRE VICTIMS, 1911/BROWN BROTHERS

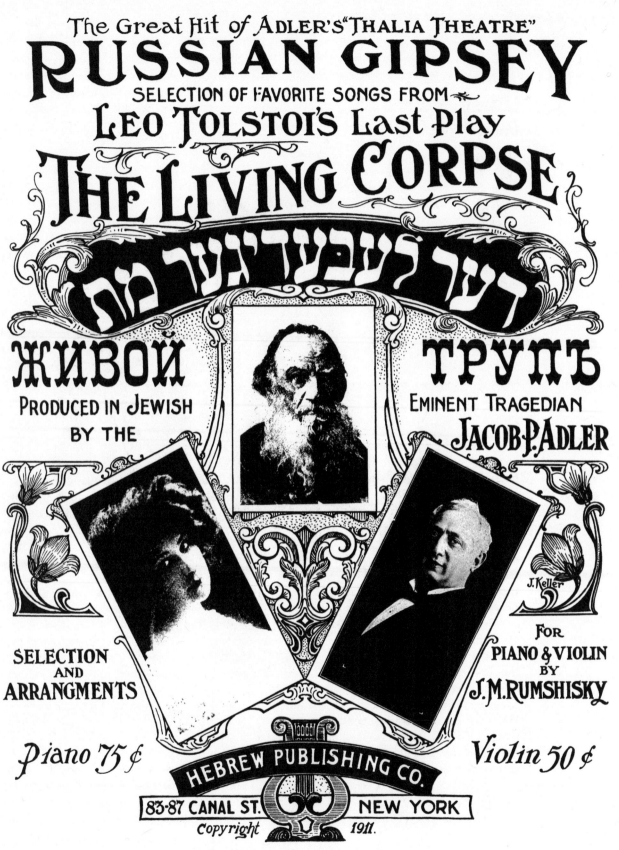

Lillian Wald's Case Notes

Visit and care of typhoid patient, 182 Ludlow Street. Visit to 7 Hester Street where in rooms of Nathan S. found two children with measles. After much argument succeeded in bathing these two patients and the sick baby. The first time in their experience. They insisted no water and soap could be applied to anyone with measles before seven days. Brought clean dresses to the older children.

Answer from dispensary doctor expresses great satisfaction of mother and says Mrs. M.'s child could be taken to a summer hospital, but on account of measles in the family this now must be given up. Spoke to the father about moving family away from the wretched house, advising country is less crowded than the city. He explained that being near people who could understand their language was sole influence on their choice of residence, professing to despise the filth and vermin. Upon his promising to seek employment elsewhere, I agreed that if he moved to the country, we would give the children shoes and assist in their respectable appearance in their new home.

Gave tickets for Hebrew Sanitarium excursion to Mrs. D. and 3 children, Mrs. S. and 5 children, for Tuesday's excursion, but five of the seven children are nearly naked. I am convinced they have no apparel in their possession, so we will make their decent appearance possible for the picnic. Visited both families and rooms, and an effort is really being made to keep them and the children cleaner.

Hannah R. visited. I explained how to reach 42nd Street hospital where truss will be applied gratis. She had actually bathed both children before I came and assures me she does it now daily.

At luncheon Miss Loeb (one of the visiting nurses) reports Mrs. L., 11 Rutgers Street, basement, consented to go to German hospital. Horrible tales of a child's immorality, her presence being a menace to the children of both sexes of the tenement. With the mother's conset, I reported her to the Gerry Society for them to act.

Next call on Hattie I., 20 Rutgers Place, basement. A girl of 17 years old with *phthisis*. The mother supports her family (old mother and five children) by a small candy store. The making of the candy, the sleeping, eating, washing of the family, the mingled odors of these and the street, in the same basement with the consumptive. The girl is not complaining but only longs to get out of the basement. I learned that the mother had had a letter written to Mr. Schiff, asking to have the girl admitted to the Montefiore Home, but her need is most urgent, so I wrote at once to the Superintendent.

Case of Mrs. G., 183 Clinton Street, rear tenement, second floor. First found by Miss Brewster, July 1st, *puerperal septicemia*, lying on vermin-infested bed without sheets or pillow cases. Husband, a peddler, had had $40 saved at beginning of illness, 3 weeks before. All had gone and none coming in, for he had been obliged to remain home to care for five children and wife. Dr. T. in attendance had been receiving 75 cents a visit. Miss B. considered the woman in bad condition, interviewed doctor. Woman's place was cleaned, beef and wine obtained from United Hebrew Charities. Carefully nursed, and husband, after much argument upon the economy of it, agreed to pay a woman three dollars a week to wash the clothes, look after the children all day, while he resumed his work. After much labor a Jewish woman was obtained for such service but impossible for less than $6 per week. We are paying the other $3. The husband is capable of making $4 a day, so they will soon be on their feet. Nursing continued by us. This and proper food soon told for the woman is convalescing. We loaned her all utensils necessary for good nursing. Started the children in Penny Provident Bank of the College Settlement. Despite their exceeding poverty, the children are being taught the thrift of penny saving.

Mrs. E., 3 Sheriff Street. Her leg has been treated by Miss B. It merely needed clean bandaging. She did scrub her rooms once, but as both husband and wife drink and they are old, Miss B. thinks time wasted to attempt reformation. Will confine herself to physical help.

Case of Hannah R., 7 Hester Street, rear tenement, first floor. Upon repeated investigation found the woman suffering from a bad hernia, and washing or earning her living of course impossible by hand labor. I fear she is hopelessly unclean, for the children are only washed and the rooms cleansed when she sees me approach. The truss was needed, and yesterday she wore it for the first time. The 42nd Street dispensary fitted her gratis at request of United Hebrew Charities.

Opposite a Russian family, name of H. The father has obtained work in Newark, but leaves family here as they have not saved money to move. Saturday, when the husband is in New York, I will persuade him to move (the wife has already consented), for I am provided with a letter from Mr. Solomon of the Baron de Hirsch Fund, who has agreed to pay transportation.

Annie P., 44 Allen Street, front tenement, second floor. Husband Louis P. came here three years ago and one year ago sent for wife and three children. From that time unfortunately, his trade, that of shoemaker, became less remunerative. She helped by washing and like labor, but two months ago he deserted her, though she stoutly maintains that he returned to Odessa to get his old work back. The youngest, Meyer P., age 5 years, fell from the table and injured his hip. He lay for 7 months in the Orthopedic Hospital, 42nd Street; he was discharged as incurable and supplied with a brace. I found them eating, as I have told in the letter to Mr. Schiff. The mother is absolutely tied by her pregnant condition; the cripple is in pain and cries to be carried. They had no rooms of their own but paid $3 a month to Hannah A., a decent tailoress, who allowed the family to sleep on her floor. The $3 cannot be forthcoming now for the woman's accouchement is in three weeks. The children are unusually attractive, and later investigation showed that they all told the exact truth. Sunday I saw them. Monday I filed application with Montefiore Home for Meyer's admission. The New York Hospital promised to look after the child until place was secured—if not too long. Tuesday I went to Hebrew Sheltering Guardian Society, saw Superintendent, and obtained promise of place for the two well children by Thursday. Necessary to procure committal first. Mr. Jenkins of S.P.C.C. made it urgent and obtained Judge Ryan's signature Thursday morning. Thursday afternoon, we washed and dressed the two children, and I left them in the afternoon at the Asylum, leaving my address for the Superintendent so that he might know their friend in case of need. They have absolutely no one in America but their mother. As soon as an answer is received from the Montefiore application, I will take the mother to the Nursery and Child's hospital where she will be cared for during confinement.

THE NEW YORK TIMES,
JANUARY 18, 1895

For Better Tenements

The Tenement House Committee submitted its report yesterday to the State Senate and Assembly. The committee consists of Richard Watson Gilder, Chairman; Edward Marshall, Secretary; W. Bayard Cutting, Dr. Cyrus Edson, Roger Foster, Solomon Moses, George B. Post, and John O. Schuchman. The committee began May 12, 1894, to gather evidence under the act which empowered it to conduct its investigation, and its report contains many recommendations, the effect of the adoption of which, it believes, would be the betterment of the condition of the poor. The first recommendation is that power be given to the Board of Health to institute condemnation proceedings for the destruction of buildings which are so unsanitary as to be unfit for human habitation, with provision for reasonable compensation to the owners in case of such destruction. Commenting on this, the report continues that nothing is more clearly shown in this report than the necessity, in the interests of public health, of destroying, under due process of law, the oldest and worst tenement houses in the city.

Under existing laws, the Board of Health is unable to compel the destruction of tenement houses, which, in their opinion, repairs or renovation can remedy the evils are so unfit for human habitation that no which they cause. Such buildings cannot now be destroyed, unless they amount to a nuisance, in which case the owner receives no compensation. This committee has, consequently, drawn a bill providing for the condemnation of such buildings and for the payment of compensation to the owner in case of their destruction. This bill has been modeled upon a similar statute which has worked satisfactorily in Great Britain.

The committee believes that more light and air are needed in tenements. To that end, it recommends that the Board of Health and the Building Department be deprived of the power to dispense with the requirements of the law concerning the amount of open space to be left on lots where tenement houses are constructed. It recommends that no tenement or lodging-house shall occupy more than 70 per cent of an interior city lot, nor more than 90 per cent of a corner lot.

The committee has prepared a bill embodying recommendations that further precautions be taken to decrease the danger from fire in tenement houses already constructed. For this purpose a law should

be passed forbidding, after the 1st day of September, 1895, (a) the storage in any tenement house of feed, hay, or straw; (b) the maintenance after that date of any bakery or place of business in which fat is boiled in any tenement house more than three stories in height, in which more than two families live on one floor, and which is not fireproof; (c) that after said date all openings into the halls or other parts of the tenement houses from bakeries or places of business in which fat is boiled shall be solidly closed with fireproof material so as to prevent the escape of fire and smoke from them into other parts of the house; and (d) that after the same date all transoms and windows opening into halls from any portion of any tenement house where paint, oil, spiritous liquors, or drugs are stored or kept for sale, shall be removed and closed up as solidly as the rest of the wall and that all doors leading into any such hall or room from a place thus used in a tenement house shall be made fireproof. A bill which contains all these provisions is ready, and there is another which would make it compulsory that ceilings of all basements occupied as human habitations be at least two feet above the level of the ground adjoining.

In regard to the present condition of things, the report says that ventilation of basements both supplies the fresh air necessary to carry on the proper functions of life and carries off the moisture which would otherwise do injury. Experience proves that, while the air will renew itself in basements having ceilings one foot above the sidewalk, there is not sufficient volume of it in movement, and every foot added to this height increases the volume of air in movement.

The following recommendations are not accompanied by bills. As one of the principal means of prevention of overcrowding of houses and districts, rapid-transit facilities should be pushed forward as vigorously as possible. In addition to the free, floating baths maintained in the summer months, the city should open in the crowded districts fully equipped bathing establishments, on the best European models, and with moderate charges. Numerous drinking fountains and sufficient public lavatories should be established in the tenement house districts. Electric light should be extended as rapidly as possible throughout all parts of the tenement-house districts. The system of asphalt pavements should be extended as rapidly as possible throughout the streets of the tenement-house districts of the city. A thorough inquiry should be made as to the condition of the older schoolhouses in New York and as to the sufficiency of school accommodations in general, and the number of kindergartens should be largely increased in connection with the public school system. A law should be passed making the offenses of soliciting and the maintenance of disorderly houses in tenement houses punishable with greater severity than when they are committed elsewhere. The present Tenement House Board, consisting of certain city officials, should be abrogated, and special commissions, with full powers of examination and recommendation, should be constituted by the Legislature at intervals of not more than five years.

After relating the conditions affecting tenement-house life in New York, the insular character of the city, its narrowness, its position as the chief port of entry, the high value of real estate, and the lack of breathing places, the report says that it is impossible to ascertain from existing data how many immigrants yearly remain in New York City. At the office of the United States Commission of Immigration, Ellis Island, New York Harbor, there are figures showing the number of immigrants coming to America who give their intended destination as New York State. Of course, a very large part of the these remain in the city, but no figures in the possession of the commissioner show how many take up their residence in New York City for a period of six months or more, as distinct from those who leave immediately or soon after for other points.

	Total immigrants to the U.S.	Total immigrants arriving at N.Y.S.	Tota immigr destin N.Y.
Year ending June 30, '91	560,319	405,664	169,8
Year ending June 30, '92	579,663	445,987	234,3
Year ending June 30, '93	439,730	343,422	153,2
Year ending June 30, '94	285,631	219,046	91,1

It will be seen that 45.85 per cent of all the immigrants who were landed at the port were destined for the State of New York. But, these figures are, to a certain extent, misleading in so far as they do not represent the actual number, or anything like it, who remain in New York, for the simple reason that New York is the distributing point for the whole country. As to the actual number of the population of immediate foreign descent, the figures, though not complete, are at least much more accurate. On June 1, 1890, the date of the United States census, of the 1,489,627 whites in New York, 636,986 were foreign born; that is, 42.8 per cent, not counting the nearly 26,000 persons of African descent born in America. At the same date 76.2 per cent had foreign-born mothers.

In the density of population of New York in comparison with that of other cities, New York, including the thinly populated annexed district, ranks sixth. New York below the Harlem has a greater density per acre than any other city in the world—143.2 per acre. Paris comes next with a density of 125.2 per acre, and Berlin follows, with 113.6. The population of New York in 1894 has been estimated by Dr. Tracy as 1,957,452, a figure which may be somewhat excessive, as the rate of increase may not have been the usual one, owing to a decrease in the flow of immigration and some emigration to Europe in consequence of the recent financial depression. According to estimates based upon the above total, Sanitary District A, of the Eleventh Ward, contained on June 1, 1894, as many as 986.4 persons to every one of its thirty-two acres. The census of 1890 gives 800.47 to this district. It may be that these figures are equaled in some parts of the world, but the only information at hand indicated but one district approaching this—a part of Bombay, which in 1881 had a population of 759.66 to the acre in an area of 46.06 acres. It should be noted that the Asiatic density is comparatively more oppressive as it is spread over much less floor space, the New York buildings having more stories. The densest small section of Europe seems to be the Josefstadt of Prague, with its 485.4 to the acre, but New York's Tenth Ward exceeds this with not less than 626.26 to the acre, and the Tenth Ward has nearly five times the acreage of the crowded district in Prague.

The entire population of the tenements in 1893, according to the Board of Health Census, was 1,332,773 persons living in 39,138 houses, out of an entire estimated population of 1,891,306. Laws touching upon tenements may, therefore, where there is no exception, directly affect 70.46 of our population. But it is estimated that of the entire tenement-house population as defined by law, only about four-fifths really belong to the class usually designated by that term, the remaining fifth living in what are known as flats, or apartment houses. The double-decker, so called, is the one hopeless form of tenement-house construction. It began with the alteration of old New York dwellings, and gradually a type was produced in some respects better and in some worse than the earlier forms of the narrow tenement. The double-decker cannot be well ventilated; it cannot be well lighted; it is not safe in case of fire. The tenement-house population of New York is crowded into tall and narrow buildings that are not of fireproof construction. The only alleviation of the ever-threatening danger from fire is the system of iron fire escapes on the outside of the buildings and the existence of an alert and well-trained Fire Department. A map prepared by the Fire Department giving the fires in all parts of the city for a single year shows that the greatest activity of the department is in the most populous tenement-house districts. In the year ending June 30, 1894,

there were 2,415 tenement-house fires, involving a loss of $608,784, and in that time fifteen occupants were killed outright and seventy-two injured. It is a startling fact that while less than one-third of the buildings in New York are tenement houses, among them occur annually more than one-half of the fires. During the half-year or more that this committee has been at work, seven fatal tenement-house fires have taken place. In each of four of these one life was lost, in one two lives, in another three lives, and in still another, seven, making a total of sixteen deaths.

The evils inflicted by tenement-house fires should not be computed in mere statistics of death, personal injury, or property destroyed. Such a fire, even when not reckoned serious, means a panic, with all the distress suggested by the word, and the unrecorded ills that follow such a calamity. The destruction of property, however slight in money value, entails sudden eviction and generally the uninsured loss of all the worldly possessions of the tenant. When it is remembered that the larger part of our population is peculiarly subject to these dangers, it becomes evident that not only should there be legislation looking to the future, but that something should be done at once to reduce the number and virulence of tenement-house fires. It is well-known that many fires originate in cellars or basements. For this reason certain hazardous occupations in these should be at once prevented or made more safe, and in future construction an unbroken fireproof floor should be required in the very lowest story. This solid floor has sanitary uses, as well as value in protection from fire. Fireproof construction is much less expensive than is popularly supposed. It is to be remembered that the greater permanence of the building, the decreased ratio of repairs with advancing age, and the saving in insurance are elements that tend to counterbalance the increased cost.

The condition in certain sections of the city caused by the overcrowding of buildings is serious and quite as menacing to health as the overcrowding of inhabitants in the tenement houses themselves. The statistics accentuate the necessity of a law providing that no discretion should be allowed the Building Department in granting permits for houses to cover more than 70 per cent of the area of any inside lot. The law has long limited the area which should be covered but has permitted exceptions to be made. These exceptions have become the rule, and a block was discovered in which nearly 93 per cent of the total area is covered by buildings. Others ran from 80 per cent to 86 per cent, and a total average for thirty-four blocks showed 78.13 of the area built upon. This greatly reduces the means of ventilation and the breathing space of those living in the rear apartments, particularly in view of the fact that the average number of stories throughout this section is nearly four and one-half. Taking this as an average height of buildings, the ventilation for at least the first three floors must be most inadequate and the air impure. Moreover, the extra risk from a fire insurance point of view in this crowded section is 12½ per cent of the entire area; in other words, one house in eight is regarded as of a seriously inflammable character—certainly a most dangerous condition both as to buildings and humanity in such a thickly populated neighborhood.

The most important evidence concerning the healthfulness of the tenement houses in this city is to be found in the statistics which show the proportion of annual deaths occurring in them to the total number of their inhabitants. The high death rate among Italians, the report says, is due to unsanitary conditions, overcrowding, and lack of ventilation, but mainly to the fact that they are affected by the change from the climate of Italy to the severe one of New York. The diet which they are accustomed to there is not suitable to this climate, and they deteriorate owing to insufficient nourishment. They conceal from the Health Department cases of contagious diseases, and they live in the most unsanitary houses.

With an average density of 57.2, i.e., an average of 57.2 tenants to the house, the highest in the city, the death rate in the Tenth Ward is 17.14, the report says. This means that while the Tenth Ward is first on the list of density in population in its tenement houses, it ranks twenty-second among the wards in its death rate, there being but two wards (the Third and the Twenty-fourth) with a lower rate. While other factors may tend slightly to affect this, it is in the main due to the nationality of its population, which is largely composed of Hebrews, whose religious laws are designed to maintain health. The mere fact that one ward has more inhabitants than another does not necessarily mean that the death rate is higher in the entire ward than in wards where there are fewer inhabitants. But the first well-known cause operating to effect an increase in the death rate is density of population.

The wards showing the greatest house density combined with a low death rate, namely, the Tenth and Seventh Wards, are very largely populated by Russian and Polish Jews. This is, in fact, the Jewish quarter of the city. The wards having the highest death rate, the Fourth and Fourteenth, the former with a house density below the average and the latter with one lower than the lowest of the Jewish districts, are largely occupied by Italians, and constitute two of the numerous Italian colonies which are distributed through the city. It is worth a passing notice that in the Sixth Ward, which is also the seat of an Italian colony (the notorious Mulberry Bend), where the house density is high, 38.8, the death rate is considerably lower than in the other wards just mentioned, namely, 27.36. This is possibly caused by the large percentage of Jews in Bayard and Baxter Streets, whose low death rate in a measure offsets the high death rate of the Italians.

Now, it is a well-known fact that human dwellings, by prolonged occupation, become so saturated with the bodily emanations of those who have lived in them, sick and well, as to be less healthy than newer houses. It has often been proposed to construct hospitals of flimsy and inexpensive material after the manner of a temporary shelter and to destroy them by fire every few years, to be replaced with new ones. The result of prolonged human occupancy is made worse in this city by the rapidity with which the character of the population in the lower parts of the city has changed and by the fact that houses built as private dwellings are not fitted to serve as tenements, either in respect to light, ventilation, water supply, privacy, or facilities for cleanliness. Another potent cause of the high death rates in the lower part of the city is the excessive number of rear tenement houses in these older wards. In the Sixth Ward, for example, 46.53 per cent of the population is housed on lots containing both front and rear houses; in the Fourteenth Ward the proportion is 44.46 and in the Fourth 30.31, from which percentage it falls off rapidly to 21.05 in the Tenth Ward, and 20.90 in the Eighth. The unsanitary character of the rear tenement houses is generally admitted. The most cursory examination shows that the death rates are very high where there are rear tenements, running up to 61.97—an enormous death rate—in the entire city, against 22.21 for the single tenements.

On the supplying of water to tenements, the report says that freer use of water by the tenement-house population would aid them very materially in their struggle for existence by assisting the elimination from their systems of the poisons absorbed in the sunless and airless dwellings. That several hundred thousand people in the city have no proper facilities for keeping their bodies clean is a disgrace to the city and to the civilization of the nineteenth century. These facilities have been used, and are abundant in many enlightened nations, and they are being increased in every way possible. The amount of money annually spent in charity in this city amounts to millions, and the question arises whether it be not greater ecenomy to spend more for the preservation of health and the prevention of disease, because less would then be required for the support and care of the sick and helpless. The cultivation of the habit of personal cleanliness has a favorable effect, also, upon character, tending to self-respect and decency of life.

The committee made special inquiries as to rentals, and says that in some cases the profits of landlords are as high as 20 per cent. From such general information as this committee has been able to obtain, it seems that when a tenement house is properly constructed in accordance with the present laws, kept in good repair and in excellent sanitary condition, one of the first class, namely, the single-flat house, produces a net profit to the owner of about 9 per cent, upon the value of the equity. One of the second class, namely, the one with two apartments on a floor, and with no improvements such as baths, water closets, ranges, boilers, and stationary washtubs furnished by the landlord in each apartment, realizes a net profit to the owner of about 8 per cent, on the value of the equity; a house of the third class realizes to the owner a profit of about 9 per cent, on the value of the equity, and one of the fourth class 10 per cent on the value of the equity.

NEW YORK TRIBUNE,
NOVEMBER 25, 1900

Landlords Permit Wickedness To Flourish

The squalor, the poverty, the hopeless drudgery, and the queer features of this foreign district are evident to the visitor, no matter how hurriedly he goes over the ground, but the crime with which that part of the city is infested has been concealed from the general public until it gained such proportions that men like Bishop Potter were compelled to step in and call a halt. The police say, and the records show, that there is less drunkenness there than in other parts of the East Side tenement-house district, that there are not many cases of assault, and that street fights are of rare occurrence. But the big tenement houses in Chrystie, Allen, Stanton, and Forsyth Streets shelter crime in its worst form, and the inmates of these apartments contaminate their neighbors and create an atmosphere in which good morals cannot exist. For years these places have been known by the red lamps which shone in the windows or hallways. These lamps increased in number to such an extent that the district became known as the "red light district," and the degraded men who lived on the vice of the inmates of the houses were known in that section as "lighthouses." The police, the landlord, and the "lighthouse" formed a combination against which the respectable element could make no headway.

A peculiar feature of the situation is the lack of interest displayed on the part of what is known as "the decent" class in the crusade against the dive and red-lamp proprietors. Nearly all the red-lamp places are on the first floors of tenement houses, and the buildings with high, old-fashioned stoops are most in favor. For that reason the places are often referred to by the police as "stoops." When an objectionable tenant moves into a "stoop," puts up lace curtains and other decorations too expensive for and not in harmony with the surroundings, a tenant or possibly several tenants usually make objection and protest. But the "stoop" pays at least twice as much rent when occupied by the objectionable people as it would if only respectable people lived there, and the objectors are told to move out if they don't like their neighbors. In a comparatively short time the children in the house, possibly those of the original objectors, become the friends of the degraded inmates, and in return for candy, cast-off clothes, "show" tickets, and other bribes they become the spies, the watchers, and agents of the people in the "stoop" apart-

ment, and are finally engulfed in the sea of vice.

All this has been known to the police for years as well as it has been known to the people who seek the betterment of the district, but the district was too good a source of revenue for some people to be purified. The law which requires the posting of the name of the owner of a tenement house has been evaded, and although owners are responsible, they have not hesitated to let their apartments to any person who would pay a high rental, regardless of the use made of them. The owners of these houses know that it is difficult to procure evidence against tenants, and until the question of purification was brought forward because of the insolence of the police to the rector of the Pro-Cathedral, the Tammany motto, "What are you going to do about it?" stared the good people in the face.

The landlords are for the most part people who made their money in the district. There are some houses whose owners have moved uptown, but the greater number live in the houses which shelter the objectionable tenants. The "housekeeper" is an institution of the district. In other parts of the city he is known as the agent, janitor or superintendent. He usually fixes the rate of rent and collects it, and with him complaints are lodged. He must know the police in order to be a good "housekeeper," and his word "goes" with many tenants as to where coal, wood, groceries, and other necessary articles should be purchased. The "housekeeper" does not hesitate to charge $30 a month for a $15 apartment when the tenant is of a certain character, but his receipt, when he gives one at all, never shows such figures. He has a wholesome fear of documentary evidence, and where he gives a receipt it is for the legitimate amount, and the signature is not often one by which the real owner may be identified. The extra rent, the blackmail which he extorts from the tenants, may be given to the owner, or he may keep it for himself or share it with the owner and others. There is no fixed rule or regulation about that point, and it makes little difference to the "stoop" tenant where the money goes or how it is divided—he or she knows that so long as it is paid promptly the red lamp may burn and the police will not see it or, seeing it, will not know what it means.

James B. Reynolds of the University Settlement said that he had endeavored for a long time to have red-light places in Rivington Street suppressed, but without success. He said, "It is hard to get sufficient evidence against the landlord, because the very power which should aid us has been on the other side. The law is deficient, and should be amended so that the landlord would become responsible for the tenant. He should be placed on a level with a common carrier; then no bad people could remain in his house, except by the consent or the connivance of the owner or his agent, and, the name of the owner being posted, as it should be, it would be an easy matter to put an end to the nuisance."

THE NEW YORK TIMES, JULY 9, 1899

Changes on the East Side

Quietly, but none the less surely and steadily, the transformation of the East Side is working. Within the past few years changes, at once gratifying and wonderful, have been made in the character and kind of buildings situated in that portion of the city bounded by Catharine Street, the Bowery, St. Mark's Place, and the East River. Many thousands of dollars have been put into new buildings there to replace the old-time, ill-constructed, poorly ventilated tenements. A walk through the district will show that in many places it seems as if it were born anew. Substantial, and in some instances handsome, new tenement houses, five and six stories high, everywhere abound, and instead of the erstwhile miserably lighted, poorly ventilated, cramped quarters, there may now be seen apartments and flats at once commodious and comfortable.

The transformation is not changing the character of the East Side residents; that promises for some time yet to be more or less a constant factor, made up as it is of all sorts and conditions of people and of diverse elements. The people themselves, however, are improving. New schools have been built, and are building in the district, and through these and the improved condition of their manner and means of living the people are becoming educated. They have learned, too, the lesson that fresh air and good light are prerequisites to health, and for that reason the cry for more and better buildings is going up. Filth and squalor, it is true, are yet frequently met with but in no such marked degree as in times past. With the building of the better tenements has come also a greater attention to cleanliness and good order.

Exactly how considerable and striking the improvements in the matter of new buildings have been may best be impressed by a reference to figures in the case. A glance over the records for the first six months of last year shows that the total outlay in the building line in the district referred to was exactly $3,598,000, by far the greater part of which was for tenements. Of this sum $350,000 was expended in Henry Street, $393,000 in Monroe Street, $290,000 in Second Avenue, $195,000 in Madison Street, $150,000 in Pitt Street, $125,000 in Stanton Street, $100,000 in Cherry Street, with the remainder scattered about in various parts, beginning practically at the waterfront itself. The figures for the last six months of the same year show that in this district the expenditure on buildings was $2,775,000. Of this amount something like $250,000 was expended in Cherry Street, about the same amount in Broome Street, $150,000 in Henry Street, $150,000 in Madison Street, $150,000 in Eldridge Street, $100,000 in

Pike, and $100,000 in Stanton, with the rest scattered. This year, up to the present time, the value of the buildings either built, under process of construction, or projected, totals $4,674,000. Of this sum, Madison Street has $400,000 to its credit, Henry $200,000, Broome, $200,000 and Rivington, Eldridge, and Stanton $150,000.

The figures for any particular district are, however, given only by way of illustration. The fact is, as has been stated, the improvements are confined to no particular street, but are general and "all along the line." If one talks to a man who, like the politician, divides the district into wards, one will learn that in the Seventh Ward the greatest improvement has been made in Monroe, Cherry, Madison, and Henry Street. In the Tenth Ward the greatest improvement has been in Eldridge and Rivington Streets, while in the Thirteenth Ward the streets most to benefit have been Goerch, Willett, and Pitt. Nor have the improvements been confined to the last year and a half. The figures for preceding years show that in 1897 the number of flats and tenements built in that part of the city lying from river to river south of Fourteenth Street was 199 at an estimated cost of $4,587,500. Of this number it is stated that fully three-fourths were on the East Side. In 1896 the number was 60 and the value $1,295,000; in 1895 the figures were 117, and $2,428,340 respectively; and in 1894, 77 and $1,548,-250. These figures of themselves contrasted with the figures for last year and this year, show how striking has been the growth in tenement-house building within even a year.

On the other hand, it is somewhat interesting to note the marked decline in buildings which for the purpose of classification are put under the head of hotels, stores, churches, and office buildings. In 1895 exactly 115 of these were built in the section of the city, from river to river, south of Fourteenth Street at a cost of $17,867,750; in 1896, 113 were built at a cost of $16,593,600; in 1897, the figures were 97 and $18,066,980 respectively; but last year they fell still further to 68 and $6,569,500 respectively. Of course the East Side shared little in these buildings, most of them being in the business and so-called downtown portion of the city. The reason for the falling off in office buildings and for the increase in tenement-house building suggests itself. In the one case so many large office buildings have been built that the supply of office room may now fairly be said to equal the demand; in the other case the demand for better tenements is still great, and the supply clearly is far from being adequate.

Nor has the work of transforming the East Side ceased. On the contrary, real estate dealers who have been approached on the subject, with few exceptions, agree that the activity of recent years will continue. Various factors will contribute to this. In the first place the owners of the old tenement houses have learned to their sorrow that the new tenement houses have constituted a drain on their tenants, the temptation being, not unnaturally, for tenants to seek those houses offering superior accommodation and conveniences. As a result the original tenement-house keepers find themselves in a quandary. In other words, they must either reduce their rents in order to retain their tenants, or they must tear down their buildings and put up new and modern ones. A reduction of rents would mean poor returns on investments; accordingly the owners prefer to build new tenement houses, which, it is said, yield on an average 12 per cent gross or 10 per cent net on the invested capital. In the second place the East Side is especially convenient to a vast army of workers about Broadway, who can, if they choose, without much inconvenience, reach their homes on that side without the necessity of paying carfare. That of itself is no inconsiderable factor in keeping a large element on the East Side—an element by the way which is among the strongest of the insistors upon good living houses.

Then, too, the improvement of the parks in the district and the building of the East River bridge will have their effect and influence on the growth of the district. The growth, however, will in the opinion of real estate men, be in the next few years in the uptown portion of the district—that is, beginning about First Street and along the intersecting avenues. The reason for this is that most of the available lots in the downtown section have been bought up and are now held, many of them it is said for speculative purposes, in the belief that the value of these lots will increase at least 25 per cent in the next three years. Further uptown, however, land can still be bought at what is considered a reasonable rate, and it is for this reason that activity for the future is predicted in that direction.

It is worth noticing that in all this improvement on the East Side few factories have been put up. The explanation for this is that the land is altogether too valuable for factory purposes. Manufacturers find that they cannot afford to pay the prices asked for land, while on the other hand, owners of land find that their best investments are in the way of tenement houses.

One of the striking facts in connection with this gradual transforming of the East Side—and it is a fact gladly attested by the Health Department—is that sickness and disease in the district are not nearly so prevalent, and as a consequence the death rate is lower. This, of course, is accounted for by the less cramped condition of the tenement-house dwellers and the better ventilation and care of the places. It is admitted, nevertheless, that there is much room for improvement. Of course with all these changes has come also a change in the condition of the sweatshop workers in the district, who now find their lines cast in more pleasant quarters, where elbow does not touch elbow, nor fetid, poisonous air is alone breathed.

Excepting the Germania Bank and the new schoolhouses of the district, it may safely be said that nine-tenths of all the money stated as expended in the district has been on tenement and flat houses, some with stores on the ground floor and some without. Private dwelling houses are a rarity.

Slums That Once Were

It was the Tenement House Committee of 1894 and the Small Parks Commission that administered the death blow to some of New York's most sodden slums. These, though only phases of the agitation extending over many years for slum regeneration, proved to be the final weapons for those who would wipe out festering spots. What was sought to be accomplished began after this committee and this commission had handed up their recommendations and had mapped out their work. It is not to be contended, indeed, that all slums have disappeared in New York, though the metropolis shares with nearly every other municipality in this country and in Europe the honor for the fact that there has been a decrease in the number and a contraction in the size of its regions of crime that stalks nakedly and causes extreme suffering. But the worst have gone. Beneath the vigorous strokes of dealers in secondhand building materials, the grimy, ancient, disease-filled structures have vanished. A round half-dozen of the localities famed malodorously in police annals and in the records of the Health Board from 1870 on are no more.

If the old slum sites have not become places of beauty, they are at least nowadays spots of comfort. No disease lurks in them; there are no shadowy haunts and recesses for the plotting and committing of crime. The regeneration has been effective and has left little behind it but memories. Memories there will always be. The traditions of the old sites are not likely to be forgotten or lost. Nevertheless, the younger generation of today, visiting these localities, will find it hard to realize what they once were, with the herding together, the noisy revelry, the wickedness, and the dirt of years. Indeed, they will never be able to realize it, for, save on a few occasions, the worst was never told. A tour through some of these slums, a revisiting of the sites of the old plague spots, has deep interest for one who remembers somewhat of their days of crime. What might be called the building regeneration of these localities is now complete. Where slums once stood there is here a park, there an open yard, here a business structure, there a street. Absolutely and definitely the old fester has been cut out of the municipality, making in spots almost a new New York.

With the sunlight shining brightly upon its sweep of green, its well-washed asphalt, and its glistening white pavilion, Mulberry Bend Park, a breathing place these days for thousands of Italians, is a remarkable change from the old "Bend" that was the abode of vileness. Not an iota of picturesqueness has been sacrificed, for the scene now reminds one irresistibly of a bit of an Italian city. The row of dwelling houses and shops in Mulberry Street, east of the park, shows a long range of quaint and foreign fronts. Even the Baxter Street buildings at the west stand out more artistically and seem less commonplace because of their new setting. This "Little Italy"— New York has at least three "Italy's"— has not lost in any manner in the change. It has gained unreservedly, for the crime and dirt of the "Bend" more than counterbalanced all its ancient-quarter charm. There are many filthy tenements in the adjoining streets, but with the abolition of the real "Bend" the most frightful have disappeared. Here, where the beautiful park now extends, is the exact site where some years ago Lady Henry Somerset, in company with Jacob A. Riis, most expert of slum guides, discovered the first thoroughly drunken and bestial woman in the city. Mr. Riis described this in an article written just at the time the "Bend" was vanishing:

"Into every place made vacant by an Irishman moved an Italian and a tramp, and when the transformation was completed the 'Bend' held two or three times as many tenants as before. . . .Lady Henry

Somerset found some of them burrowing in their underground dens, the stale beer dives, when she went the rounds of the 'Bend' in the small hours of the morning with the writer. She had been congratulating New York upon its freedom from drunken women until she went down there and changed her mind.

"The police sometimes took as many as seventy or one hundred men and women tramps out of the stale beer dives of the 'Bend' alleys at a single raid. On such nights every window in the Elizabeth Street station stood open all night, and the policemen smoked the strongest cigars to be got by way of disinfecting the house."

That was the old Mulberry Bend, of which police tradition recalls that there were nearly six hundred ways, by actual count, by which a desperate criminal or petty thief, pursued by officers, could escape. All the ramshackle, aged buildings communicated with one another, above, below, in cellars, and over roofs. There were scores of grim, underground passages and a dozen or so winding alleys piercing the block. When the Italians came, herding two or three families to a small room, armed with pistol and knife, prepared to settle their difficulties by stealthy stabs instead of by application to the courts, it was indescribably bad. Added to all this there were Jews of the lowest type on the Baxter Street side. Here was Ragpicker's Row. Bottle Alley, which held the city's record for fights for many a long year, was one of the chief inlets from Mulberry Street. Another byway led to Bandits' Roost, the refuge of real bandit mountaineers from Italy. Dirty stable lanes hemmed it in, as, indeed they did every spot. What the famous fights were is too long a story to tell here.

"The Bend" went the way of the older Five Points four years ago. Park building is slow work. It was not until last summer that Mulberry Park began to show its real charm and to stamp itself a success. This year the grass has come out velvety, the seats are filled day and evening, and after the colony has finished its supper huge crowds congregate here. Though these Italians are growing gradually Americanized, this is not evident in their costumes. As a military band plays in the pavilion, the scene is deliciously picturesque. Not one single reminder lingers of the old slum. Even the Mulberry Street houses opposite the park, now thrust into the broad light of day, have been forced to be cleaner than before.

From the "Bend" to Cherry Hill is a long walk through Chinatown, the lower end of the Jewish quarters, and the haunts of the few Irish yet left on the far southeast side of New York. Turning down from Roosevelt Street into Cherry Street, one comes across a big yard in the midst of the block. Blocks of sidewalk stones are stored there, huge piles of worm-eaten, dirty lumber wagons stand out in what might be called the roadway. In one corner there is a tottering shed made to serve the purposes of a stable for two old horses. The yard is certainly not prepossessing. It is utterly uninteresting—a junk shop in the open air. But at least the four winds of heaven can blow over it and purify it, which was not the case until two years ago. Until then the fresh air only filtered in, losing all its purity and becoming vitiated before it had gone a dozen feet. In the old days the air that struck the famous Oak Street Police Station was laden with horrible odors, telling the nose only too plainly that here were crowding people who were little better than brutes, perhaps worse. For this was Double Alley and Single Alley, the Gotham Court of an earlier day, and Mullin's Alley where the "Swamp Angels" of years ago rioted, stole, fought policemen, committed murders, and, when followed, hid in the great sewer beneath Double Alley, crouching on the coping safe in ten cases out of ten from the iron hand of the law.

New York never had worse slums than Double Alley, Single Alley, and Mullin's Alley. The overcrowding may be judged from the fact that dwellers on opposite sides of these alleys could, by leaning a little from their windows, shake hands across. Not that they ever wanted to shake hands under any circumstances, for war reigned between all the households. In Single Alley two men could hardly walk abreast comfortably. In Double Alley it was a little better. Heaps of rotting refuse were in every corner of the courts, and the odor of stale beer arose above all.

The story never changes; each filthy slum of New York always comes to Italians for tenants. The last lessee of these alleys bundled out what Irish there were remaining. Why should he not? It meant to him at least 50 per cent more rents. The Italians merely accepted the situation. They were getting their rents close to nothing, for each of the small rooms now came to be occupied by two or three families, where one Irish household had found it a tight squeeze for themselves alone. At a bound the population of this slum came near to doubling. There were fewer fights now that Italy was installed here, the police reserves did not have to tumble out of bed and rush around at the double quick so often, but the filth and immorality increased, and even with the "Swamp Angels" dead and gone, these alleys had dropped a peg lower.

Why they were left standing so long is one of the city's mysteries. The rear-tenement agitation waxed and waned, and yet Single Alley and Double Alley remained. Their deathblow came two years ago this spring on an order of the Board of Health. And yet even now the old slum is not entirely demolished. The dirty tenement of Single Alley has been left, though it now faces on the open, broad yard. With nearly every window gone and everything that could be torn away out of it, there is to be seen still an Italian family or two in some of the rooms. But the air can now get a chance at the gloomy, shallow building for the first time in its history. It is understood that a big warehouse will rise eventually on this site, blotting out finally and thoroughly all traces of one of the vilest of plague spots. Meantime, however, the wood and stone yard does well. It has laid to rest for all time the ghosts of filth and crime.

Gone, too, and its site now a playground for children and a breathing place for older people of evenings, is what long was the worst strip of the ghetto. Hester, Norfolk, Suffolk, and Rutgers Streets, poor as they were, did not sink into a helpless, apathetic state until the invasion of the Russian Jews, beginning in 1884, as a result of the exile because of the May Laws. With their coming in masses, shrewd landlords began to put in flimsy rear tenements and, because of the demand, to raise rents until one family had of necessity to huddle in a single room and even to take in boarders. There may have been worse blocks in the ghetto than those bounded by Norfolk, Suffolk, Hester, Jefferson, Rutgers, East Broadway, and Canal, but if there ever were, the writer never knew them.

In truth, these blocks were bad enough. Huge, malodorous "barracks," smelling of fried fish and unclean persons, filled their centers as well as fronted on the streets. In these blocks is said to have been the most overcrowded spot in the world, far surpassing the ill-reputed ghettos of European cities in the number of souls clustered to the square rod. Every room at one time was a workshop as well as a sleeping and living apartment. A series of miniature factories honeycombed them all, and here were indescribable dirt and odors. The people gave no heed to their condition; they were unwilling to change. Over all was the sign of the gabardine, the wig of the matron, the *shul* on many a tenement floor. The light of day never came to the ghetto; literally, there were many rooms it hardly visited at all.

And now? Where these festering tenements were, a broad field stretches itself, unshaded and blazing hot at noonday, dusty and rough, but still an open place, instead of the many score of tenements. Some day it will be made into a beautiful shady park, with such a greensward as slum dwellers love. That will take a long time, however. Meanwhile, city and educational authorities have thrown open the ground, surrounding it only by a slight fence, to keep some semblance of order.

The Hester Street open-air drygoods market to the west looms out on an altogether unaccustomed sight. It sees in place of a line of scowling tenements an open-air gymnasium, a running track, a basketball field, two covered sand playgrounds for the smaller children, a tented platform on which fifty miniature women of all ages at one time play kindergarten games. And, what is still stranger and more wonderful, it sees croquet actually being taught. This is the regeneration of the worst corner of the ghetto slum, viewed at its crudest now because, though the old buildings have gone, there is as yet little that is attractive to succeed it. But already it has become a paradise for the children and the perfection of resting places at evening for those older. No slum of the town was ever transformed to better uses.

Jacob A. Riis, for this authority on the New York tenements must be quoted again, has spoken many a time in print of the filth of Cat Alley and its buildings, directly under the nose of Police Headquarters—in front of it, in fact. Cat Alley grew to be a well-known locality among police reporters, who constantly had it before their eyes. There was much to disgust, to horrify, about Cat Alley, for it was always a haunt of lawlessness as well as filth. The knell has sounded over that as well. The widening and extension of Elm Street are what brought about its tearing down. A slice of the block bounded by Mulberry, Houston, Crosby, and Bleecker Streets has been torn away for the Elm Street lengthening. By rare good fortune this demolition took the course of the little slum. Only the extension of the street was being considered, but the work could not have resulted better. It razed every vestige of the slum, leaving only a broad street, with a semisquare where Bleecker Street and Mulberry Street meet it, and Cat Alley, with all its turbulence, its crime, its police record, and, it must be confessed, its picturesqueness, is now only a name.

LEWIS W. HINE/COMBINED BATH AND LAUNDRY IN A TENEMENT SINK, c. 1907–1915/GEORGE EASTMAN HOUSE

JESSIE TARBOX BEALS/IN THE KITCHEN, 1915/COMMUNITY SERVICE SOCIETY, NEW YORK

LEWIS W. HINE/REAR TENEMENT BEDROOM, c. 1910/GEORGE EASTMAN HOUSE

LEWIS W. HINE/COMMUNITY FAUCET, 1910/GEORGE EASTMAN HOUSE

LEWIS W. HINE/WASHING DISHES, c. 1907–1915/GEORGE EASTMAN HOUSE

UNKNOWN PHOTOGRAPHER/TENEMENT LIFE, c. 1905/BROWN BROTHERS

LEWIS W. HINE/TENEMENT LIFE, c. 1910/THE GRANGER COLLECTION

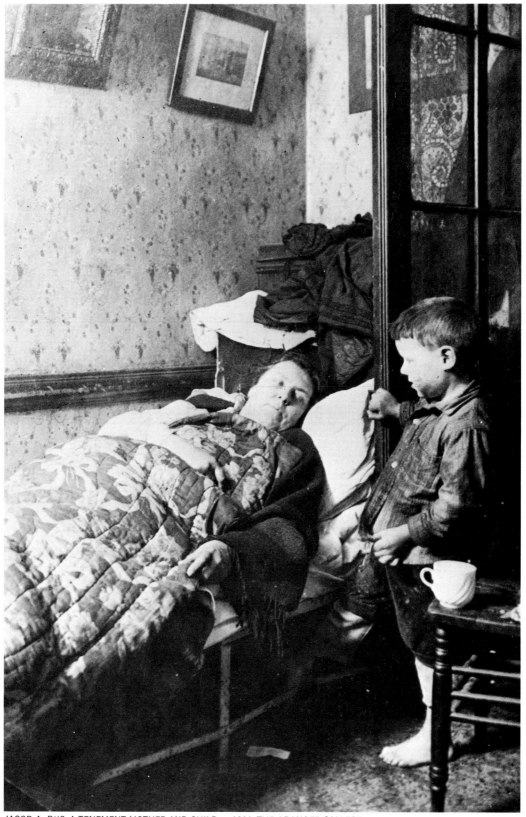

JACOB A. RIIS/A TENEMENT MOTHER AND CHILD, c. 1890/THE GRANGER COLLECTION

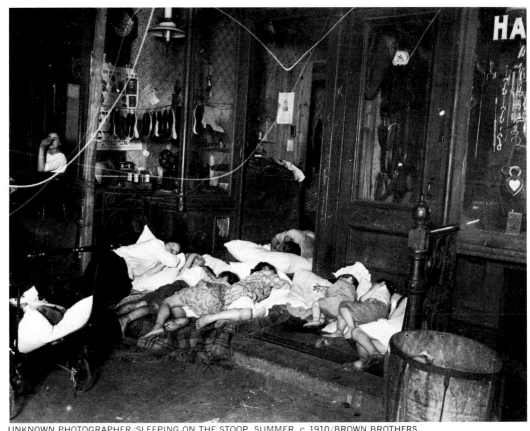

UNKNOWN PHOTOGRAPHER/SLEEPING ON THE STOOP, SUMMER, c. 1910/BROWN BROTHERS

JACOB A. RIIS/CHILD OF THE TENEMENTS, c. 1890/THE GRANGER COLLECTION

JACOB A. RIIS/PRAYERTIME IN A FIVE POINTS ORPHANAGE, c. 1889/THE GRANGER COLLECTION

JACOB A. RIIS/MAKING READY FOR THE SABBATH, c. 1890/THE JACOB A. RIIS COLLECTION, MUSEUM OF THE CITY
OF NEW YORK

JACOB A. RIIS/UNDER THE DUMP, RIVINGTON STREET, c. 1890/THE JACOB A. RIIS COLLECTION, MUSEUM OF THE CITY OF NEW YORK

JACOB A. RIIS/SLEEPING ON THE STOOP, c. 1890/THE GRANGER COLLECTION

UNKNOWN PHOTOGRAPHER/TENEMENT DWELLERS, UNDATED/AMALGAMATED CLOTHING WORKERS OF AMERICA

JACOB A. RIIS/MULLEN'S ALLEY, c. 1890/THE JACOB A. RIIS COLLECTION, MUSEUM OF THE CITY OF NEW YORK

UNKNOWN PHOTOGRAPHER/ATTORNEY STREET, c. 1904/PICTURE COLLECTION, NEW YORK PUBLIC LIBRARY

JACOB A. RIIS/THE SHORT TAIL GANG, AT CORLEAR'S HOOK, UNDER THE PIER AT FOOT OF JACKSON STREET. c, 1889/
THE JACOB A. RIIS COLLECTION, MUSEUM OF THE CITY OF NEW YORK

JACOB A. RIIS/BANDIT'S ROOST, 39½ MULBERRY STREET, c. 1890/THE JACOB A. RIIS COLLECTION, MUSEUM OF THE CITY OF NEW YORK

JACOB A. RIIS/BATHTUB IN AIRSHAFT, UNDATED/THE JACOB A. RIIS COLLECTION,
MUSEUM OF THE CITY OF NEW YORK

JACOB A. RIIS/BOTTLE ALLEY, 1889/THE JACOB A. RIIS COLLECTION, MUSEUM OF THE CITY OF NEW YORK

JACOB A. RIIS/BAXTER STREET COURT, c. 1890/THE JACOB A. RIIS COLLECTION, MUSEUM OF THE CITY OF NEW YORK RESIDENCE/242

UNKNOWN PHOTOGRAPHER/BACKYARD SCENE, UNDATED/NEW YORK CITY POLICE DEPARTMENT

UNKNOWN PHOTOGRAPHER/LAUNDRY DRYING,
UNDATED/LIBRARY OF CONGRESS

שלום עליכם

SHOLOM ALEICHEM

שלום עליכם

(פֿון די חזנים)

ווערטער פֿון ב. טהאמאשעפֿסקי

מוזיק פֿון י. רומשינסקי

געזונגען פֿון מ. שווארץ

SHOLOM ALEICHEM

Words by
BORIS THOMASHEFSKY

Music by
J. M. RUMSHINSKY

Sung by
MORRIS SHWARTZ

HEBREW PUBLISHING CO.
50 ELDRIDGE S?   NEW YORK

J. KELLER

Dear Mr. Editor of the
Forward:

I read the troubles of family life in your
"Bintel Brief" each day very attentively.
But my own troubles are so great, so
enormous, that I will not even ask you
for your permission to print my few words
in your paper, as others do, but simply, I
ask you right on the spot: Help!

Your Constant Reader

FEBRUARY 8, 1906

Dear Mr. Editor:

My own daughter, who was born in Russia, married a Hungarian–Jewish young
man. She adopted all the Hungarian customs and not a trace of a Russian–Jewish
woman remained with her. This would not
have been so bad. The trouble is, now that
she is first–class Hungarian, she laughs at
the way I talk, at my manners, and even
the way we cook. She does not avoid me.
On the contrary, since her marriage, she
has been calling on me even more than
before. Not an evening passes without
quarrels, without mockery and ridicule.

I therefore want to express my opinion
that Russian Jews and Hungarian Jews
should not intermarry; a Russian Jew and
an Hungarian Jew are in my opinion two
different worlds and one does not and cannot understand the other.

The Russian Mother

MARCH 6, 1906

Dear Mr. Editor:

I am a greenhorn. I have only been five
weeks in the country. I am a jewelry
maker. I left a blind father and a step-
mother in Russia. Before my departure
my father begged me not to forget him. I
promised that I would send him the first
money I should earn. I walked around two
weeks and looked for work. But at the
end of the third week I succeeded in getting a job. I worked a week and received
eight dollars for the week. I am working
the third week now. I paid for my board
and bought certain necessities, such as a

hat, shoes, and some small items, and I
have a few dollars, too. Now, Mr. Editor, I
want to ask you to give me some advice,
as to what to do. Should I send my father
a few dollars for Passover, or should I
keep them for myself? Because the work
at our place is at an end, and I may have
to be without work. So that I do not know
what to do. I hope that you will give me
some advice, and I shall obey you just as
you tell me.

Youah Mednikoff

JANUARY 20, 1906

Dear Editor of the
Forward:

Permit me to express in our workers'
paper my broken feelings. I am a greenhorn, being only five months out of Odessa,
and I cannot forgive myself for being in
America now. My head and heart ache
when I read in your paper that thousands
of workers stand on the barricades in Russia and fight like lions. Who can feel it
more than we who have just come from
Russia, from just such an army which is
now doing battle? I cannot express my
feelings, the steam from the iron in the
shop destroys my feelings. I do not know
myself what to do; I know that I have
committed a crime, that I am deserter, I
ran away from the battlefield. I would like
to stand again with my brothers on the line
of combat. I walk around now as one pos-
sessed; when we hear that the end of Czar-
ism is near, that in a day or so the final
blow will be dealt against the Russian government, oh, how I would like to be there
in the midst of battle, to stand shoulder
to shoulder with my comrades that my
blood too may make our flag red. But the
great ocean does not permit one to flee
without a ticket, and the boat and railroad
do not want to know of my thoughts, and
they say that without the dollars they will
not take me. Money to pay I have not.
What shall I do? To save a few dollars is
impossible; all I earn is five dollars a week,
and a few days a week there is no work.
I cannot go on living any longer; I do not

sleep nights; I do not know what to do.

I beg you, dear Editor, answer me, what shall I do? And I think there are many, many like me.

Joseph Thest

Dear Editor:

A novel could be made out of my life. I am 49 years old, and I loved twice and was married once. More than 20 years ago I fell in love with a girl in my town in Lithuania. We loved each other passionately. The girl's father was a government official, an inspector, who was supposed to see to it that no tobacco or whiskey was sold without a license. Once when his own wife sold tobacco without a license, he handed her over to the government. He also ruined many Jewish families.

I used to meet my sweetheart outside the city at a place where there were many lumber mills. Once we were caught there. When my father found out about this, he was very much incensed over it. But I told him that I loved her and will marry her. My father beat me and drove me from his house. I wandered over the face of the earth.

Many years passed. I found out that my sweetheart married and that she was living in Odessa. I went there and only through great effort discovered her house. I did not dare go to her. I would pace back and forth in front of her house, and this made me happy. One day, a little girl of about 12 years came out of that house. It was her little daughter. She was so like her mother that I forgot where I was, and it seemed to me that I was seeing her, my beloved, in my native town. I walked up to her and talked to her. I stroked her cheek and taking a silver coin from my pocket gave it to her.

Who are you? she asked. Why do you give me money? One mustn't accept money from a stranger.

You little fool, I am no stranger, I am your uncle, I told her.

If you are my uncle, then why don't you come in to see us? Come in, I am running to tell mama that an uncle came.

I attempted to keep her back, saying that I had no time now, that I shall come later. But she refused to listen and ran into the house. I immediately went away. Later I used to await her in front of the school and would accompany her a few blocks. She kept on asking me why I do not come to see them. I would give her excuses.

Once, when I waited for her at school, her mother suddenly came. I am incapable of describing how I felt then. She too was terribly upset. She begged me not to wait any more for the child, because the whole affair seemed odd to her husband; he actually had asked her to see who was this "uncle" who waited for the child each day at school.

I promised her that. I went to America. There I forgot my troubles somewhat. I took to business, and I was very successful. But I did not stop thinking of my former sweetheart for one moment. Several years later a friend came from Odessa and told me that my beloved had died. Later the husband too died, the house a heap of ruins, the daughter living with her father's relatives. I immediately wrote a letter, in which I made her a proposal if she would like to come to America to her "uncle." She wrote me that she would come to America, and she came. When I saw her, it seemed to me that it was her mother come to life. In. short, after a while we were married. We were truly happy. I also loved her mother in her—my first sweetheart. But my happiness was wrecked shortly afterwards. Death robbed me of it. My dear one died from an inflammation of the lungs.

Kaufman Ongel

Dear Mr. Editor:

I am yet a very young woman, and I do not want to praise myself, but anyone who sees me admits that I am very pretty, tall, healthy and strong, and full of desire to live. But notwithstanding my good qualities I remained on account of various circumstances lonely, without friends. But by chance I met a man who is not only a very kind person but quite an educated man as well, whom I came to love greatly for his precious qualities, so I married him.

But after living with him a short time, I realized that he is my direct opposite. I am tall, and he is very small, short. I am healthy, strong, and he is nebach slim and slight like a splinter: I am pretty and attractive and he is a horror: hollow cheeks, twisted teeth and so on and so on. Just as he is enchanting spiritually so is he disgusting physically.

Living with him a short time, I learned to hate him. When he was not home, I loved and respected him; as soon as he would enter the house I could not look at him. And as I could no longer go on living a dual life, I separated from him.

And here a worse tragedy began with me. My two sisters butted in and do not let me live, and torment me and torture me for the great crime that I committed against this man.

I therefore turn to you dear Editor, you shall tell me the truth, if I truly deserved to be condemned for separating from the man as I am condemned by my sisters or whether it is possible to justify me somehow.

Do not print my name and my city and this is really because I do not want to cause any grief or humiliation to that man, whom I love and honor as a human being but not as a husband or a life companion.

Anonymous

APRIL 1, 1906

Dear Mr. Editor:

My trouble consists of this: I am a married man. I have been in this country six years. I am in business, and I am not badly off. In my old home, in Russia, I was also very well off. I was a merchant and always did a good business. Then why did I go to America? This is indeed my trouble. I married a very nice girl. Her parents were among the most prominent citizens of the city, we led a very happy life after our marriage. But a snake sneaked into our home and embittered our lives. This snake is no other than my mother-in-law. If I wanted to write you all about her, it would take up whole sheets of paper. I will only describe to you briefly the sort of creature she is. My father-in-law was not home almost the entire week; he used to travel to villages, where he conducted his business. So the mother-in-law would stay at my home the whole day. She got busy with my wife and began pointing out the faults she had found with me. My wife, quiet and kind by nature, tried to prove to her that she was mistaken, but that was of little use. At first my wife did not tell me anything. Later I somehow began to notice, that my mother-in-law was interfering too much with my home affairs, as if my wife did not count with me at all. I talked to my wife about it, and she told me that her mother was constantly inciting her against me. She asked me not to make any fuss over it, that I should not hurt her mother. My mother-in-law, seeing that my wife was with me, lost control of herself and began to embitter the lives of both of us. When I was not home, she vexed my wife. For instance: she is no housekeeper, she does not know how to deal with me, with the maid and so on. No maid could stay more than two weeks at my house; she got their goat. And when I came home, she would sit on me. Now she had this against me. Now that I am no business man. I am a bad husband, and so on. In short, there was darkness and misery in the house. Even on the Sabbath, when my father-in-law was home, I had no rest. At first I wanted to please my wife and did not say anything, but finally I lost my patience and told my mother-in-law, that if she did not stop making rows in my house, I won't let her cross my doorstep. Well, you can imagine, what took place then at our home. I realized that it would come to no good, because my wife suffered terribly on account of it, so I decided to go to America. At first my wife was against that. She did not want to part from her parents. She wanted us to move to another city. But I knew that that would scarcely have been a solution; my mother-in-law would have been our guest frequently. In short we went to America. As I have already said before, I should have no complaint to make as far as America is concerned, were it not for my trouble. Half a year ago my father-in-law died. He was a very kind man, just the opposite of my mother-in-law. And now my mother-in-law writes me that she wants to come here. Well, what is one to do? I know, that should she come here my home would again be turned into a gehenom.

Dear Editor! Give me some advice, as to what I should do. My wife, although she knows her mother well, insists that we bring her over. And that is natural, isn't she her child? But I would rather that she should stay at home, and may she prosper there. She has a married son there, who is very well, and she will want nothing. But my mother-in-law wants to come here. I answer, that if I were to be obstinate, I would win. But my wife will suffer very much on account of it, and that I do not want. And so, give me some advice, dear Editor, I shall do as you will advise me.

With respect,
A Despondent Son-in-law

MARCH 11, 1906

Dear Mr. Editor:

I have been married 9 years. I have two children, one of 7 years and the other of 3 years. I am a working man and earn 14 dollars a week. I am strong enough and not old. My wife too is the same. Ten years ago, when we met, we were equals in education and also in finances. We truly loved one another's company. We had no other ideal in life than to try and save a few dollars that we might be able to provide ourselves with a small business so that I would not have to go to the shop and suffer so many hours there. As for religious matters there was disagreement between us, but this was only before Yom Kippur, because she always wanted to go to the synagogue and fast the whole day. It would take a few weeks, and everything would be as before. I had to stand this for 4 years, when one bright morning my devoted wife told me, that she understood very well now, that religion was nothing more than humbug and so on. She told me how she suddenly came to her senses. She went to a meeting of the recently organized society where the speakers proved black on white the futility of religion. Now all manner of things began to happen daily. She demanded that I become a member of the new club, that I take lessons in English, that I have nothing to do with my acquaintances—the ignorant workers —and that I don a hat befitting an educated man. To cut it short, she wanted that I do only that which she ordered.

I cannot describe to you how my life was upset through these new ideas which this woman got. I simply did not know what to do. I could not devote myself to education while at work. The few free hours which I had in the evenings were spent entertaining new acquaintances.

I turned to my wife with questions: company costs money, the children are neglected, the house is in a dilapidated condition, I never find any supper cooked. She answered that she was a different person now. She no longer believed in the family life which she led before. She got after me more and more. At least I should become an insurance agent to get away from the "ignoramuses" in the shop. I told her that I am satisfied with the shop, and that she can go on as she pleases, but without company. She told me plainly, that if I am not in accord with her behavior, we must separate. These were the final words of a woman who has two children. Two months later I became convinced that she was really in earnest. I found all my things packed, and she told me to move.

I went to my parents. When they found out about it, they compelled me to take the children from her and sell all the furniture from the rooms. That is what I did. What else could I do?

Hoping that you will have compassion

on a father who loves his children dearly, and will advise him as to what to do, I remain with kind greetings,

An Unhappy Father

Dear Editor of the
Forward:

It will surprise you perhaps, that along with the letter from my mother you also receive a letter from me, her son. After my mother had a discussion with me concerning the usefulness and necessity of getting married and after I proved to her that now was not the time to get married, she wanted me to write to you because the Forward certainly understands such problems. I can imagine what my mother has written about me, but of one thing I am certain, that she wrote no evil of me. She has no cause to complain about me.

I need not tell you, what is going on on the other side of the ocean. The revolution is blazing in full force. Since the revolution began in our old home, I became an entirely different person. I do not enjoy eating, drinking, I do not miss a single meeting, which is called for the purpose of aiding the Russian revolution. Besides attending all meetings and mass gatherings I undertook some work which takes at least a few hours each night. After all, I am only a human being. One wants to read the local revolutionary literature and the great mass of new, free newspapers and journals, which come from Russia. During the day one has to work for a living. I suppose you understand now that simply no time is left for other matters. My bride is, fortunately, also a comrade. She attends all the meetings with me and takes part in the movement. From her I have not heard that we should get married. She understands that this is not the time for it. The only one who demands that I get married is my mother. She cannot understand how it is possible to be engaged and not marry. How can I satisfy her? My soul and my bride's soul are eager for the struggle, not for the marriage canopy. I do not give up the idea of marriage

entirely. When the revolution will be at an end and will be victorious over the autocracy, we will start thinking about ourselves. Now, in the midst of things in the middle of the stream, there is no time.

I should be very thankful to you if you will print my letter. My mother thinks very highly of your newspaper. When she sees my letter printed too, she will understand that I too am right and she will not consider my and my bride's waiting a crime.

Your reader,
S. G.

Dear Mr. Editor:

Our boss is an honest man, but being a boss it is naturally to his interests to exploit us. He is really very poor. He is a very poor businessman, a poor manager, but that does not concern us here. One of the workers in our shop is a miserly fellow. His whole life is wrapped up in his bank book. Nothing in the world interests him. He hates music, the theater, and socialism. He is a man without any feeling. In a short time I am convinced that this worker will be a boss or a landlord, or simply a capitalist sucker, and then he will be one of the worst. The question now is: To whom shall I be more faithful— to the poor, honest boss, or to this miserable future exploiter? I am not more loyal to my boss than are other workers to their bosses, but in comparison to my co-worker, I must maintain, that I am loyal to my boss. Once there was a question of a strike, I voted against it only because of that worker. To strike in order that this worker should have more money to deposit into the bank? . . . What is your answer?

Raphael Kislikoff

Dear Mr. Editor:

With this letter a poor mother with a bitter heart turns to you. And as I know that your paper does not refuse space for the letters of the unfortunate, the worried, and the embittered, I am certain that my words too will be printed in your worthy paper.

My trouble consists of this: I have a son, who is otherwise quite a good child, devoted to his family, but. . .he is too much of a socialist. I am by no means opposed to that; let him be whatever he wants to be, especially when socialism teaches him to be a good man and a devoted child. But socialism hinders my son from becoming a husband and a father of children. My son has a bride, a very dear child, but he is so devoted to the movement that it is not possible to persuade him to get married. Since the revolution in Russia began, he is so caught up in it that it is simply impossible even to talk to him about marriage. My heart is broken. I cannot bear the pain of the bride. Perhaps you will advise me, dear Editor, how to influence my son, that socialism is socialism and getting married too is a human affair.

The Troubled Mother

MARCH 27, 1906

Dear Mr. Editor:

My wife is one of those types who loves when passing someone to rub her shoulder, so that one may feel that she is present. She is a great preacher of women's rights. Women, she says, stand on a much higher plane than men, and the woman who cannot control her husband is an animal. Wherever she puts her foot, there you find accidents. She is very nervous. She has a big mouth, cries easily, and hates to listen to anyone. Such is my wife. I myself am a peace-loving, quiet man. I conduct a small business, a two-by-four grocery store. My wife is the business lady in the family. This is how she talks to me: "What can I do when I have a dummy for a husband, such a schlemiel." And so, she is the head of the business, and I am the arm. Work for me, says she, she has plenty, a steady job for day and night. If there is no work for me in the store, says she, then do the housework. For me, home is a prison. I am out in the open just once a year: on Yom Kippur when the store is closed and my old woman is in the synagogue. During the entire year, when there is any time, she is the first to go out. And when she goes out she sees to it that I have so much work that I cannot go out even. There is always quarreling in the house. If I order goods, it's all wrong. If I charge high prices, I drive away customers. If I sell cheap, I waste her money. If I am sick, I am lazy. If I want to read the paper she argues, "Why should a businessman read a paper? You have to help conduct Russian politics? Aren't you ashamed of yourself, just like a little boy. . . ."

In short, I smuggle in a paper. Just listen how it is done: In the morning, when my wife is still sleeping, the first thing I do is to twist and wrinkle the paper in such a way that it should appear in case of danger like yesterday's paper. Then I unroll it slowly that no sound be heard, I hastily glance at the headlines, and I check the most interesting ones where they are found. All this I do with the greatest caution, not losing for a moment the thought that she might hear. Then I bury it somewhere and breathe freely.

How can one stand for so much? I have children whom I love, and their fate frightens me. A divorce can be of little use to me. I see no way out.

Do not publish my name; also pardon me for writing so much. This is not even a tenth of my heavy heart.

The Woman's Husband

MARCH 9, 1906

Dear Mr. Editor:

I am a working girl of 18 years and live with my parents together with an older sister and brother. We all work, and my father is a very good man. He would do everything in the world for us, in order that we may lack nothing. So seemingly everything is all right, and it may seem that I lack nothing. But I am here to tell you about this "lacking."

I lack the most important thing in the world, the feeling of "mother-love." My mother is a very mean woman. From the time when I was able to stand on my feet, she gave me only one thing—curses, curses, curses. And so I thirst all my life for mother-love. When I was but a small child and saw how mothers kissed their children and called them by the most endearing names, I would shed rivers of tears out of pain, out of grief, because my mother did not kiss me. Now I no longer cry because my mother does not kiss me. I cry now because my mother is not a true mother to me, because she is not even a friend to me. It is well known that one does not play around in the shops. The work there is hard and bitter; still when we come from the shop she wants me and my sister to wash clothes or clean the house, and when I tell her that we tire ourselves out the whole day and want to rest in the evening, she says that when one sits at a machine the whole day one rests sufficiently. And if I feel bad sometimes and lie on the lounge for a second, my mother does not even come to ask me what the trouble is and this makes my pain still greater. We are children who love a home, but home is curses and screams. We have no place to go to; we do not like dance halls. My brother goes there, and he wouldn't go but how can you help yourself, when it is impossible to stay in the house. Believe me, dear Mr. Editor, that when I am in the shop, I think how well it would be to be able to go home, but when I come home and take a look at the person, whom I ought to love and honor, but whom I hate for her ugly character. She is such a mean woman that not only is she unfriendly to her own children, but there is not a single person to whom she is a friend. We hate capitalists, she likes capitalists. What we do not like, she likes, to spite us. My sister and I have a girl friend who visits us often and understands us and sympathizes with us, well, so mother drives her out and she says, that our friend leads us astray. I feel very unhappy, for having to avoid my mother, but I cannot help it, because I haven't a spark of child-love or friendliness toward her. When I talk to her she answers me with curses and when I do not talk to her, she yells

that I am a bad daughter. . . .

So, dear Mr. Editor, give me some advice as to how to deal with my bad mother, how I can avoid her horrible curses. Hoping that you will print my words, I remain your friend.

The Peculiar Daughter

FEBRUARY 2, 1906

Dear Mr. Editor of the Forward:

Allow me a little space in your worthy paper to tell your honorable readers what took place at my home a month before my wedding. As is probably well known to you, a bride whom God has blessed with many good friends receives various gifts at her wedding. I am getting married, and I have many friends and landsleit I am acquainted with. A week before my wedding they gathered at my mother's home. At the rooms which I have already taken, they brought a whole loadful of wedding gifts. Among my landsleit there was also one whom people considered something of a crank. I have not considered him as such, only my landsleit. When he saw the presents which were brought me, he was seized with a fit and he began to shout: Fools! What have you brought together here? Four tables, ten lamps, three beds for one couple. . . .Come, let us rather go into this room and decide, that each one bring that, which the young couple needs, not that, which she does not need.

However, as my wise landsman is of course a "crank", his proposal was not accepted.

Therefore I turn to you, Mr. Editor, you shall answer me, as to who is right, the crank with his proposal to give me one bed as a wedding gift or the other landsleit, who brought me three beds.

Miss Gussie Frug

MARCH 22, 1906

Dear Mr. Editor:

On a terribly horribly frosty morning I found a man of sixty or seventy years sitting on the steps of No. 21 Eldridge Street, and shivering from the cold. My heart was touched and I asked him why he sits here —if he were waiting for someone or perhaps a few pennies from a passer-by. He answered me that he does not beg and may God keep him from stretching out his hand for pennies. I took him into a hallway with me. He was nebach overjoyed, because he would warm his frozen limbs, and we talked. I would really like to write you every detail at which my hair stood on end, but I am afraid that his children would read these lines and that, God forbid, might hurt him. He has several children who are well off, and yet he must roam the streets hungry and frozen. One son has his own stable and carriages. A second son is an operator on cloaks and makes good money, and a daughter is a waitress in a saloon and also makes a fine living. And with all this he stands on the street and waits for the door of a certain woman to open, who gives him each morning a few glasses of tea and bread and thus keeps him alive. It is outrageous, when such a thing is passed over.

Dear Mr. Editor, cry out against it in your paper. Perhaps the children will find out that the world knows. Here is the name of the woman who gives him tea and bread each day: Mrs. Pearlman.

I am your constant reader.

G. R.

FEBRUARY 20, 1906

Dear Editor:

Working for a very long time with a Gentile woman in the shop, I came to know her very intimately, and we began to go out together very often. In the end, we fell in love with each other. Naturally, we decided that I should not be a Gentile nor she a Jewess. But in the course of a year I realized that we were not compatible. Whenever an acquaintance, a friend, comes home, I note a great dissatisfaction on her face. When she sees me reading a Jewish paper, her face changes color. She does not tell me anything, but I see that the woman is wasting away like a candle. I feel that she is very unhappy with me

although I am certain she loves me. On top of that, she is to become a mother soon. Her tie to me becomes stronger. Only a few weeks ago Christ awoke within her. Every Sunday she rises at dawn, hurries to church and comes back with eyes swollen from crying. Whenever I go out with her and it happens that we pass a church, tremors seize her.

Give me, dear Mr. Editor some advice as to what I should do. To convert to Christianity is out of the question. She will not stop going to church. What can be done, that there may not be so much trouble in our home?

Hyman Frumkin

FEBRUARY 26, 1906

Dear Mr. Editor of the Forward:

I have been a servant girl these two years. I came to America six years ago. For four years I worked in a shop and I got sick, but I was still strong enough to be employed as a servant. I worked here, but a poor person must work hard nowadays in order to make a living. But my emotional trouble, which I had to endure being a servant, made me thin and emaciated. This is my story. I contracted consumption while working in the shop and had to go to Denver, Colorado. There are no shops here, so I have become a servant. My first job was in the household of an upstart real estate operator and a Gentile to boot. And here is what happened: Not an evening passed, when the house was not full of guests. The tables were set with all good things, and I, tired out, broken, sat in the kitchen at the table with the dog and cat. If the son or the mistress wanted to spit they found no other place to spit but the kitchen and exactly at the time when I was eating. In short, I quit and I am now with rich German Jews. So I tell you that I feel even more depressed and more unhappy than when I was with the spitting Gentiles. I am writing you this letter, in order that servants the world over might understand their plight, as I do, and might understand, as I do, to who it was that humiliated them and brought them to such a horrible position. And then if they only knew it, they would have united and our position would then have been greatly bettered.

With socialist greetings
Trilby

FEBRUARY 15, 1906

Dear Mr. Editor:

The life of a poor worker's family must be well known to you, and just imagine, when the poor worker's wife takes sick and is confined to her sick bed for nine whole weeks. On top of that the woman is a mother of three tiny children, and the husband is in the shop the whole day, and his wages are such that one cannot afford to hire a maid in the house to attend to the children, and only benevolent neighbors come in now and then and with tears in their eyes wash up and dress the children. And picture to yourself how, suddenly, the door of my rooms opens unexpectedly and the landlady comes in. I told her I was dangerously ill and that I must go to the hospital to be operated on and I cannot pay her the rent that month.

The landlady however did not take the rent and said she does not want any sick poor tenants in her house. When I asked what I was to do with my three unfortunate children, she told me to put them in an orphan asylum, where they will be well attended, and at the same time I will be rid of extra mouths and at the same time she will be rid of begging tenants. Her words made a horrible impression on me and certainly it was no cure for me.

I therefore ask you, you should answer me, if it is the right thing to do for a Jewish landlady, who was perhaps herself once a poor girl, only her husband has good luck with real estate and he bought a house in Brownsville? I want to ask her through your paper, which she certainly reads, what is the matter with her, that she prides herself so upon her riches? May it not happen that the poor will regain his health and become rich and she, the rich landlady, will be reduced to our state?

Dear readers: I write this letter on my sick bed and ask for some advice as to how to carry on the struggle against such a murderous landlady. The paper, on which I write, is steeped in tears. One does not want to part from children. I am afraid she might make it so that the children will be taken from me by force.

Answer me, good people, what shall I do?

An Unfortunate Woman

MARCH 15, 1906

Dear Mr. Editor:

The story I want to tell you is this. I have two little girls, one 10 years and the other 13. Both go to school. A few months ago a friend of mine told me, that he saw one of my girls walking about arm-in-arm with a little boy, who probably goes to the same school with her. I happen to be a busy man, I have a stationery store and am always occupied, I cannot even get away for a minute. Of course my wife is busy with a new one, and she too cannot leave the house. So with tears in my eyes I begged my friend, to stop working for a few days at my expense and watch my two girls. My friend did not refuse me this favor, and he spied on my two girls on the other sidewalk, as soon as the children left school. And he saw something horrible. As soon as my daughters walked out of school, they walked up to the corner of the street and stood waiting. . . .About fifteen minutes later two boys from the same school met them. My friend followed them, and he saw how the boys took candy, chocolates and peanuts from their pockets and treated my daughters. The girls would take the presents and for this would drag around for many hours through tens of streets. It would not have grieved me, because they walked around, but my friend saw such wicked behavior on the part of the boys, who are very much like the "gang" of the great bandits. At each street corner they would go into a hallway. My daughters would laugh out loud, and my friend heard both times how they agreed to meet in the evening at a certain spot in Hester Street Park. My friend watched them in the park too, and his face burned for shame at what he saw the little bandits do and at the indifference of the two girls. Walking home from the park, they several times walked into other hallways. What they did there, this my friend did not see, because I told him, not to show himself to my daughters since they know him.

I cannot keep them in the house: And so I can find no way out. I am afraid to turn to the police, lest they be given over to the Gerry Society and even there, I think, they do not turn into nuns.

What is to be done, dear Editor?

The Unhappy Father

MARCH 13, 1906

Dear Editor of the
Forward:

My married life consists of the following: We are living in a room and bedroom on the top floor on Allen Street. We cannot pay more than eleven dollars a month. I have two children so they are pale, without a drop of blood. More than once the doctor told me I should move, because the children haven't enough air. Lately, however, I realized that many of my acquaintances, who are not better off than we, live nevertheless in nice, comfortable rooms and in a better neighborhood. They have each several boarders, and in this way the rent does not come to much. I began to reason with my husband that we ought to do the same, so he does not want to listen. He does not want to have any boarders, because he fears, that on account of them there would be quarreling between us. He is simply afraid that I would become jealous, if we were to take in a female boarder, and that he would become jealous if a male boarder is taken in. "Who can tell what may happen!" he says. I laughed at it, but he is like steel and iron and does not want to hear of it. He is in the shop the whole day and when he comes home, he eats and goes somewhere or goes to bed. But I want to work hard, wait on boarders so that I may have comfortable rooms for my children, and for myself too.

Mr. Editor, which of us is right?

Rose Eisenberg

FEBRUARY 11, 1906

Dear Editor of the
Forward:

It was reported in your Bintel Brief that the parents of the couple at 9 Pitt Street had separated the young wife from her husband because he fell in their disfavor. I ask you, what more can parents do than they have done? We paid the young couple's rent for fully sixteen months, with food and clothing we always provided them. The husband did not make a living, so we tried our best. It is out of reason here in America in these times for one to get one's board eternally. Do not believe what the husband writes. This is how it happened. We wanted to do something with him. It came to a pass where they wanted to throw him out on the street, and we could not help him any longer. We went to the Rabbi on Broome Street, he told us to take him into our house for a month. We obeyed, but so found out that he had a railroad ticket and was getting ready to leave the next morning. We had to put an end to it. How could we do any better when we saw how a young man was bringing misfortune upon a whole family?

I hope, that with this statement my guilt is washed away.

B. Silberstieg